THISTLE AND BAMBOO
THE LIFE AND TIMES OF
SIR JAMES STEWART LOCKHART

Echoes: Classics of Hong Kong Culture and History

Series General Editor: Robert Nield

The life of Hong Kong and its region has been explored in a vast number of books. They include ground-breaking scholarly studies of great standing, and literary works that shed light on people, places and events. Many of these books, unfortunately, are no longer available to the general reader.

The aim of the *Echoes* series is once more to make available in paperback the best of those books that would otherwise be lost. The series will embrace not only history, but also memoirs, fiction, politics, natural history and other fields. The focal point will be Hong Kong, but the series will extend to places that were connected with the city or shared some of its experiences. In this way we hope to bring a growing number of classic publications to a new and wider readership.

Other titles in the Echoes series:

Power and Charity: A Chinese Merchant Elite in Colonial Hong Kong
   Elizabeth Sinn

A Biographical Sketch-book of Early Hong Kong
   G. B. Endacott

Chinese Christians: Elites, Middlemen and the Church in Hong Kong
   Carl T. Smith

Edge of Empires: Chinese Elites and British Colonials in Hong Kong
   John M. Carroll

Anglo-China: Chinese People and British Rule in Hong Kong, 1841–1880
   Christopher Munn

City of Broken Promises
   Austin Coates

Macao and the British, 1637–1842: Prelude to Hong Kong
   Austin Coates

A Macao Narrative
   Austin Coates

The Road
   Austin Coates

The Taking of Hong Kong: Charles and Clara Elliot in China Waters
   Susanna Hoe and Derek Roebuck

THISTLE
AND
BAMBOO

The Life and Times of
Sir James Stewart Lockhart

SHIONA AIRLIE

with a foreword

by

Carol G.S. Tan

香港大學出版社
HONG KONG UNIVERSITY PRESS

Hong Kong University Press
14/F Hing Wai Centre
7 Tin Wan Praya Road
Aberdeen
Hong Kong

© Hong Kong University Press 2010

First published in 1989 by Oxford University Press
This paperback edition published by Hong Kong University Press
in 2010

ISBN 978-988-8028-92-4

British Library Cataloguing-in-Publication Data
A catalogue entry for this book is available from the British Library.

Secure On-line Ordering
www.hkupress.org

Printed and bound by Prepress Co. Ltd., Hong Kong, China.

For Michael and Benjamin Gill

CONTENTS

PLATES

THE photographs are reproducted with the consent of the copyright holders, The Merchant Company Education Board.

FOREWORD

Lockhart Road on Hong Kong island is known to most residents of Hong Kong and, indeed, to many of its visitors. Most would guess correctly that the road is named after a British colonial official. Few would know that there was once another Lockhart Road, further north, in Weihaiwei in Shandong province. The two roads reflect the two appointments in the career of James Stewart Lockhart.

At the time Lockhart was a young man leaving school and contemplating his future, the system for recruiting men to the civil service in India and elsewhere had already experienced its first major reforms, with a second tide of change still to come at the end of the nineteenth century. Around the middle of the nineteenth century, opinion favouring a liberal, generalist, education had triumphed. In a reversal of the earlier pattern, specialist education in the languages and cultures, sometimes including the laws, relevant to the place of appointment would follow rather than take the place of a general education. Although men were no longer being recruited at the age of seventeen or eighteen, the time had not yet come for the age limit to be raised sufficiently for men to complete their university studies. Thus it is of no surprise that James Stewart Lockhart would have attempted the examinations for the India Civil Service before the time he might have completed his first degree studies at Edinburgh. Neither is it surprising that the man who was to spend his career in the Far East first attempted the examinations for an appointment in India; the examinations for the Home, Indian and Eastern civil services were only amalgamated later. A man thus had to make a definite choice of where he wished to spend his lifelong career before presenting himself for the examinations. Reasons for the popularity of the Home Civil Service rested on other grounds but, if it was a career overseas that was sought, the Indian Civil Service possessed prestige. It also held out greater opportunity for promotion and, in this regard, contrasted greatly with the more limited opportunities of the small and separate services of Hong Kong, Ceylon and the Straits Settlements. Even though there was a common examination for the Eastern cadetships — posts first begun in 1862 and the result of influences borrowed from the system of training and recruiting members of the consular service in China — the regulations insisted that a cadet was to seek promotion in the colony where he had served as a cadet. A transfer to another Eastern colony or state required the approval of the Secretary of State. What is surprising, given his excellent academic record, is that Lockhart should have twice attempted the examinations without success. It may be that he did not seek the help of an experienced teacher in one of the crammers that had become popular with examinees and almost essential for success: it is thought that four out of five successful candidates had gone to a crammer. The pervasiveness of the use of crammers was one of the reasons why further reforms were later instituted to introduce an examination system that accorded more with the degree examinations at Oxford and Cambridge.

As a Hong Kong cadet, Lockhart was required to first spend time in London for the purpose of acquainting himself with the work of the Colonial Office and in order to begin learning Chinese. In November 1879, having acquired some knowledge of the Chinese language, he arrived in Hong Kong and, before long, proceeded to Guangzhou to continue his study of Chinese and to learn Cantonese. His time in Guangzhou ending during 1882 and, once again in Hong Kong, he rose quickly through successive posts to hold what was later to be renamed the post of Secretary for Chinese Affairs. Of his time in the government of Hong Kong, the first brief biographical account of Lockhart singles out his wisdom and prescience in seeing the need to involve resident Chinese elites in local affairs and his success in encouraging prominent Chinese residents to respond positively. Institutions familiar to Hong Kong residents even today such as the Tung Wah Hospital, the Po Leung Kuk and the perhaps less well-remembered District Watchmen Force all bore Lockhart's imprint. By the eve of the leasing of the New Territories, he was undoubtedly one of the most important officials in Hong Kong. In preparation for taking over control of the New Territories, it was Lockhart who was sent to visit the area and who wrote a report surveying the territory's socio-economic conditions. It was Lockhart who, after the initial disturbances of 1899, was responsible for laying the foundations of the system of administration in the New Territories. In so doing, he used the area's natural village boundaries to form the basis for a division of the territory into districts and sub-districts. Local leaders were identified who were made 'committee-men' to act as a conduit between the administration and ordinary villagers. The basic method of trying, as far as possible, to use pre-existing social and other structures is one he would again use a few years later in Weihaiwei.

Lockhart was Weihaiwei's first civil Commissioner from 1902 until his retirement in 1921, a period which, as it turned out, was nearly two-thirds of the period of the lease. The territory of Weihaiwei had been obtained by a lease from China in the same year as the New Territories and on very similar terms. However, between 1898 and Lockhart's arrival there, very little had been done by the interim authorities to exercise administrative authority over the territory. So it was a rather clean slate that he inherited and on which he established his administration. He drew on his experiences of the New Territories with the difference that in Weihaiwei, occupying the top post in the territory, he had a freer hand in deciding how best to arrange the affairs of the territory. In fact, Weihaiwei, because it was only at the periphery of Whitehall's gaze, gave Lockhart greater opportunity to put into practice his own beliefs on governing a territory of rural Chinese villages.

No account of Lockhart would be complete without mentioning his abiding interest in Chinese culture, which he cultivated and expanded throughout his career and well into his retirement. It can be stated briefly that, though his scholarly contributions may be of lesser value, he has been mentioned in the same breath as Herbert A. Giles, E.H. Parker, E.D.H. Fraser, and other scholar-officials. Perhaps Giles' trenchant criticism of Lockhart's first major sinological work is reasonable evidence of his membership of the contemporary sinological circle; his first book did not meet with unqualified praise yet it merited serious critique. In his own mind he was clearly a contender for a Chair in Chinese at the School of Oriental Studies in London; there was no shortage of people willing to provide supporting statements of his knowledge, abilities and reputation.

Viewing his career as a whole, Lockhart appears to have very rarely acted in self-aggrandisement or to have pandered to popular sentiment. He was efficient in carrying out his duties but, rather than any bureaucratic tendencies, it was effectiveness, together with genuine interest in the Chinese, that was at the heart of his style. He believed in governing with firmness but, at the same time, also believed in minimal interference with the local community. He also never tried to legislate change based on his personal views of particular cultural practices. His actions may not have strictly accorded with law and procedure at every turn but, for the most part, such departures were done in the context of good relations with the Chinese and with consultation and persuasion. It is a fair summation of Lockhart to say that he impressed the people he governed more than his superiors because he cared more about them than he did of the bureaucracy of which he was a part.

Since the publication of *Thistle and Bamboo* over twenty years ago, interest in the life of Sir James and in the history of Hong Kong during the period of his career in China has grown with the publication of a number of works on the New Territories. There has also been a growth in interest in Weihaiwei's history, stemming principally from the efforts of the local archive bureau in the city of Weihai to recapture and present the history of their own city. Furthermore, as interest in China's role in the First World War has grown in recent years, so too has interest in Weihaiwei and the part played by that territory and its officials in the embarkation for France of many thousands of Chinese men. These developments make republication of *Thistle and Bamboo* both appropriate and timely. They should not, however, detract from its inherent excellence and significance. Shiona Airlie's biography of Sir James is a fine example of painstaking, empirically-based, historiography of the sort that provides scholars with a case study with which to avoid sweeping generalisations about the nature of British rule and Empire. Its republication by Hong Kong University Press and the Royal Asiatic Society Hong Kong Branch now is, on this ground alone, more than justified.

Carol G. S. Tan
School of Oriental and African Studies
University of London
August 2010

PREFACE TO THE PAPERBACK EDITION

I finished writing *Thistle and Bamboo* late one night, tears streaming down my cheeks. Years of research were over. I'd told Sir James Stewart Lockhart's story to the world. It never occurred to me that the published book would fill the next twenty years of my life in an extraordinary manner.

Thistle and Bamboo appeared, and as it was my first book I was astonished when pleasant reviews appeared. People sent me kind letters and I was invited to speak at important conferences. At a time when British imperialism was being condemned as a great force of evil by so many historians, I had had the temerity to suggest that not all imperialists were bad. It was wonderful to hear from one of the former governors of Hong Kong that I'd done a good job in describing their service. It was equally gratifying to have the book accepted in China. During my research I had visited Hong Kong, but Weihai was still a closed area at the time.

As more and more began to be written about Hong Kong and Weihai, I was contacted by increasing numbers of historians. The collection of papers in the National Library of Scotland became known through the book; Sally Harrower, the person in charge of them, and I have lost count of the number of times we have been asked for access to them. The photographs were moved to the National Galleries under the stewardship of Sara Stevenson and again, just like the papers, the book made their existence known to the wider world. People started asking to use them in their books.

Then some people from the Weihai Archives Bureau came to Edinburgh to see the collection. The director, Zhang Jianguo, historian, Zhang Junyong, and interpreter, Ma Xianghong, first visited when they were setting up their local history resource in Weihai. Thanks to Sir James's magpie instincts, the Weihai team discovered a wealth of information about the period of British rule. It was difficult at first for a Scottish historian and a Chinese archivist to agree over what we were reading, but Zhang Jianguo and I got to know each other over the years, and I am proud to call him an elder brother.

It was fifteen years after the publication of the book before I finally managed to reach China. Sir James's daughter, Mary, had suggested that I write a biography about his great friend Reginald Johnston once I had 'finished' her father, and I had written a long biography about Johnston, who turned out to be as fascinating as Stewart Lockhart. Unfortunately, only a shortened version finally appeared, but it was a start.[1] With my friends in Weihai and Xi'an I looked forward to seeing the country for the first time. Weihai did not disappoint. One of China's green cities, it was easy to understand why Stewart Lockhart and Johnston had loved it so. And the Archives Bureau showed me all the old remaining buildings. I swear I could feel the ghosts of every officer who had worked there swirling around me. I visited the island of Liugong, saw old Chinese streets, met the mayor, and was treated quite royally. They even arranged for me, under the guidance of Miss Ma Xianghong, to travel up to Qufu, just as Stewart Lockhart and Johnston had done. There was no Duke Kong to meet, of course, and I was somewhat taken aback by the vivid colours of the temple, which I had only known until then from old black and white photographs, but it was a wonderful pilgrimage all the same. In return, I gave a lecture to the students at the university in Weihai about Sir James, Johnston and their links to the Confucian clan.

As a museum curator, I had mounted the first exhibition in Britain of the Xi'an terracotta warriors, so a visit to the museum there was another imperative while in China. Once more, I was shown great kindness in Xi'an. I was given the honour of standing beside the terracotta warriors, and taken on a tour of the entire museum complex. Then the Terracotta Museum decided that I needed to see some of the other sites in the province, and for a whole week I was driven from one museum and temple to another across Shaanxi Province. The museum

---

1.   *Reginald Johnston, Chinese Mandarin* (NMS Publishing, 2001)

gave me one of their top guides as an interpreter, Han Dong Hong. Like so many of the people I have met in China, she has remained a firm friend.

Two years later the Weihai Archives asked me back to speak at a conference there. This time, I chose 'Johnston and the Chinese' as my topic. I wanted to show how we could learn from his example and how bridges could be built from the most unlikely partnerships. A contingent from Hong Kong had come to attend the conference, and I was amazed to find some of them had brought copies of *Thistle and Bamboo* for me to sign. One of them, Robert Nield, suggested it was time to see the book in print once more. The first edition had sold out within a couple of years of publication and copies were fetching very high prices on the rare book market. It is largely thanks to Robert's efforts that you are reading this now.

The Weihai people had brought others to the conference, including Sir James's great-grandson, Clive, and businessman Duncan Clark's grandson, Duncan. What a joy to sit down of an evening in Weihai having a drink with these two men. Sir James would have enjoyed the connection. There were other surprises in Weihai. My driver's father had been Johnston's gardener when he was Commissioner. Another delegate had actually attended the rendition ceremony. Unfortunately, he was just five at the time and only remembered the swagger of the soldiers' kilts. It was a wonderful visit, which allowed me to see the surrounding area, and I only hope it is not my last time in a very special part of China. It also led to the Archives Bureau publishing my first book in Chinese: a translation of the full Johnston biography. How ironic that it can be read in its complete version in Chinese but not in English! I cannot help feeling, however, that Johnston would approve, and, as it has the seal of Chinese governmental approval, it is available throughout China. Not a bad achievement for a Scottish lass.

While in China, I took the opportunity to return to Xi'an, where I spent a happy time exploring Shaanxi, especially the places Johnston had visited. I have wandered on the silk road and stood in temples he stayed in, all thanks to the hospitality of the Terracotta Museum. I then ventured alone into Sichuan Province and traced his steps up sacred mountains, monuments and temples. Johnston does not mention seeing pandas there, but I did.

I love China and the Chinese with the same passion that Sir James and Johnston had. But I do not think I could have visited the country with my eyes quite so open had I not studied their lives so closely. One final, extraordinary, friendship has occurred because of this book. An exhibition of the Qufu photographs from the collection was shown in Dulwich, London. As a result, the gallery was asked to put Jeni Hong in touch with me. It sounded intriguing. It was far more than that. Jeni is the mother of the newest generation of the Kong clan. Her son, James, will one day perform the rites for his illustrious ancestor, Confucius, in Qufu. What a pleasure it was to be able to invite them to my home! I know Sir James would have been so proud to see us together.

The book has not only enriched my life. Mike and Ben, to whom it is dedicated, have also enjoyed many of the wonderful connections I have made because of *Thistle and Bamboo*. So, thank you Sir James and Sir Reginald. You have filled my life with friendships and experiences I never dreamed I would have.

Shiona M. Airlie
Lanarkshire, Scotland
August 2010

PREFACE TO THE ORIGINAL EDITION

SERENDIPITY brought me to Stewart Lockhart when, more than a decade ago, a charming gentleman who knew of my interest in Chinese art invited me to see some Chinese paintings held in an Edinburgh school, George Watson's College. The paintings were of great beauty and inspired me to delve further into the collection, discovering as I did so that the works of art were only one small part of a much larger whole which reflected the life of an extraordinary man: Sir James Stewart Lockhart. Since that first afternoon of discovery, the Stewart Lockhart Collection and my guide to it have remained an absorbing part of my life. The charming gentleman became my husband and the collection of papers, paintings and coins the mainstay of my research ever since.

The Stewart Lockhart Collection is indeed a strange one, and encountering it for the first time is rather like rummaging through someone else's attic: one is never sure what will next appear. James Stewart Lockhart was obviously a man who found it difficult to throw anything away, and his magpie instincts today serve historians well. It is a collection which tells the tale, in a most vivid way, of one man's life in China through the objects, papers and ephemera he gathered together over the years. It is also a collection about life; nowhere does one find a single mention of his death. For example, there are no obituary notices and no letters of condolence. For these pieces of information one has to search elsewhere. It is almost as though, in an effort to keep his memory alive, his family deliberately destroyed anything which signified the end of James Stewart Lockhart. They need not have feared, for Stewart Lockhart's name is one unlikely to fade into obscurity.

That a colonial official's collection of personal papers and art should end up in an Edinburgh school is a tale in itself. The final placing of the collection — indeed, the very existence of the collection in its present intact state — owes much to the efforts of Sir James' daughter, Mary. Mary adored her father and it was to his daughter that Sir James bequeathed his collection of Chinese paintings. The remainder of what is now known as the

Stewart Lockhart Collection, including his papers and vast numismatic holdings, passed to his wife, Lady Edith, and on her death to Mary. In 1967, Mary decided to donate her father's collection to his former school, George Watson's College. The school's governing body, The Merchant Company Education Board, formally accepted the gift and lodged the collection in the school. It is The Merchant Company Education Board who placed the bulk of the papers on loan to the National Library of Scotland, thereby facilitating access for scholars, whilst the school retains the collection of paintings, coins and photographs, as well as the papers relating specifically to those particular aspects of the collection.

Just before her death in 1985, Mary Stewart Lockhart gave the remainder of her father's papers to The Merchant Company Education Board as well. This final gift includes all the family's personal letters to survive from Sir James's lifetime and is deposited with the art collection at George Watson's College. The Stewart Lockhart Collection owned by The Merchant Company Education Board has been the foundation for much of my research into the life of Sir James. Though uncatalogued, the seventy boxes of papers in the National Library of Scotland and the various chests and cases of papers at George Watson's College provide a vital, and quite comprehensive, range of information about Sir James. Included in these are his personal letters which exist in sufficient quantity to give a marvellous insight into his life and times.

I have been particularly fortunate to have had the unstinting support of The Merchant Company Education Board in my research, for they have given me the opportunity to spend an unlimited amount of time working with the collection they now own. The former Principal of George Watson's College, Sir Roger Young, was equally supportive of my efforts and untiring in his assistance, spurring me on to dig deeper and learn more. His successor, Mr Frank Gerstenberg, continues to make access to the collection readily available to me, for which I am most grateful. My gratitude also goes to the staff of the National Library of Scotland, and in particular to Dr Thomas Rae, Keeper of Manuscripts, who offered me every assistance throughout this long project.

But the Stewart Lockhart Papers are only one bank of source material. Few scholars seem to have tapped another major source in Edinburgh, that of The Stewart Society. Mary Stewart Lockhart gave certain family papers to them, and although most of the papers concern the Stewart heritage, and include many early family manuscripts dating from the seventeenth century, nuggets of information regarding Weihaiwei and Stewart Lockhart's friend and colleague, Reginald F. Johnston, are also to be found in this particular trove. In common with The Merchant Company Education Board holdings, the papers lie uncatalogued in folders and I am grateful to Mr Douglas Stewart, former Honorary Secretary of The Stewart Society, for so readily granting me access to their collection.

The main collection of official papers lies in the Public Record Office at Kew where the various Colonial Office and Foreign Office Series provide a fascinating insight into official machinations during Stewart Lockhart's career in Hong Kong and Weihaiwei, and are a perfect foil to the personal papers in Edinburgh. I am indebted to the staff at the Public Record Office for all their courtesy and help; their enthusiasm for the manuscripts and records in their care make it one of the most pleasant working environments imaginable.

Useful duplicate material relating to Hong Kong is also available in the History Department at the University of Hong Kong, and I likewise wish to thank the staff at this institution for the assistance they gave me when I first began my research.

Every effort was made to trace the copyright holders of letters belonging to the Stewart Lockhart Collection. Mary Stewart Lockhart passed her possession of copyright to The Merchant Company Education Board when she gifted them the collection. Mr Tse Kwok Cheong, descendant of Tse Tsan T'ai, and General Ho Shai Lai, son of Sir Robert Ho Tung, are thanked for their generous permission to reproduce family papers held in the Stewart Lockhart Collection. General Ho and his wife, Hesta, are due special thanks for their support in this project and I shall treasure the memories of our meeting in Hong Kong when they freely gave information to me about the Stewart Lockhart family.

The copyright of the Stewart Lockhart papers, his photographs, and art collection belongs to The Merchant Company Education Board, and it is a pleasure to record my thanks to them for their permission to use both photographs and letters from the collection. As copyright holders of all the work from the hands of Sir James, Lady Edith, and Mary Stewart Lockhart, this volume could not have been written without their support. In this area, Mr William McDonald, Secretary and Chamberlain to The Company of Merchants of The City of Edinburgh, is due particular gratitude for the patient way in which he has coped with my many requests for assistance.

Countless individuals have assisted me in numerous ways as I have continued my research. I particularly wish to acknowledge the assistance given to me, in myriad forms, by Mr Maurice Berrill, Miss Margaret Shaw, Mr Iain Airlie, Miss Elizabeth Airlie, Miss Caroline McAuley, Mr Neil Sutherland, Mr Michael de Havilland, Reverend David Day of St Adamnan's in Duror, and Jane and Robert Taylor, who now own Ardsheal House.

During the final years of her life, Mary Stewart Lockhart gave me every help and encouragement. When a fact needed verifying, she was there to conjure up from her astonishing memory the required information. It is through her father's collection that her own reputation lives on and I pay tribute to a great and remarkable lady.

My husband and son must be thanked for their patience and support which I hope is repaid in some small way by my dedication of this book to them. I am also truly indebted to Norman and Jill Macdonald. They gave me a haven in which to write when I needed it. That this book has reached fruition is as much due to the serenity of their cottage 'Half of Two' as it is to my own efforts.

Throughout this book, the Pinyin system of romanization is used for all Chinese terms, except for Cantonese proper names. The Wade-Giles system appears in brackets after the first usage of each word in the main text. The romanizations from both systems may be found in the index.

In July 1989 the Merchant Company Education Board plans to disperse the Stewart Lockhart Coin Collection through public auction, by selling the coins in individual lots.

Shiona M. Airlie
Edinburgh
April 1989

Chapter 1

GOOD ABILITIES
(1858–1879)

'THE measure of a man's success is not only his words nor even his popularity but largely the example he leaves behind. In your dealings not only with us but with the Chinese you have left behind an example which it will be difficult to follow and which won't be surpassed.'[1] Words of high praise are not easy to earn, and, perhaps, even less easy to live up to. Yet this compliment was only one of many given to a British colonial official who considered, one suspects, that he had just been 'doing his job' for Britain in Asia for almost half a century. Exactly what made James Stewart Lockhart so different, so special, and so deserving of esteem from his colleagues and acquaintances was that he set an example as a colonial civil servant which few could equal. Throughout his life, he strove to be best — not necessarily a merit in itself — but, more importantly, he did so with a firm set of ideals which, while not to be equated with missionary zeal, had a profound effect on the territories in which he worked.

In an age when it is fashionable to criticize nineteenth-century British imperialism and to deplore the attitude of many colonial officials towards the people in their charge, it is invigorating to encounter a man who lived during the height of imperialism, was part of that system, and yet was refreshingly different in his outlook. Respected by his colleagues, admired by the people with whom he worked, James Stewart Lockhart was not only a sinologist of considerable repute, but also a member of the British Colonial Service in Hong Kong and China for forty years. A hard-working Scot, he was to see his career blossom as Hong Kong's flourished under British rule, and his ambitions fade, as Britain's did, in China, during the faltering years following the fall of the Qing (Ch'ing) dynasty. One of a band of extremely able Britons whose administrative and intellectual ability were to prove to be the backbone of the British Colonial Service, his background was similar to those of countless others who had expanded and consolidated the British Empire since its inception; but his talent, particularly as a colonial servant, was a rare one.

The British Empire at its height provided an enormous employment market for young men in trade, the army, or in government service. A complex governmental system had developed from the seventeenth century onwards: from the time when the foundations of the British Empire were being laid. In the early days of empire-building, the British Government and the Crown took little direct action themselves to establish the colonies which were instead largely the work of 'court favourites on the make, chartered companies in search of profits, or protesting groups looking for sanctuary'.[2] In succeeding centuries, British rule of foreign territories gradually became regularized under the control of government bodies; and although the merchants and adventurers were still of immense importance in an empire which thrived upon capitalism, government departments, such as the Colonial Office, required the continuous export of large numbers of able young men from the shores of Britain to her colonies in order to ensure the smooth running of these territories. Merchants and administrators worked hand in hand, though not always with total amiability, to establish a British base of operations in the farthest flung parts of the globe. Frequently working in immensely trying conditions, these men had to be quick witted — and often quite ruthless — to survive, let alone succeed. Their backgrounds were as varied as their talents, but large numbers were Scottish in origin. 'Education in Scotland was better than in England ... but the younger sons of the lower gentry had fewer opportunities to make an acceptable living in their own country than their counterparts in England.'[3] Having received all the benefits a Scottish education system could bestow, with its well established system of village schools serving all, the sons of the middle classes, as well as the younger sons of the impoverished Scots nobility, flocked to join one of the available colonial services, or one of the many companies trading within the empire throughout the nineteenth century.

A declining Scottish economy helped to establish a tradition of emigration from Scotland, a tradition which varied in extent with each decade's varying fortunes from the seventeenth century and beyond. As a result, the idea of settling half-way across the world was treated with an acceptance not necessarily found in the more affluent parts of Europe. Some areas of the British Empire became miniature Scotias, with traders and administrators being linked not only through nationality but also in many cases through family and school connections. The Scottish scholastic system served its pupils well in preparation for civil service examinations; and in some Scottish schools a higher percentage of pupils entered the British civil service, either at home or abroad, during the last three decades of the nineteenth century, than entered almost any other profession.[4]

The early life and career of James Stewart Lockhart was to follow the course taken by many of his contemporaries: a comprehensive and intensive education in Scotland followed by a move to the other side of the world to work with his countrymen in the service of Britain. In his life can be seen the reflection of countless other British administrators, but in his attitude to the people over whom he held power, he was very different.

Stewart Lockhart was born on 25 May 1858 at his maternal uncle's estate of Ardsheal in Argyll, north-west Scotland. The fourth son, and the sixth of nine children, he was born into a family of some wealth and social status, and his first two christian names reflected this, originating as they did from a paternal relation, the Reverend James Haldane, Bishop of Argyll and the Isles. His paternal grandfather had been a successful London banker with the firm of Ingram, Piggot and Lockhart, and his father, Miles Lockhart, had no need of a career, having sufficient private means at his disposal to enable him to be a gentleman of leisure. In his youth, Miles spent some time in Europe, including an extended stay in Holland where 'he lived at Haarlem ... and there spoke Dutch like a native!'[5] Later, a good marriage was made with Anna Stewart, niece and heiress of Charles Stewart, last Laird of Ardsheal.[6] Whereas the Lockharts were a family of financial standing, the Stewarts had something more to offer: they had history in their blood and were related to the ancient and noble Stewart clan with its strong Jacobite associations.

The Stewart ancestry was deeply important to Stewart Lockhart, so much so, that when he became married, he incorporated his Stewart forename into his surname. To this day, his surviving family are known by the name 'Stewart Lockhart'.[7]

Miles Lockhart's marriage further enhanced his social standing, but it also had one unfortunate consequence. Presuming (incorrectly) that his son had married a woman of considerable private means, Miles's father left him very little money when he died. As a result, the younger sons of the next generation had to go out into the world to earn their living when they reached adulthood, for their Stewart mother's inheritance was composed largely of memories and mementos rather than of money.

James's early life, however, was hardly one which could be described as deprived or impecunious. Much of his childhood was spent in the Stewart family home of Ardsheal where a large, twelve-bedroomed house sat on the shores of Loch Linnhe, surrounded by 800 acres of forest and hills. Ardsheal was a treasure-house of Jacobite relics belonging to the family. Few of these passed to James Stewart Lockhart, but amongst the Jacobite heritage which surrounded him as a child, and which he did inherit, was the ring of Charles Stuart, Pretender to the British throne, a Jacobite snuff box, the Commission given by James VIII of Scotland to Charles Stewart of Ardsheal, and a multitude of documents relating to the history of the Stewart clan.[8]

James Stewart Lockhart's initial education probably took place at Ardsheal, where he was brought up like a young highland laird, speaking Gaelic as his first language.[9] However, when the Lockharts moved southwards, some time before 1868, James was sent to a Dame's School.[10] By August 1868, the family were living in Clifton House on the Isle of Man and that summer James was enrolled at one of the major schools on the island, King William's College. This independent school for boys had been founded in 1833 from an existing theological college with the intention of 'establishing a place of general education in the island'.[11] James was to stay there until July 1872 and studied, in accordance with the initial purpose of the college, a broad academic curriculum. The school day was filled with the study of Classics, English, French, and Mathematics, and in addition pupils undertook scientific experiments in a newly opened laboratory. Progress reports for each of the 115 pupils were issued every quarter by the college and Stewart Lockhart's show that he was a bright child who displayed a particular aptitude for languages.[12] When he left King William's, his headmaster wrote about him in terms of unqualified satisfaction: 'his conduct was uniformly satisfactory and his progress in his studies rapid and great. He was most diligent and attentive, possessed of good abilities, and carried off at different times several prizes against considerable competition'.[13]

Although his stay at King William's was a relatively short one, and forms only a small part of his long life, this school meant much to him. Ultimately, the Stewart Lockhart Collection of personal papers, art, and artefacts was to be given to the administrative body of his senior school, George Watson's College. As a result, it is easy to underestimate the strength of his feelings for King William's. The island school, however, had its own old boy network which extended to China and in later years some of these former pupils were to band together to provide a gift for the college. The story is related in a school magazine:

Four men found themselves in conversation in a well-known Club in China. A remark by one led to the discovery that each had been educated at K. W. C. To celebrate this remarkable coincidence, they decided to present the College a cup to be called the 'China Cup', which is now presented to the best 'all-rounder' in the school.[14]

Stewart Lockhart was one of those four men. When the China Cup was first presented in 1907, the group of four had contacted several other former pupils and finally ten donors subscribed to the trophy.

The network of people who had a former school or university in common was one which bound British officials and merchants together even in the most remote parts of the globe. It was rare, for example, for 'new men' arriving in Hong Kong to be without any contacts created through the education system, and many such connections were further strengthened by family ties. These links did not necessarily increase one's opportunities for promotion or advancement, but they did grant an automatic acceptance from, and entry into, certain social circles.

In the summer of 1872, the Lockharts left the Isle of Man and moved back to Scotland. Initially, they lived on the outskirts of Edinburgh, although it was not long before they acquired a house within the city boundaries. Edinburgh contained several good schools and James was enrolled at one of the largest, George Watson's College, situated near the centre of town. With a school roll of over a thousand boys, this large establishment might have overwhelmed many a boy. Yet Stewart Lockhart flourished in the busy environment provided there. Like King William's College, Watson's had a fine academic tradition and it also encouraged a strong competitive spirit on the sporting field. Stewart Lockhart was able to make full use of both the physical and academic opportunities. Although he never forgot King William's, the impression given by Stewart Lockhart himself was that it was George Watson's which made the most lasting mark upon him. In 1909, he wrote to the school magazine, *The Watsonian*, enclosing a photograph of himself and his schoolmates of 1874 and including some reminiscences from that time. The memories of his masters must have been tempered by the years, but as a schoolboy he had flourished under their care and he recalled them with great fondness:

Those were the days of Ogilvie the Great, whose sweetness of disposition, extraordinary knowledge of the boys, and genius for organisation have left behind them an influence and a memory that will never die. Of the many masters who so ably assisted him I remember 'Jimmy' Blyth, skilled in mathematics and science, upon whose good nature some of us too frequently imposed: 'Traddles' Wilson who drove arithmetic into us with a ruthless but clever hand: MacClennan, whose kindly nature and literary gifts were not appreciated as they should have been by 'the young barbarians all at play' in his class: Calder with flashing eye who made the geography of South Africa a living terror, and who first revealed to us the existence of the Limpopo: Robson, the polyglot, as benign as he was linguistic: Oudet, 'the gentleman of France', whose culture made him respected even by those who were inclined to regard a teacher of French as 'fair game'! Sellar, the athletic, who was almost better at football and cricket than at Classics. But of all the henchmen of Ogilvie the Great, he who had the greatest influence on those under him was 'Tommy' Stewart, the senior Classical master.[15]

The subjects at which he excelled were Classics and Games. It seems, however, that he was highly competitive in all subjects, and once told his daughter Mary that 'I always liked to be top of my class'.[16] Noted above all for his ability in Classics, he attained the highest academic honour the college could bestow when, in 1874, he became joint dux of the school.[17] A contemporary of his from Watson's later wrote that 'He was an excellent Grecian and gained prizes and medals galore.'[18] But his achievements were not limited to the classroom alone, and in the same year that he became dux, Stewart Lockhart not only had contributions accepted by the school's literary magazine but also captained the first teams in both cricket and rugby. To this day, he is considered to have been one of the best all-round sportsmen the school has ever produced.[19] In James Stewart Lockhart, George Watson's College found a boy who was the embodiment of all that was best in the school.

His schooldays wreathed in glory, Stewart Lockhart left Watson's to embark upon a course of study at the University of Edinburgh. He enrolled there in September 1874 and chose Greek as his main subject, with Rhetoric and English Literature as a subsidiary course. By the end of his first year, he had gained certificates of merit in all subjects, and during the following session gained further academic distinction when he was awarded the Gold Medal for first prize in Greek. The same year, 1876, he also gained a first class merit from the English department, an indication of his potential to achieve a first class degree.[20] In addition to his studies he continued to play sport with enthusiasm, representing the university in their rugby football team from 1874 to 1876. He could have sat his degree examinations in the 1876–77 session, but did not enrol at the university that year, and seems instead to have unsuccessfully entered the open competition for the Civil Service of India. Nowadays, students generally prefer to complete their further education before seeking employment, whereas far less emphasis was placed on the possession of a degree in the late nineteenth century. Today, it is virtually impossible to reach a senior professional grade in the British civil service without a university qualification, but in the 1870s the recently introduced competitive examination was the most common form of entry into the service and, as a result, some young men with proven academic ability halted their university careers mid-way when given the opportunity to compete for a position in one of its many branches.

By this time, Stewart Lockhart was eighteen — an adult in the eyes of many — and he would have been well aware that it was imperative to find a career for himself if he was to survive financially in the long term. Perhaps his father was also pressing him to begin a move towards financial independence and the result was this year away from university attempting to gain admittance into his chosen field: the Indian Service. India seems to have been chosen partly because some of Miles Lockhart's family were already working there. This was not unusual, as huge numbers of upper and upper-middle class Britons were involved either commercially, militarily, or diplomatically in the Indian subcontinent. (The Indian connection was also to continue in the next generation of Lockharts, with one of James's brothers, Robert, who spent the greater part of his working life there.)[21] The subcontinent must have had further attraction for the young Stewart Lockhart as it was undoubtedly, in the 1870s, Britain's premier colonial outpost. By then, the British Empire had reached its commercial high point and was continuing to expand its colonial administration. For a youth with the academic potential Stewart Lockhart clearly possessed, the India Office was an obvious choice as it offered the possibility of excellent career advancement. However, given the career potential and prestige of working for the civil service in India, competition for places (which were very few) was extremely fierce.

After this first unsuccessful attempt to enter colonial administration, Stewart Lockhart returned to Edinburgh where he lived in the fashionable Georgian New Town, once more enrolling at Edinburgh University where, in September 1877, he commenced a further year of study. The twelve-month lapse in his academic career appears to have had an adverse effect on his grades, for no merits or prizes were collected by him during this session. It is not even certain that he completed his final year, as the university records show no examination passes for him during it. It is known from civil service results that he once more attempted the entrance examination for the Indian Civil Service in April 1878, in the middle of the university year, and the renewed attempt to gain admittance into this profession is the likeliest explanation for his failure to complete the degree in Greek. Once more, he was unsuccessful in the highly competitive examination, ranking only thirty-seventh in a field of sixty-nine candidates.[22]

The home civil service, the Civil Service of India and the Colonial Office were open to applicants through a system of examinations. Young men presented themselves for examination in a variety of subjects, both compulsory and optional, and Stewart Lockhart's results show him to have been rather unprepared for the high standards which were expected in the Indian Civil Service examinations. He failed all eight papers he attempted, and even in his strongest subject, Greek, achieved only 143 marks out of a possible 750.[23] A career in India may have been his first choice, but Stewart Lockhart was sufficiently realistic to realise that other options might be more easily accessible to him. Although the India Service was, at that time, the premier one within the British Empire, other areas were offering equally promising career prospects to men of suitable ability, though they lacked the cachet of colonial India. Three months after his failure in the India exam, Stewart Lockhart turned to pastures new and applied to sit the examination for entry into the Colonial Office as a trainee official in either Hong Kong or Ceylon, for which a single examination was to be held.[24]

The Colonial Office did not emerge as an independent government department until 1854. For half a century before that it had been incorporated into the Department of War and it was not until it became an office in its own right that rationalization of administration in British colonies was dealt with in any systematic manner.[25] Throughout the decades following 1854 the various parts of the British Empire were introduced to forms of administration which accorded as closely as was feasible with those used in the home civil service; and in 1862, in line with a general move towards administrative reforms within the empire as a whole, Hong Kong Cadetships were created 'with a view to supply Interpreters and other Civil Officers in Hong Kong'.[26] Sir John Bowring, Governor of Hong Kong from 1854–9, was the first to promote the idea of 'a cadet scheme to supply the Consular service in China with the necessary language training'.[27] This scheme was introduced into mainland China almost immediately, but it was not until Bowring's successor, Sir Hercules Robinson, took office, that a similar system was introduced into the Hong Kong administration. Robinson used Bowring's scheme as the basis for the structure of Hong Kong Cadetships. The objective for these was that men should come from Britain and learn the Chinese language to a sufficiently high standard to work without the aid of an interpreter. The idea was approved by the British Government in 1861 and the first cadets arrived in Hong Kong the following year.

With a population which was dominated, in numerical terms,

by the Chinese, the Hong Kong administration was, by 1860, in desperate need of officials who could work with the local Chinese without always requiring an interpreter by their side. The judiciary were particularly hard pressed and it was intended, when the Cadet Scheme first began, that cadets should work within this department and thereafter become eligible for senior posts within the broader administration.[28] It is some indication of the need within the territory for Chinese-speaking officials that when, in 1860, the posts of Chief and Assistant Magistrate were abolished and replaced by two Police Magistrates, a knowledge of Chinese was deemed of greater importance than a knowledge of law for appointment to these positions.[29] As a result, when cadets were appointed, their services as Chinese speakers were required so urgently that few cadets completed their Chinese studies without having to combine them with some administrative post.

With the exception of the first few cadets, who had travelled to Hong Kong as soon as they were appointed, cadets commenced their training in London where they spent a year learning Chinese at King's College in central London. There, on Tuesday and Friday evenings, intensive Chinese language courses were taught.[30] Simultaneously, the cadets, who had to be aged between 20 and 23, spent 'some hours daily at the Colonial Office in the work of the Department'.[31] It was an exacting first year, and for their labours they received an annual salary of £100; just enough to sustain them above subsistence level. At the end of the year they were examined in Chinese and, given a successful result, were sent to Hong Kong where they continued their study of the language. In both London and China cadets were housed, tutored, and provided with books at the government's expense. In return they were expected to sit and pass an examination in Chinese every six months while at the same time undertaking some small duties within the administration, thereby preparing themselves for full-time work in the Government of Hong Kong once their two years or so of cadetship were completed.

The introduction of the Cadet Scheme marked the beginning of a new phase in Hong Kong's government, initiating a structure for the training of professional government personnel and greatly reducing the administration's reliance upon untrained and often unreliable men who were employed by virtue of the fact that no one else was available. In time, the Cadet Scheme was to result in 'a quota of officials much more interested in the affairs of the Chinese community and in the language, culture, civilization, and history of China than was true of their predecessors'.[32] In no instance is this observation more apposite than with regard to Stewart Lockhart.

In the autumn of 1878 an examination was held for two Ceylon Writerships and two Hong Kong Cadetships. Stewart Lockhart, in obtaining fourth place in the examination, was offered a posting as a Hong Kong Cadet, the first two candidates having elected to enter the service in Ceylon.[33] The examination involved a series of tests. His compulsory papers included exercises in Handwriting, English Composition and Précis Writing, Arithmetic, Latin and French. (One of the options for the compulsory language paper was Greek and it should be noted that he chose not to be examined in it, perhaps as a result of his poor showing in the India examination.) He was also presented in four optional papers in History, Constitutional and International Law, Political Economy, and Geography. He scored a pass mark or better in all but the last two papers.[34]

The cadet post must have held considerable attraction for Stewart Lockhart as the regulations stipulated that he would have to learn Chinese, and he had already exhibited a talent for languages, the occasional exam lapse in Greek excepting. Hong Kong may itself have seemed appealing, for although it was half-way across the world and was recognized as a place of uncompromising climate and unhealthy conditions — complete with regular visitations of the plague — it was also an area in which a number of Scottish entrepreneurs, including some distant relatives of his, had already staked successful economic claims. He can, however, have had little access to specific public information about the territory or his appointment. India and Africa generated far greater interest with the British public in the 1870s than did the rocky trading post on the edge of China. Even the British parliament rarely debated China, concentrating its parliamentary energies instead on India and South Africa. The notes of guidance issued by the Colonial Office gave no information about the territory; indeed, they provided only the minimum of information about the Cadetship, relating merely the bare essentials regarding pay and conditions. As only seven cadets had previously been appointed, and the last of these as far back as 1867, Stewart Lockhart must have felt that he was to some extent venturing into unknown territory.

His appointment was confirmed by Sir Michael Hicks Beach, Disraeli's Secretary of State for the Colonies, on 25 November 1878,[35] and followed the reintroduction of Cadetships after a decade's lapse under Hicks Beach's predecessor, Lord Carnarvon. The appointment of cadets from Britain had been halted in an effort to save money and Sir Arthur Kennedy, Hong Kong's Governor from 1872–7, had actually gone so far as to propose the disbanding of the scheme. Chinese-speaking officials were still, of course, required within the administration, and Kennedy intended to recruit men locally to fill the appointments. The first of the locally recruited interpreters was the son of a missionary in Guangzhou (Canton), J. Dyer Ball. A Cantonese speaker, Dyer Ball carried out his tasks efficiently,[36] but Lord Carnarvon eventually overruled Kennedy's plan of using local men, being of the opinion that, while reasonable interpreters might indeed be recruited from Hong Kong and Guangzhou, few would have sufficient education to assume senior posts within the government. He therefore reinstated the Cadetship scheme. Carnarvon also made a few amendments to the training of cadets, the main reform being that instead of going directly to Hong Kong as soon as they were appointed, cadets now had to spend a year in London learning Chinese. Accordingly, Stewart Lockhart was informed that although he now bore the title 'Hong Kong Cadet', he would 'not be called upon to proceed to that Colony for at least a year'.[37]

Stewart Lockhart began his training as a cadet on 1 January 1879 in London, where he attended the class for students of Chinese at King's College. There, the Professor of Chinese, Robert Douglas, taught him the rudiments of the language, although the young student had also to spend much time in the Colonial Office in Whitehall, acquainting himself with the techniques of the British civil servant. Stewart Lockhart was installed in the West Indian section, part of the same division which had responsibility for Hong Kong, where his duties involved logging daily despatches and arranging for their reply.[38] Part-time lecturing not only suited the Colonial Office, whose overstretched staff were always able gainfully to employ an extra pair of hands;[39] it also permitted Robert Douglas to continue his work at the British Museum where he was a Senior Assistant in the Department of Printed Books. His student was an enthusiastic one who threw himself wholeheartedly into the subject. Determined to prove himself, almost from the start as a sinologist, Stewart Lockhart began by being elected as a member of the illustrious Royal Asiatic Society in the summer of 1879.

He would have expected to remain in London until the early part of 1880, but his aptitude for languages was undiminished and by September 1879 he had progressed sufficiently in the study of Chinese to have passed an initial examination in the language. As a result, on 2 October 1879, he sailed out of Southampton on the S. S. *Khedive* on the six-week journey to Hong Kong, the colony which was to be his home for the next twenty-three years. He was moving into one of Britain's most isolationist civil services. In both the China Service and the Government of Hong Kong, a thorough knowledge of Chinese was an essential prerequisite to promotion. The cadet system ensured officers were well trained, but a knowledge of Cantonese or Mandarin was generally too good to waste in another part of the world, and Stewart Lockhart must have been aware from the outset that in passing the entrance exam for the Cadetship, he was moving towards a lifetime's career in the Far East, a completely foreign land.

Chapter 2

A RIGOROUS TRAINING
(1879–1884)

STEWART Lockhart's entrance into Hong Kong on 18 November 1879 could hardly have passed unnoticed by the European community there. New arrivals were announced in the newspaper and the arrival of a cadet after so many years without any of these junior officials in the colony was a particularly newsworthy event. *The China Mail* of 17 November 1879 disclosed 'the arrival by the English Mail Steamer of Mr Lockhart, a young gentleman who has been studying Chinese in London for sometime and who comes out here as a Cadet for the Hong Kong Government'. His first action was to report to the Colonial Secretary who informed him that he would begin his duties, as was customary, by spending a few weeks in the colony becoming acquainted with the administration as a whole. In addition, Hong Kong's newest cadet would have been introduced to the other 'young bloods' of the island — a mixed bag of young men, no doubt, encompassing a variety of occupations ranging from the military to the mercantile. However, Stewart Lockhart had little opportunity to indulge himself in Hong Kong's emerging social scene for, after a brief respite from the rigours of travel, he was on his way once more; this time to Guangzhou to continue his Chinese studies.

The regulations regarding his Cadetship were laid out quite clearly in the notes sent to him when he first applied for a Cadetship. Quarters, books and teachers were supplied by the government, which gave him an annual allowance of HK$168 for a teacher of Chinese and HK$540 for his Guangzhou lodgings.[1] Provided he passed his half yearly examinations, the Governor, his ultimate superior, need show no concern. Meanwhile, the cadet could enjoy life in the Chinese city to its full, a life which included 'the varied attractions of two fair missionary damsels ... whose charms I had to resist by frequent doses of Confucius and Mencius'.[2]

Guangzhou is approximately eighty miles north-west of Hong Kong, and cadets normally lodged there in a yamen within the city walls.[3] Life for Stewart Lockhart, given his sense of adventure, must have been relatively pleasant, despite the sordid and filthy state of the city.[4] Invitations to dinner lightened the serious business of study, added to which he must have found it quite exhilarating to be in this new environment. His colleagues in Guangzhou were to remain close friends for the rest of his life and they included some illustrious names. Sir John Jordan, later the most senior official, as British Minister, in Beijing (Peking), started his working life as an assistant in Guangzhou and is referred to as 'my old friend ... whom I knew more than 25 years ago at Canton'.[5] Other friendships cemented in Guangzhou were with Sir Charles Addis, who became British Consul in Tianjin (Tientsin) and, latterly, Chairman of the Hongkong and Shanghai Banking Corporation, and E. H. Parker, an official in the China Service who became Reader of Chinese at the University of Manchester and then at the University of Liverpool after his retirement from the service in 1895.

It is Parker who provides the greatest volume of information about those days in Guangzhou, and it was he who organized a Cantonese teacher for Stewart Lockhart.[6] In 1874, Parker had employed a certain Ouyang Hui (Ou-yang Hui) as a private tutor of Cantonese. This arrangement had continued when Parker returned to Guangzhou in 1878 and was still in existence when Stewart Lockhart arrived in the city at the end of 1879. Balding, but with a long queue, the ageing tutor was to make a great impression on the young Scot who was later to describe him as 'my faithful old teacher'.[7] Addis and Stewart Lockhart called their tutor Old Au; Parker employed the different spelling 'Ow' and described this formidable teacher at length.

He was a little, thin man with a tremendous nose and deep, raucous voice, through which instruments he emitted with clarion precision the then still but half-understood Cantonese syllables; and above all the tones — eighteen of them: it was almost like the braying of a jackass ... He had once been employed as a ... secretary, in Hu Nan; but apparently his rigid and Diogenes-like virtue had failed to advance his material interests. He was, in one sense, a sort of Chinese Carlyle, always denouncing humbugs and pretenders; extolling the ancient sages, and full of ceremony, funerals, reverence for 'bones', and all manner of Confucian characteristics such as the 'superior man' ought to delight in.[8]

Parker's recollection of Stewart Lockhart's arrival in Guangzhou is vivid and, as both men remained in regular contact into the twentieth century, one can assume that Parker's reminiscences are accurate; certainly, Stewart Lockhart never contradicted them. Following the new cadet's arrival in Guangzhou, Parker remembers: 'I lent him 'Old Ow', who took the youngster up country and taught him Cantonese very well. A year or two later the old man was carried off by his new patron to the barbarian stronghold of Hongkong, and given employment in the Registrar General's department.'[9]

Apart from several trips back to Hong Kong to work for short periods in the administration, Stewart Lockhart remained with Ouyang Hui until 1882. Old Au was a hard task master; Parker remembers him beginning lessons at 5 a.m.,[10] and it may be that this habit of rising early and beginning work early was first learned by Stewart Lockhart from Old Au in Guangzhou. Certainly, during his life in Hong Kong and later in Weihaiwei he was noted as being an early riser. His daughter, Mary, recalled how he would be up at 5 a.m. in the summer and would immediately set out to work on the verandah of their home before going to the office to begin his official duties.[11] It should be noted, however, that this praiseworthy existence had its lapsed periods. On his return to Hong Kong as a Passed Cadet, Stewart Lockhart admitted that as he was 'at the office from 9.30 a.m. to 5 p.m. there is not over-much time for my Chinese studies'.[12] This loss of stamina did not last long and he was quickly recognized within the Colonial Office as displaying 'wonderful industry'.[13]

Not only did Old Au insist that pupils work long and hard, he also expected them to give him the respect due by every pupil to his teacher in China. Pupils were taught to treat their tutors with extreme deference and this custom extended to all pupils, no matter how exalted their rank. Reginald Johnston, at one time a Scottish tutor to the last Emperor of China, explained how the system worked in the imperial classroom.

Another mark of respect shown by the emperor to each of his tutors — even the barbarian from overseas — was to rise when the tutor entered the room. The tutor advanced to the middle of the room, bowed once, and emperor and tutor then sat down simultaneously in their proper places. If the tutor, in the course of the lesson-hours, had occasion to rise for the purpose of fetching a book from a shelf or for any other reason, the emperor rose too, and remained standing till the tutor returned to his place.[14]

Old Au retained the same code of respect, and no pupil would dare talk to him until he was seated. The months spent with this daunting teacher were Stewart Lockhart's first experience of Chinese etiquette and custom, and these early lessons were ones which he mastered with meticulous care. In later years, his knowledge of Chinese etiquette and manners for every occasion was to help him immeasurably in his dealings not only with important Chinese in Hong Kong but also with the various Governors and senior officials he met in Shandong (Shantung) Province during his career in Weihaiwei. He would study the smallest detail of correct etiquette and made copious notes regarding the acceptable custom for every conceivable event, applying this knowledge when appropriate circumstances arose.[15] Even the Colonial Office realized the importance of such studies, and cadets sat one of their final exams in the etiquette of Chinese society as recorded in ancient texts.[16]

Ouyang Hui was, of course, not only important because of his insistence upon industry and etiquette. Most crucial was his teaching of Cantonese. According to Stewart Lockhart, his teacher 'enjoyed a high reputation among several distinguished foreign students of Chinese for his power of ready and lucid explanation',[17] a sentiment shared by Parker. Robert Douglas, who was later knighted, had initiated the first forays into the study of Chinese, and for this Stewart Lockhart was always grateful. The two men maintained contact with one another during Stewart Lockhart's life in China, and Steward Lockhart continued to receive letters from him until 1907, when the health of his former teacher began to fail. It was Old Au, however, who introduced him to the joys of Chinese literature and Stewart Lockhart revered the man for giving him the key to this knowledge. It was a key which was to open many doors for the Scot, and for the rest of his life Stewart Lockhart was to be an avid student of all things Chinese. Old Au's tuition was to instigate a lifetime's sinological research, extending far beyond the confines of literature, language, and poetry to the history, custom, and culture of China. Stewart Lockhart began with all the advantages intellect and linguistic facility can bestow, but without the inspired wisdom of his Chinese tutor he might never have crossed the gap which separates an interested student from an expert sinologue.

Au's tuition was very broadly based. Under his watchful eye, Stewart Lockhart began by translating simple phrases from English into Chinese. Some of these early exercises survive in notebooks kept throughout the various collections of Stewart Lockhart's papers and show his early attempts at translating literary gems such as 'Lok gave Ow a book.'[18] At the same time, Au was introducing his pupil to Chinese thought and custom, and notes on the writings of Confucius and Mencius abound. It was Au who introduced Stewart Lockhart to the *Analects*, a text which was to be of immense significance to the young cadet who was to continue to study the great philosopher's ideas for the rest of his life. Notes were made about Confucius' life, his influence, his opinions, and his views on government. Confucius' ideal that an official should act as both father and mother to the people under his care was one which Stewart Lockhart took to heart, and, when he reached the higher ranks of officialdom — particularly in Weihaiwei where he had the opportunity to administer the territory himself — he regulated his official dealings with at least part of his mind fixed upon Confucian ideals. Simultaneously with the lessons on language and philosophy, Au introduced Stewart Lockhart to the customs and culture of Chinese society. Many of the earliest notes made as a result of these lessons concentrate on the rites surrounding marriage and death, areas of research which would be greatly expanded by Stewart Lockhart in later years.

As a break from the study of the ancient texts with their elegant turns of phrase, Au provided his cadet with the Chinese language newspapers. By 1881, Stewart Lockhart's knowledge of Chinese was sufficiently fluent that he could translate, admittedly with numerous corrections and alterations, the latest gossip from the Chinese press in Hong Kong and Guangzhou. Many of the articles concerned the Hong Kong administration, at that time headed by the controversial Governor, Sir John Pope Hennessy.[19] In his previous gubernatorial postings, which had ranged from Labuan in the East to the Bahamas in the West, Pope Hennessy's administrations had, without exception, been turbulent and eventful. His appointment as Governor of Hong Kong had been a surprising choice, for 'in the view of the Colonial Office, and of the local merchants, Hong Kong needed few improvements, and could offer small scope for Hennessy's revolutionary mind, and for his gift of stirring up a hornet's nest of opposition'.[20] Indeed, it seems likely that he had been given the posting for the very reason that Hong Kong was 'an unusually peaceful and prosperous Colony',[21] and therefore there would be little Pope Hennessy could do to upset the status quo. The Colonial Office were to be proved badly misguided in their assessment of the situation, and by the time Stewart Lockhart arrived in Hong Kong, the Governor had established himself as one of the most unpopular administrators the Colony had had in its short history. Because of his efforts to achieve greater equality for the Chinese, he had alienated most of the British merchants in Hong Kong although he had at the same time won the respect of some of the Chinese community there.

Towards the end of his career in Hong Kong, the news of a scandal between Pope Hennessy's wife and a local lawyer called Hayller broke in the local newspapers. In the autumn of 1881, the Governor made a visit to Beijing and before he left, gave his private secretary, Eitel,[22] permission to reveal private correspondence relating to the Hayller scandal. The scheme to discredit the lawyer backfired: Hayller served a writ on Eitel, and Eitel accordingly offered to resign from his post. The British community, who disliked Eitel as a foreigner (although he had become a naturalized British citizen in 1880), approved of his resignation, but the Chinese view was quite different; and in October 1881 Ouyang Hui gave his pupil the task of translating the Chinese view of the affair as reported in the Chinese press.

Chinese Secretary Eitel is a man of extensive literary acquirements, high talent, eminent ability. He has for long been looked up to by all literati. Governor Hennessy holds him in very high esteem and especially appointed him Chinese Secretary in order to secure his assistance and help, and so relies upon him as his right or left hand. Govr. H. treats the Chinese kindly without any distinction of race and Dr Eitel is extraordinarily well acquainted with Chinese matters, ready to promote good and remove evil ... The day before yesterday, the Govr. returned from Peking. Before he had almost arrived, an idle rumour went abroad that he had addressed a communication to the Chinese Secretary that he had ceased to employ him. Where had the rumour its origin! No doubt among that class of scandal mongers, who make mountains out of mole-hills. Of the scandals of society none has ever been worse than this. The great thing is to be able to correct such stories.[23]

Eitel's resignation eventually had to be accepted by Pope Hennessy, to the immense satisfaction of the British community. In accepting his resignation Hennessy ironically gave Stewart Lockhart his first promotion within Hong Kong as a result of the reshuffle caused by Eitel's departure.

One must admire Au's percipience for introducing, at regular intervals, the Chinese view of current affairs to his British pupil. It seems certain that Stewart Lockhart's view of equality was not dissimilar to Pope Hennessy's, and any bias against the Governor must have been tempered by his knowledge of the Chinese view of this controversial figure. Even so, Stewart Lockhart, like many others in the administration, knew of the Governor as 'His Holiness', a punning nickname also derived from Pope Hennessy's apparent belief in his own omnipotence.[24]

Whilst the lessons in translation from the Chinese press served the additional purpose of providing light relief from Au's more solid linguistic exercises, Stewart Lockhart was not sufficiently fluent at this stage that the complexities of the Chinese language did not sometimes perplex him completely. One phrase in an article he was given the task of translating nonplussed him totally until Au explained that 'Oi-li-sz' was merely the Cantonese way of spelling 'Irish'![25] In Au's care, Stewart Lockhart was totally immersed in the study of Chinese language and culture. He never forgot these early lessons, and indeed spent the rest of his life working on from them. The process initiated by the old Chinese scholar in 1880 was to develop in the young official until it finally flowered, two and a half decades later, as a unique combination of British administrator and Chinese mandarin. It is perhaps some indication of Stewart Lockhart's relationship with his teacher that he managed to procure for Old Au a clerical post within the Registrar General's Department, a post which the Chinese held until his retirement in 1885.

It is difficult to appreciate the impact this single man had upon his pupils. Parker wrote that Stewart Lockhart 'always cherished a noble veneration for his memory',[26] and Sir Charles

Addis described with equal fondness how 'Old Au looks down from the wall and reminds me sweetly and sadly of old times.'[27] Addis was not alone in possessing a portrait of his teacher. A second portrait hung in Stewart Lockhart's office in Hong Kong. When he retired to London it was hung in the place of honour in his study and was seen there by a neighbour who noted:

As you sit on the comfortable Chesterfield, beside an open fire, your gaze is riveted to the portrait of a Chinese gentleman — a dignified seated figure in butcher blue gown, dark silk sleeveless jacket, and black silk shoes, and skull cap — the expression is at once benign and shrewd — this place of honour is reserved for the teacher who introduced Sir James to Chinese culture.[28]

Ouyang Hui died around 1890, but his memory was long cherished by Stewart Lockhart and his instruction never forgotten.

It was also in Guangzhou that Stewart Lockhart, like so many other Britons in the Far East, began to collect items of Chinese art. Although he did not accumulate works of art with any intensity until much later, the foundations of what was to become a significant private collection were laid in these early years. His Stewart ancestry and his childhood days at Ardsheal ensured that he was brought up surrounded by objects of beauty and value. From an early age, his eye had certainly been taught to appreciate such items for their historical importance, if not for their aesthetic value. This tradition was to stand him in good stead when purchasing oriental works. Indeed, one of the finest pieces of porcelain he ever acquired was bought, according to his family, whilst in Guangzhou as a young cadet.[29] This early acquisition was an enormous porcelain dish with green celadon glaze, dating from the late Ming dynasty. Made from a lump of clay weighing almost sixty pounds, it has a diameter of sixty-eight centimetres and was bought from a Cantonese family who had fallen on hard times. The simple, flawless shape and perfection of the glaze mark it out as a first-rate example of Ming porcelain; and to acquire such a magnificent ceramic piece so early in his sojourn in China might be considered mere luck were it not reinforced by equally significant purchases in later years which confirmed Stewart Lockhart as a collector of refined taste.

The cadet years were not, however, all work and no play.

Trips to Hong Kong were fairly frequent, giving Stewart Lockhart plenty of time for socializing. Despite the fact that men greatly outnumbered women in the colony, eligible men were in short supply and a great deal of harmless flirting — as well as manœuvring by mothers eager to advance their daughters' futures — took place within the colony's society. The pressures on any young unmarried men must have been considerable, and Stewart Lockhart was well aware of the dangers. He was, however, undoubtedly confident that he could escape the matrimonial trap for at least a few years, and promoted his confidence by means of a light-hearted wager which he wrote down: 'Marriage Bet: if I make an ass of myself in less than 6 years, I pay Mrs Masters per 'Grainger' 3 doz. gloves: If I preserve the state of single bliss other way round.'[30] No note was made as to whether or not he received the three dozen gloves, for he won the wager and remained unmarried until 1889.

Months of study in Guangzhou were interspersed with some extended spells of work within the administration in Hong Kong. Although it was the Colonial Office's intention that the cadet should concentrate almost exclusively on his Cantonese studies, Governor Pope Hennessy, typically, had other ideas, which could have ended Stewart Lockhart's studies. He was intent on setting up a fully independent Interpreters Department with Dr Eitel at its head, a move calculated to diminish the authority of the Registrar General and increase Eitel's influence. Pope Hennessy intended to make Stewart Lockhart Eitel's first clerk, despite the fact that the cadet had not completed his studies.[31] The Colonial Office was swift to disabuse Pope Hennessy of his plans, declaring that 'Mr Lockhart must not be brought down from China, where he is working hard on Chinese, for the purpose of making him do clerical work.'[32] Accordingly, Stewart Lockhart continued his studies with Ouyang Hui, passing his final examination in Chinese in September 1881.

Under normal circumstances, he would have remained in Hong Kong to begin full-time work in the administration, but Tonnochy, administrator of the Board of Examiners, decided that although Stewart Lockhart had passed all five exams,[33] he was not sufficiently fluent in translation from Chinese to cope with all documents. Tonnochy's decision illustrates the confusion there was when it came to detailed consideration of the training of cadets: the administration had simply not the practice in passing cadets to have clearly defined ideas of standards. Eitel, the chief examiner, pointed out that no one could attain Tonnochy's desired level of fluency in less than five or six years and the matter was referred to London, with Stewart Lockhart writing to his colleague there, Charles Lucas, for support.[34] The Colonial Office overruled Tonnochy's decision to return the cadet to Guangzhou for a further six months, but the time taken to contact London and receive their response still meant that it was November before their decision reached the colony. Stewart Lockhart did not therefore start his first attachment in the Colonial Secretary's office until London's decision had been received. For the next four months he worked there 'chiefly translating Chinese into English'[35] before returning briefly to Guangzhou to upgrade his spoken Cantonese and become, in August 1882, a Passed Cadet.

For the next two months he held the post of Clerk of Councils and Chief Clerk in the Colonial Secretary's office, a post which introduced him to the day-to-day running of the senior department in the colony's administration. As one who had been trained for rapid career advancement within the colonial service, his early career is significant for the way in which each posting gave him a successively broadening insight into the organization of the administration. After two months involvement in the taking of minutes and the daily administration of the colony, he was moved to the Registrar General's office. Here he 'had many opportunities of investigating all kinds of cases arising amongst the Chinese and ... the means of obtaining considerable practice in the methods of enquiry which a Magistrate in this Colony must adopt'.[36] Less than six months later, while being retained by the Registrar General's department to translate documents of all types, he received further advancement when he was appointed Superintendent of Opium Revenue. This was followed by another promotion when, in August 1883, he was appointed as Hong Kong's first Assistant Colonial Secretary and Auditor General. A man of undoubted talent, his progress was not due solely to his administrative ability, but also lay in the fact that Hong Kong in the 1880s possessed relatively few British officials who understood Cantonese. Given that the administration as a whole was tiny, with only twelve officials forming the government secretariat,[37] there was plenty of scope for promotion, and plenty of work to keep one occupied, whatever one's capabilities. The quality of the young officials in Hong Kong was, however, generally very good. One Governor of the colony later noted that, 'the work of the Governor here is generally made much easier by the excellence of the cadet officers'.[38]

Pope Hennessy, the first Governor under whom Stewart Lockhart served, had arrived in Hong Kong in 1877 and remained there until March 1882 when Marsh, the Colonial Secretary, became Acting Governor for twelve months. As has already been noted, Pope Hennessy was a controversial figure, and he tried to some extent to allay the misgivings of the European community on his arrival in Hong Kong by declaring that his primary aim was to protect Hong Kong's trading interests.[39] The mercantile input was, naturally, crucial to a colony which by this time was considered to be the British Empire's most important port after London. Despite his initial aim, Pope Hennessy was less than successful in gaining the wholehearted support of the European trading community, and one contemporary observer noted that during his tenure 'the Legislative Council Chamber was the arena of almost perpetual strife.'[40] One major point of contention was that Pope Hennessy wished to give the Chinese community greater equality than it had enjoyed under any of his predecessors. Although non-discrimination of the races had been declared in Governors' instructions as early as 1866, in accordance with British colonial policy generally, the intent was — as is so often the case — far removed from the fact. In Hong Kong, despite the 1866 declaration, Europeans and Chinese lived in separate areas and this segregation was enforced by clauses inserted into land leases. Pope Hennessy tried hard to redress the balance in favour of the Chinese by treating them as equal partners, and though the policy was an enlightened one, it found little support amongst Europeans.

A particularly vigorous point of contention was Pope Hennessy's attitude towards the treatment of prisoners, most notably his insistence that Chinese criminals should have the same punishments as those which were meted out to Europeans. This view caused a great deal of concern amongst the European community, many of whom argued that the Chinese in Hong Kong expected the same type of punishment — such as branding and public flogging — as was given on the Chinese mainland, and that to reduce the severity of punishments for crimes committed by members of the Chinese population was tantamount to desisting from all deterrents. Although Pope Hennessy's reforms of the Hong Kong penal code were eventually ratified by the British Government after he had left Hong Kong, the view which so dominated public opinion during his Governorship was to remain in currency for more than twenty years after his departure from the colony. Even at the beginning of the twentieth century, some authors considered: 'The population of Hong Kong is not normal in its composition, for it contains an undue proportion of criminals. This is due to its undue proximity to Canton, and to the extreme mildness of the English criminal law as compared with that of China'.[41] Given this kind of resistance to change, and given Pope Hennessy's abrasive and uncompromising style, which has been described as 'highhanded',[42] it is perhaps not surprising that he was so unpopular in the colony. On the other hand, Pope Hennessy was to set an example which Stewart Lockhart was himself to follow, for in every place where this controversial Irishman administered, 'the natives of these colonies believed that here, at last, was a Governor who put their welfare and interests before those of British commerce'.[43] Stewart Lockhart also sought equality for the Chinese in British-held territories, but he followed the example set by his first Governor with a deal more diplomacy and expertise than Pope Hennessy had ever been able to muster.

One of the many radical proposals made by Pope Hennessy in Hong Kong was that a non-European should be appointed to the colony's Legislative Council. The Governor of Hong Kong was assisted by two non-elected councils; the Executive and the Legislative Councils. In the early 1880s, the Executive Council contained only government officials. The Legislative Council, however, had at that time four unofficial members. With characteristic lack of consultation, Pope Hennessy, in 1880, appointed Ng Choy, a non-European, as an unofficial member of the Legislative Council. The fact that he had pushed through this proposal without even discussing the matter with the home government, caused no small amount of uproar in Hong Kong.

It is likely that, had the Governor approached this problem more sensitively, the choice of Ng Choy would have been less controversial. His selection was quite a sensible one, for he was a British subject, born in Singapore, and educated in England. As far as the Governor was concerned, non-European representation was essential in a colony where less than ten per cent of the population was European, and where the revenue and prosperity of the colony depended upon Chinese entrepreneurial skills to a very large extent. Sir Michael Hicks Beach, Secretary of State for the Colonies, was less sure of the Governor's judgement, and decided to let Ng Choy's appointment go ahead, but only for three years' duration instead of for the usual life tenure.[44]

The Colonial Office was worried that, were Britain's relations with China to deteriorate markedly during any period, Chinese unofficial members of the Legislative Council might find their loyalties lying with China, rather than with the administration in Hong Kong. Thus moves towards a power base, however limited, for the Chinese in the Colony, were often mistrusted. In addition, Pope Hennessy's motives were by now being questioned at almost every turn by those working in the Colonial Office who felt — understandably, given his past record — that he was not a Governor in whom one could invest unquestioning faith. On the other hand, Pope Hennessy was a humanitarian who, within the existing framework, was striving for a fair deal for the Chinese and who believed passionately in racial equality. He had followed this course throughout his career. In Labuan, for example, in 1867, he was the first Governor ever to ask Chinese, Malays and Indians to a Government House party,[45] and even as a junior official, Stewart Lockhart must have been aware of the liberalism of the Governor's policies. As we have seen, Ouyang Hui was carefully presenting the pro-Hennessy point of view held by most of the Chinese population, and it is impossible to believe, given his later career, that Stewart Lockhart was not influenced by Pope Hennessy's views, much as he may have disliked the man himself.

It is not inconceivable that the Governor's example provided Stewart Lockhart with the encouragement to pursue the ideal of equality when he himself held the reins of power, for Stewart Lockhart earned the friendship and admiration of the Chinese in Hong Kong through his attempts to extend and consolidate the Chinese power base within the colony. But before Stewart Lockhart could wield any great influence, he had first to grasp the techniques of the administration within Hong Kong, and his first years as a Passed Cadet in the colony were spent familiarizing himself with the complexities of the governmental system.

Hong Kong was designated a British colony on 26 June 1843, and by 1844 an administrative structure for the territory had been organized. Throughout the remainder of the nineteenth century, Hong Kong was administered by a relatively small number of officials with the Governor at their helm. The Colonial Secretary was the Governor's 'right-hand man' and the administration was supported by a number of other officials. Of these the Treasurer, Auditor-General, Registrar General, Chief Justice, and Attorney-General were responsible for the majority of the decisions within the colony. Most departments were run by only a handful of staff and the Governor was assisted in his work by the Executive Council and the Legislative Council. Most of the policy decisions were made by the Executive Council which was composed of only official members until 1896. The Legislative Council contained both official and unofficial members. Officials were appointed to each council by virtue of the posts they held: the Colonial Secretary, for example, was a member of both councils. The governor was chairman of both, and also held the casting vote. It was he who was ultimately responsible for the appointment of unofficial members, although such appointments were also sanctioned by the home government. These were appointed by virtue of their own credentials, rather than because of any post they held. Occasionally, in the early history of Hong Kong, unofficial members were in fact government officials, but increasingly these posts were filled by men representing the major commercial interests within the colony, and lawyers and other professionals were also included.

This administration, complete with clerks and interpreters, ran the small island which was generally considered to be Britain's key to the East. The British Government's attitude was neatly summarized by the Governor, Sir George Bowen in 1883, when he wrote

... Hongkong has been aptly named 'the Gibraltar of the East' ... Of course, it will not be forgotten that Hongkong is not only an Imperial Fortress but also an Imperial Emporium; and that the tonnage of the shipping which annually enter this port ... is nearly equal to the tonnage which entered the Port of London in 1837 ... at a period when this Island was a desolate rock ...[46]

That Hong Kong was an amalgamation of fortress and emporium, of commercial and political considerations, was the prevailing view of the day. In less than forty years, a barren island had been converted into one of the great commercial successes of the nineteenth century. Strategically, Hong Kong was the extension of Britain's chain of power which stretched from Africa, India, and along the Straits Settlements into Asia. At the time, China was seen to be ripe for a commercial takeover, and by holding Hong Kong, Britain had her own firm foothold in China as Hong Kong was well placed for commerce, having an excellent, sheltered, deep-water harbour.

The territory had originally been acquired by Britain for both mercantile gain and military advantage, and it was every official's duty to administer it in accordance with these aims. At times, officials had to place the administration's military objectives above commercial considerations even though commercial considerations were never far from their minds. This was a source of conflict between the administration and the British traders who naturally wanted the bulk of any trade with China to come to them and who placed constant pressure on officials to this end. The traders favoured minimal official interference in their commercial dealings and low taxes, whereas officials had to set taxes at a level which would cover the running costs of the colony and its defence. In addition, a rift had developed between the traders and the administration during Pope Hennessy's time owing to his liberalist policies towards the local Chinese and his constant interference with every aspect of the colony's life.

Sir George Bowen, Pope Hennessy's successor, did much to heal this rift but it was against this background of Pope Hennessy's liberalism and the administration's dual priorities of mercantile gain and military strength that Stewart Lockhart commenced his career as a colonial official. The halcyon days spent studying with Old Au over, he began his long administrative career as a clerk under Pope Hennessy, his appointment to the post of Superintendent of Opium Revenue coinciding with Governor Bowen's arrival in Hong Kong.

Opium was one of the mainstays of British commerce in India, Hong Kong, and China. Throughout the second half of the nineteenth century, opium production was the second largest source of revenue for the British Government in India. Grown in quantity in the subcontinent, it was then traded — via Hong Kong — to China in return for tea, silk and other goods. From the British point of view, this was an excellent commercial arrangement as the Chinese preferred to be paid in silver for goods, and by using opium as a means of trade exchange, British silver reserves were not depleted. Morality was not a consideration, although there was an anti-opium lobby in Britain which was vociferous from the middle of the century. Opium smoking was viewed as something Chinese, spurned by Europeans and accepted as a vice. The fact that there was a long tradition of opium smoking in China did not help to counteract the commonly held opinion that 'the taste for opium is a congenital disease of the Chinese race'.[47] Nevertheless it was generally considered that if the Chinese wished to use opium, it was not the British merchant's task to curtail this desire; particularly when fortunes were to be made from its sale.

The Chinese Government levied a duty on opium entering the country through Guangzhou in 1678, by which time two hundred chests a year were being imported legally through that port.[48] As the trade in opium grew, the Chinese Government made various feeble attempts to prohibit its import, but such attempts did little to stem the flow from India. Tea and silk, the main commodities traded for opium were, at the time, in enormous demand in Britain. The demand for these — plus the purely monetary profits to be made — meant that there was always a strong commercial reason for pushing the opium trade as hard as possible;[49] so much so that by the mid 1830s, opium accounted for at least three-fifths of all British imports into China, with at least 20,000 chests being imported annually. Given that one chest contained approximately 120 lbs. of opium, one can gauge the considerable quantities being exported from India.

When the British administration in Hong Kong was first established, the opium farm in the colony was immediately seized upon as a revenue generator. From 1844, the exclusive concession for selling opium in quantities of less than a chest for consumption within Hong Kong was put up for auction at a monthly rental. By 1847, a number of licences were being auctioned for the concession, and at the same time, Hong Kong traders were continuing to supply opium to China. In 1853, the Chinese Empire, desperate for finance, legalized the import of opium and imposed a heavy duty on it: a legalization which provided the traders with further impetus. Stewart Lockhart, as Superintendent of Revenue, had to administer the opium concession within Hong Kong. Quite what his personal opinions on the opium trade were then are unstated. But he did have to contend with opium farming later when he administered Weihaiwei during the first two decades of the twentieth century when it is clear that he viewed the opium farm as a commercial concern which should therefore be run as efficiently as possible. He held this view in spite of a condemnation of the opium trade by the House of Commons in 1891.

The Anti-opium Society had been formed in 1874 and throughout the 1880s the lobby was gaining in strength in Britain, but it had a great deal of prejudice to overcome. For example, in 1882, Sir George Birdwood wrote: 'opium is used in Asia in a similar way to alcohol in Europe ... there is just as much justification for the habitual use of opium in moderation as for the moderate use of alcohol'.[50] He concluded his article by declaring that he judged opium smoking to be absolutely harmless.

Stewart Lockhart remained in the Superintendent's post for only five months and, if he did record his views on this rather murky part of his career, they do not survive. It is, however, to his shame that he continued to be acquiescent about the production of opium when, as a senior government official, he continued to permit its open trade in Weihaiwei. As a junior officer starting his career in Hong Kong it would perhaps have been unrealistic to expect him to take a strong moral stance on the subject, but it is not to his credit that he later ignored eminent men such as Lord Charles Beresford, whose views on the subject were clearly stated following a visit to the Hong Kong opium farm in 1898:

The present opium farmer has a contract with the Government for three years at a rent of £3,100 a month. He sells an average of eight to ten tins of opium a day. The tins are about 9 in. by 6 in., and contain about £30 worth of opium, thus making from £7,200 to £9,000 a month. The trade would appear a very lucrative one.

The opium farmer is known to be the largest smuggler of opium into the country. If he did not smuggle he could not afford to pay the large rent demanded by the Government.

Thus, indirectly, the Hong Kong government derives a revenue by fostering an illegitimate trade with a neighbouring and friendly Power, which cannot be said to redound to the credit of the British Government. It is indirect opposition to the sentiments and traditions of the laws of the British Empire.[51]

Stewart Lockhart was taken from the superintendency in August 1883 and promoted to the dual post of Assistant Colonial Secretary and Assistant Auditor-General. This was the first time anyone had filled this post in a permanent capacity in Hong Kong and it was an important position in that, providing he acquitted himself well, he was assured of continued promotion to the upper ranks of the administration. Indeed, the post of Assistant Colonial Secretary was once described as 'the seed plot of future governors',[52] a fact which the astute and ambitious young Scot must have held firmly in his mind. As the Assistant, Stewart Lockhart was the link between the upper and lower levels of the administration. He was the channel through which all papers arrived at the Colonial Secretary's desk. His immediate superior, Colonial Secretary Marsh, was a man of considerable administrative experience, having already held the post of Registrar General as well as that of Acting Governor between the Governorships of Pope Hennessy and Bowen. Marsh required an assistant who was both quick-witted and efficient, and one who could deal with official correspondence in a manner which enabled the executive to function with the minimum of fuss and confusion. Stewart Lockhart proved himself equal to the task, and learned much from Marsh. In return, Marsh thought highly of his assistant 'appreciating the readiness with which he adapted himself to and speedily mastered the work of the different Departments in which he was called upon to serve also the cheerfulness with which he always undertook, when requested, work that did not properly belong to his office'.[53] In addition to the valuable administrative experience which he gained, Stewart Lockhart had the opportunity to learn in detail the financial arrangements of all the offices within the Hong Kong Government. Within a year, this training was to equip him to run his own department.

In addition to following his career, Stewart Lockhart continued to pursue the twin loves of his life — sport and academic research. Sport was a major preoccupation amongst the Europeans of Hong Kong, and, as a result, a number of thriving clubs and societies had been formed by the 1880s. In common with all the other colonies to which Scots had emigrated, a St Andrew's Society had been founded as soon as there were sufficient Scots to support it. This provided a base for the organization of Scottish celebrations on St Andrew's Day, (always an excuse for a grand ball which was one of the great social events of the year), the Burns' Supper, and the inevitable Hogmanay celebrations at New Year. Stewart Lockhart was a committee member of this society in Hong Kong, and was eventually honoured with life membership.

Life for the Europeans in the colony seemed to revolve around a huge number of clubs and societies. As early as 1848, the Amateur Dramatic Corps had been founded, and within a matter of months its foundation was followed by that of the Victoria Regatta Club and the Cricket Club. The premier sporting club in the colony emerged in 1872, with the formation of the Victoria Recreation Club, an amalgamation of the boat, gymnasium, and swimming clubs. Stewart Lockhart was an enthusiastic member of this society, fulfilling the duties of Honorary Secretary from 1883–1888. He swam, played rugby and soccer, rowed and hunted. One can imagine that his immense enthusiasm and boundless energy must, at times, have quite exhausted the more faint-hearted members of Hong Kong society. Sport, of course, would have been a welcome relief from the heavy workload with which Stewart Lockhart was burdened as a member of the administration. The camaraderie of sporting life must also have helped a little to take his mind away, however fleetingly, from the oppressive climate and the ever present threat of disease which was part of life in Hong Kong in the 1880s. Horse-riding was a pastime he particularly enjoyed, and, naturally enough, he was a member of the Royal Hong Kong Jockey Club. In addition to the thrill of the races, there was also quite often the opportunity to hunt within this small territory. It is some measure of his enthusiasm for sport that he reached his lowest psychological ebb in Weihaiwei when his health failed him and he had to forgo his rides in the surrounding countryside for several months. Even after he retired, Stewart Lockhart skied and walked whenever the opportunity arose and his health permitted.

Clubs and societies were also the place where government officials, however junior, had the opportunity to meet informally with both the business and military communities. Stewart Lockhart's circle of friends was extremely wide, but his closest acquaintances were drawn almost exclusively from the business and academic spheres. The officials he met during his cadet days were to become lifelong friends, and he also maintained close contact with a number of members of the great commercial establishment, Jardine Matheson, with whom he shared some family ties. The firm's compradore, Robert Ho Tung, one of the wealthiest men in the colony by the end of the century, was a man whom Stewart Lockhart first met in 1880, when Ho Tung had just joined the company. That particular friendship was to remain a strong one until Stewart Lockhart's death, and at one point Stewart Lockhart acted as guardian for Ho Tung's son, Ho Shai Lai. From the beginning of his career the Scot, it would seem, chose his friends for the quality of their company, and not for their racial origins.

Whilst pursuing his career with vigour, and at the same time enjoying the sporting and social facilities of Hong Kong to their fullest, Stewart Lockhart somehow managed to find time to continue his research into many aspects of Chinese culture. Surviving notebooks from the period demonstrate his continuing interest in the Chinese language, and it is obvious from them that his desire for knowledge was as strong as ever. Much later, he was to write of his study of China and the Chinese, 'I find the more I learn about the country, the more there seems to know! The subject is really endless.'[54] The foundations of an illustrious academic and administrative career had been laid.

Chapter 3

PROTECTOR OF CHINESE
(1884–1889)

No sooner had Stewart Lockhart begun to grasp the complexities of the Colonial Secretariat, than he was moved, albeit temporarily. Less than a year after his appointment as Assistant Colonial Secretary he was given the new appointment of Acting Registrar General, the established post at that time being held by Dr F. Stewart. Dr Stewart, a former Inspector of Schools and Acting Colonial Secretary, was Registrar General between 1883 and 1887, and it was during his absences from the post in 1884, 1885, and 1886 that Stewart Lockhart deputized for him. Only twenty-five years old, the young Scot was running one of the most important departments in the administration. His achievement contrasted sharply with the period six years earlier when he failed so miserably to enter the Indian Civil Service. The second choice, of a career in Hong Kong, by now must have seemed to have been extremely fortuitous.

The Registrar General's office had been founded in 1844 to look after Chinese interests in Hong Kong. Its early history had been a turbulent one: the office was abolished as an economy measure in 1848, and only revived under Bowring's administration. In 1858, the Registrar General was given the additional title, 'Protector of Chinese', and although this has a rather paternalistic ring to it — indeed, the department was renamed the Secretariat for Chinese Affairs in 1913 — it was, in fact, a rather good description of the Registrar General's job. He was the official channel of communication between the Chinese and the government. It was he who was responsible for disseminating government ordinances to the 150,000 or so Chinese who were living in Hong Kong in the 1880s and it was he, first and foremost, who dealt with this community's grievances. Just as the Colonial Secretary, as part of his remit, had charge of European affairs within the colony, so the Registrar General trod the parallel course for the Chinese. It was therefore crucial that he had a good knowledge of Cantonese and a sympathy for the people with whom and for whom he worked. Stewart Lockhart entered the Registrar General's office at a time when there was a general move towards increasing the participation of the Chinese community in the administration by, for example, giving them a seat on the Legislative Council.[1] The Chinese were by no means considered by the Europeans to be equal partners in the colony; but the first tentative moves towards equality were at last being made.

The department was a testing ground for cadets, and one in which their fluency in Cantonese and their administrative skills were stretched to the limit. In the 1840s, it had been a common complaint that Hong Kong was a haven for the worst elements of Chinese society. By the 1880s, however, an increasing number of wealthy and sophisticated merchants of Chinese origin were to be found living in Hong Kong, and they were unwilling to be treated in the same manner as Chinese who were less well placed had been until then. Several, in fact, opposed the existence of the Registrar General's department. Ng Choy, the first non-European member of the Legislative Council, believed that the segregation of Chinese and Europeans which forced each group to refer to their own separate departments constituted racial discrimination.[2] He was not alone, and it was not until Stewart Lockhart's appointment as Registrar General proper, that the former secretary to the Viceroy of Guangzhou, the intellectual, Ku Hung-ming, revised his reservations about the department when he wrote:

I cannot here help remarking upon the extreme danger of entrusting the functions of dealing with the Chinese to inferior men whose only qualification used to be that they could speak the language which no Englishman of superior education would condescend to learn. But now I am told that there are many Englishmen in this Colony who are not ashamed to be able to speak the languages of the natives.[3]

Ku Hung-ming had a superior opinion of his own abilities, but the sharpness of his tone nevertheless underlines the mistrust of British motives and British abilities within the Registrar General's department.

Undaunted by the task ahead of him, Stewart Lockhart tackled the post of Acting Registrar General with apparent enthusiasm. Obviously ambitious from the beginning, he very soon had his eyes on the post proper, rather than merely the deputizing role. In the summer of 1884, he wrote to Sir William MacKinnon, a Hong Kong colleague who became Director General of the Army Medical Corps, requesting his support in securing the Registrar General's post on Dr Stewart's retirement. MacKinnon's reply held out little immediate hope for him, however: 'I am afraid I cannot do very much for you at the Colonial Office as I only know some of the Junior swells. However, I will do all in my power to speak in your favour. I know no man better fitted to succeed Dr Stewart.'[4] Stewart Lockhart must have realized, surely, that Acting Registrar General was better than no promotion at all.

The Governor, Sir George Bowen, was a rather pompous man who had arrived in Hong Kong with the task of mollifying the traders who had been so ruffled by Pope Hennessy's administration. He was not a bombast in the Pope Hennessy mould, and one suspects that he permitted his officials to perform their duties with the minimum of interference. This was a great change from his predecessor who had not been well liked by his senior officers. Bowen satisfied himself, after careful enquiry and study, that the three subjects of most pressing importance to which he should first give his special attention were: '(a) the reconstruction of the Legislative Council; (b) the commencement of the much needed works of water supply and sanitation; (c) the land defences of the Colony, which had hitherto been almost entirely neglected.'[5] He made minor changes to the Executive and Legislative Councils, which included a timetable for regular meetings, and the land defences were somewhat improved, but the water supply and the problems of the insanitary condition of much of Hong Kong were to remain thorns in the flesh of several of his successors. Under his Governorship, the colony moved along fairly sweetly, and little that he did affected Stewart Lockhart's position in the administration, or his mode of working. Bowen must, however, have been quite supportive of his young colleague, for he 'was determined that the Chinese should receive perfect justice at the hands of the Government,'[6] and this aim accorded with that of the Registrar General's department.

Clouds were gathering on the horizon which were to make Stewart Lockhart's task, as the official who had to consult and act upon Chinese opinion in a sympathetic manner, an uneasy one. The upset came with the start of hostilities between France and China. Trouble had been brewing between the two countries for some time and came to a head in 1884, when their dispute flared into a short war. Bowen was immensely pleased that he managed to maintain British neutrality throughout the war, and wrote long memos to the Secretary of State describing how, amongst other things, he had been extremely careful to invite representatives from both China and France to dinner at Government House, thereby incurring no-one's wrath! There was a deal of unrest in Hong Kong, always sensitive to events on the Chinese mainland, which included a riot in October 1884 when the military had to be called out. This was followed shortly after with a strike by the colony's coolies and, as Collins, a historian of Hong Kong later noted: 'As generally happens when there is trouble in China, a number of Chinese came to the Island, and in this case many were armed and waiting for an opportunity to plunder.'[7] Although unrest did not truly cease until the end of the Sino-French war in April 1885, it was never of such severity as to concern the Governor himself over-much,[8] and while testing Stewart Lockhart's ability to the limit, he acquitted himself without causing any lasting damage to his relations with the Chinese.

It is interesting to note Stewart Lockhart's reaction to coping with the troubles which beset Hong Kong in 1884. He had already lived in the colony long enough to know that, while there was good and bad in every race, the vast majority of the people in Hong Kong wanted to get on with their business in a peaceable and, if possible, legal manner. Much of the rioting was instigated by Chinese from outside Hong Kong who were taking advantage of the generally unsettled situation, but these troublemakers could only organize riots and full-scale strikes with the help of some sort of organization. Thus it was that Stewart Lockhart began his research into the Triads, the secret organization which, he believed, lay at the root of all the strife. By the beginning of October 1884, he had compiled a series of detailed notes on the organization, which included an estimate that 10,000 Triads were active in Hong Kong.[9] Typically, his research was meticulous. It may not have helped him to curtail the riots and strike any more efficiently or quickly, but it certainly gave him a much more informative insight into the perpetrators of the trouble. This approach was characteristic of him — he always sought to know the true nature of a problem by reading far beyond official papers, thereby finding a solution which would be as pertinent as possible. The statement that he 'gave his whole life to this search for knowledge',[10] is not an inaccurate description of Stewart Lockhart, even as a junior official.

His research into the Triads was eventually to prove of great value in official circles. Governor Bowen reported to the Colonial Office that he had been told by Stewart Lockhart, following his private research 'that the enquiries he had made led him to believe that the subject was too serious and important to be dealt with by him alone', with the result that Stewart Lockhart suggested that 'I should appoint a Committee to make full enquiries and report'.[11] Two years after Stewart Lockhart had first begun his own investigations, the committee found widespread Triad involvement amongst the Chinese police force, and, as a result of their findings, a Triad purge was instigated and eighteen ringleaders were banished from the colony.[12]

In 1887, under a new Governor, Sir George William Des Voeux, Stewart Lockhart at last received the promotion he so longed for and so richly deserved: the post of Registrar General. The vacancy arose because Stewart Lockhart's former senior colleague, Dr Stewart, was appointed Colonial Secretary. During his terms as Acting Registrar General, the young Scot had familiarized himself with the multiplicity of duties he had to perform, liason with the Chinese of the colony being just one of his tasks. In addition, he had to register all births and deaths, supervise the decennial census, and chair a number of Chinese societies and committees. He could not effectively perform these latter tasks without first gaining the confidence of the Chinese community. This he achieved before he ever set foot in the Registrar General's office as a fully fledged senior official by means of a winning mixture of Scottish charm, fluent Cantonese, and a great measure of firmness and diplomacy. Because of his experience, he was the obvious man to succeed Dr Stewart, and the Governor urged his appointment to the Colonial Office, reckoning Stewart Lockhart's Cantonese to be 'better, probably, than any other English Official at Hongkong'.[13] It is easy, because Stewart Lockhart's relations with the Chinese were generally so harmonious, and because he gained such a great deal of respect from senior members of the

Chinese community both in Hong Kong and in Shandong Province, to underestimate his achievement in crossing racial boundaries. The early historian of Hong Kong, E. J. Eitel, gave a fairly typical description of the average European's view of the Chinese when he wrote:

The persistent refusal to adopt European costume or English ways of living, the uniform aversion to participation in local politics coupled with a deep-seated anxiety to keep on good terms with Chinese Mandarindom even when it blockaded the port to throttle their trade, the steady increase of Chinese joint-stock companies from which foreign investors were jealously excluded, the readiness of secret combination to retaliate against unpopular Government measures by a general strike, — all these symptoms of Chinese clannish exclusivism ... clearly indicate that on the Chinese side there is, as yet, no desire to see the chasm that still separates Chinese and European life in this Colony, bridged over.[14]

Eitel had, unavoidably, absorbed the biases of his day but, even so, his assessment gives one some indication of the problems Stewart Lockhart was to encounter in his work. Racial ignorance did not fall solely on the European side, and the Chinese at times displayed an equally astonishing ignorance of European habits. For example, when the Pope Hennessys visited the former Hoppo of Guangzhou, Lady Pope Hennessy was questioned closely about the habits of foreign women, the female members of the Hoppo's family never having encountered a non-Chinese woman before.[15]

During his tenure in the Registrar General's department, Stewart Lockhart dealt with a great variety of work. The post required enormous quantities of tact, as his predecessor Dr Stewart had discovered when, in 1886, one particular ordinance was passed in an attempt to halt armed smuggling. The ordinance specified that all Chinese should be forbidden to carry arms. The home government disliked the legislation on the grounds that it seemed to be directed purely against the Chinese (which it was) and instructed that the word 'persons' be substituted for the word 'Chinese'.[16] At times, it required an outside force to ensure that the Hong Kong administration was brought back to the reality of two races living together, and the Registrar General, above all others, had to be particularly careful about terminology for it was his job to act as a virtual 'linkman' between two races. Perhaps his Scottish ancestry helped Stewart Lockhart in working with a people so totally alien in culture from his own. The 'existence in Scotland itself of two races and two languages made Scots less sensitive than many Europeans to differences of race and colour and therefore readier to establish and maintain good relations with the natives'.[17] This would seem to have been at least part of the reason that Stewart Lockhart was quite so successful during his career in China. It cannot be said, however, to be the complete story; a further look at his continuing career is required before that can be ascertained.

Each month, myriad problems arrived on the Registrar General's desk. Daily, petitions and deputations came in from various groups, and it was Stewart Lockhart's duty to see that Chinese customs and traditions were respected at all times and that, whenever possible, the ordinances issued by the Government did not upset or contravene the Chinese moral code. He never shied away from asking the advice of others and by the mid 1880s his range of friends and contacts was sufficiently large that he could usually find someone to offer an intelligent opinion, though he ensured that the final decision was his alone and that no one was ever compromised because they had proffered him advice. In 1887, for example, Stewart Lockhart tried to act against some of the more outrageous performances which were taking place in some of the Chinese theatres on the island. He hoped to dilute the impact of their indecency by banning women from appearing in them, thereby removing as much sexual innuendo as possible. Ku Hung-ming was at that time in Hong Kong, and his advice on the advisability of permitting women to perform in these lewd stage plays was sought. Ku's reply was characteristically lengthy, and he finally made no specific proposal, pointing out that 'what is already coarse and vulgar in their own country, becomes a great deal more so when brought to be exhibited in British Colonies'.[18] He did, however, admit that the situation had improved since Stewart Lockhart had 'recently done something to purge Chinese theatres of the more offensive part of their indecencies'.[19]

A training in Classics is generally accepted as one which teaches the mind to work with logic and clarity. It certainly aided Stewart Lockhart when he was preparing reports and analysing data. His governmental memoranda are crisply written, meticulously conceived, and always give the impression of having been thoroughly researched. They demonstrate a sharp intellect, finely tuned to points of detail, which never overwhelm the major focal point of any case. During his tenure as Registrar General, he was asked to compile a memo relating to the question of the torture of Chinese prisoners, a situation which arose when wrongdoers were extradited from Hong Kong to China for crimes committed in China. Chinese law incorporated some grisly punishments into its penal code, and so it was no easy task to extradite a felon, in the knowledge that one was sending him to the mainland to be decapitated or mutilated. In his memo Stewart Lockhart points out that to refuse to send a criminal back to China would be to contravene the 1858 Treaty of Tianjin between Britain and China, and that this, in his opinion, was something which no self-respecting government would do, however distasteful the consequences. Having stated all sides of the argument, he concludes:

Generally, the question is a political and not a humanitarian question: or rather, it is impolitic to let humanitarian consideration affect the political aspect of the question. There are few probably who do not deplore the use of torture as part of the adjective law of China, and lawful efforts made towards ameliorating that criminal law are most laudable: but there is a right and a wrong way; and I judge it to be wrong, even ethically, to justify a breach of Treaty or of law on humanitarian grounds.[20]

The harshness of the judgement that humanitarian considerations should not be paramount shocks today. Few people in Hong Kong in the 1880s, however, would have disagreed with him, criminals excepted. Stewart Lockhart was proposing, in effect, that the colony apply the rule of law and the terms of the treaty in their strictest form.

The problem concerning the repatriation of criminals came to a head with the case of Lo Jen Chi, who was accused of stealing examination papers.[21] The Chinese requested his extradition in accordance with the Treaty of Tianjin, but the authorities in Hong Kong were reluctant to release him, aware that he awaited torture — enshrined in the Chinese penal code — on his return. Because of cases like this, the Foreign Office finally recommended that Hong Kong introduce legislation which, in effect, modified the treaty,[22] and in 1889, the Chinese Extradition Ordinance was passed, permitting extradition from the colony so long as the offence was not political. It did not assist the ill-fated Lo, but it did bring Hong Kong into line with practices current between other states.

Stewart Lockhart's approach to the extradition of criminals illustrates the fact that his long support of existing Chinese structures and organizations in Hong Kong and Weihaiwei was not due to altruistic humanitarianism as some might suppose. In fact he was a legalist, rather than a humanitarian, and upholding the existing rule of law, for him, meant preserving the status quo and retaining all that was good about an existing regime even if that involved sanctioning the bad. The bad could only be altered by democratic process, and until that time, bad laws and bad things implicit in them had to be upheld, whatever the consequences. Change had to be peaceful, and if it ever came to a choice between a bad law and physical disruption, his preference would always lie with the unjust law. (This is why he upheld the rights of the decaying Qing dynasty, hoping for peaceful change — which he saw as essential for China — rather than for violent revolution.) Such fatalism was to do him little good in Weihaiwei, and it is fascinating to see the seeds of his destruction sown at such an early stage in his career.

Occasionally, Stewart Lockhart had to investigate situations which had ramifications far from Hong Kong. One notable instance was the thorny problem of Chinese emigration from the colony. The first great wave of Chinese emigration via Hong Kong had taken place in the early 1850s when, as a result of the Taiping rebellion, Chinese had flooded into the colony: a common situation when there was trouble on the mainland. From Hong Kong, large numbers then emigrated abroad in search of employment. Several thousand went to California at this time, with an estimated 30,000 men leaving for San Francisco alone in 1852, spurred on by the discovery of Californian gold in 1849, and providing the passage organizers with a huge one and a half million dollars in passage money.[23] Many of these people signed illegal work contracts which resulted in their literally signing their labour away for a period of years in return for free passage, board, and employment. The levels of abuse within the system were extremely high, and in 1866 Britain, France, and China signed a convention regulating coolie contract labour. The abolition of slavery within the British Empire had, in its turn, created a market for cheap, forced labour — particularly in mining, and in the cotton and sugar plantations — with Chinese coolies fulfilling this need for the greater part of the second half of the nineteenth century. As Registrar General, it was Stewart Lockhart's task to ensure that abuse was kept to a minimum.

Throughout the 1880s the main problem was not so much the quantity of emigrant traffic, as the difficulties experienced by colonies which found that emigrant Chinese were arriving in such numbers that they threatened to swamp the native population. Honolulu was an area of particular strife. In 1886, 20,000 Chinese workers were living in that area,[24] and their relations with the local populace were not always smooth: 'The Chinese were declared to be a public menace, and their competition with the artisan class caused disquiet. The sugar planter capitalists, however, favored cheap labor [sic].'[25] When the Germans applied to the Hong Kong Government to send Chinese to the Sandwich Islands, Stewart Lockhart was asked to investigate any problems which might arise in relation to such emigration. Naturally, he was already aware of the problems caused by mass emigration to Honolulu, and having read various statements from Chinese working in those islands, he rather surprisingly concluded that 'the Chinese in Honolulu are treated as the countrymen of other nations there, their status being exactly the same as in Hongkong ... the Chinese are comparatively more numerous than any other nationality in Honolulu; and there are over thirty flourishing and respectable firms'.[26] One can only assume that these somewhat startling conclusions are the result of his reading petitions written primarily by Chinese merchants in Hong Kong and south China, people who would naturally wish to protect their business interests above all else. It is an object lesson in drawing one's conclusions from only one side of the case. Stewart Lockhart was to encounter the problems of coolie emigration in slightly different forms during his administration in Weihaiwei. Fortunately, he was in greater possession of the facts second time round.

Stewart Lockhart was at his best, and most effective, as Registrar General, when he was working with senior members of the Chinese community within their own organizations. He had particularly close involvement with three groups — the

Tung Wah Hospital Group, the District Watch Committee, and the Po Leung Kuk — and through them he helped to give the Chinese a solid base of power within Hong Kong, while at the same time consolidating Chinese control over Chinese affairs. He would lend his support to any organization which furthered these aims, wholeheartedly applauding, for instance, the establishment of a Chinese Chamber of Commerce in 1888.[27] This support process was by no means complete at the end of the 1880s, but the fundamentals were laid in this decade, and therefore merit some discussion here.

As a people with a strong racial identity, governed by British administrators who did not always understand the customs and habits of the Chinese, the vast bulk of the population of Hong Kong had little or no say in the type of administration by which they were governed. Time and again, ordinances were passed which discriminated — directly or indirectly — against them, and the lack of any voice in their own affairs must have been particularly galling for the many wealthy and educated Chinese who lived in Hong Kong by 1870. Immediately prior to this date, and throughout the succeeding decade, these men gradually evolved a number of institutions which both satisfied the needs of the community at large and gave them the administrative status, however informal, which they required. In each committee — in the District Watch, the Po Leung Kuk, and the Tung Wah Hospital Group — members had to maintain a close contact with the Registrar General. Thus it was that Stewart Lockhart became involved in these groups, supporting their work during the 1880s, and assisting in the strengthening of these organizations in the 1890s.

The District Watch Committee was the first of the organizations to be formed. In 1866, senior members of the Chinese community banded together to form a committee which organized and paid for Chinese to keep a guard within the Chinese residential areas of Hong Kong.[28] 'Before long it developed in effect into the chief consultative body for Chinese affairs.'[29] It was the Registrar General's duty to oversee the work of the committee, but the connection between this official and the Chinese on the committee was much closer than that. The District Watch Committee was composed of respected members of the community, was listened to by other Chinese, and was therefore an excellent 'sounding board' for the Registrar General when he wished either to gauge the feeling of the Chinese population on a particular subject or to obtain advice of any sort from the community. The closeness of contact between the committee and this senior government official likewise reflected well upon committee members, giving them added prestige within the community.[30]

No sooner was the District Watch Committee firmly established than another committee was set up, this time that of the Tung Wah Hospital Group, 'the pioneer of charitable organizations in Hong Kong'.[31] Although the Tung Wah was not founded until 1870, its origins lie in an earlier building, a small temple built to hold ancestral tablets in 1851, commonly called I-tsz. Because this temple was open to all, it quickly became a shelter for vagrants and the dying, with a corresponding decline in its decor and status. Apart from having insufficient space for these people, there were also no facilities to treat any ailments from which they might be suffering. True, a hospital had been built in Hong Kong, but it offered only Western-style medical treatment, and many Chinese were naturally suspicious of the alien remedies employed there. It is astonishing that, for almost thirty years following the ceding of Hong Kong to Britain, no adequate medical provision for the Chinese in the colony was made. Fortunately, Governor Macdonnell, who was Governor from 1866 to 1872, was sympathetic to the proposals which two leading members of the Chinese community drew up in 1869 for a hospital which would practise Chinese medicine. The government granted land for the project and contributed HK$15,000, the equivalent of half the sum raised by the Chinese themselves. While the hospital was being built, I-tsz was used as a temporary surgery for out-patients, reverting to its original function when the Tung Wah Hospital was opened in 1872. The organization of the hospital committee was remarkably democratic. One became an associate member by donating HK$10 to the hospital funds, and in return, became eligible to vote in the elections for committee members, who had to be people 'high in the esteem of the Chinese community'.[32] The Tung Wah did not confine its efforts to medical treatment, but performed a number of other social welfare functions, including the creation, from 1880, of free schools run on traditional Chinese lines which depended on a Confucian code of principles.

The extension into social welfare was continued with the

establishment of the Po Leung Kuk in 1878. Adopting children
into the family was a practice common in China, and it had thus
spread to Hong Kong. There were, however, numerous abuses
of the system, and numbers of young girls were bought: a type
of domestic slavery. In addition, prostitution in the colony was
rife.[33] Conditions were not made easier by the British view of
these practices, which maintained that 'this domestic slave-girl
system is a very mild form of slavery'.[34] The Po Leung Kuk had
no objection to the tradition of adopting young girls, but it did
set out to eradicate the kidnapping of young girls and women
for purposes of domestic servitude or prostitution, a practice
closely linked to domestic adoption (and sometimes indistin-
guishable from it) in nineteenth-century Hong Kong. Accordingly, a committee was set up on the same lines as that of the
Tung Wah Hospital Group, with members being given voting
rights on payment of a HK$10 donation. Two detectives were
hired, and the Tung Wah assisted with the provision of
premises.

The Registrar General maintained close contact with all three
committees although, in effect, this meant that he was dealing
with a limited number of people, as the same respected members of the Chinese community tended to be representatives on
more than one committee, and all three organizations kept in
close contact. One was expected, as a committee member, to be
willing to make large donations towards the upkeep of the
organizations and thus the wealthy Chinese merchants held the
main positions of power. Not only were these men wealthy,
they had proven organizational skills, and by the 1880s, the
Chinese of Hong Kong had strong internal organizations to
cater for health and welfare, education, and security. In effect,
there existed a sub-administration specifically for the Chinese
people of the colony. These committees gained in strength and
influence throughout the 1880s, but it was during the 1890s that
circumstances caused all three to be further strengthened and
reorganized: positive reforms which were all either initiated or
carried through by Stewart Lockhart, and which should be
considered to be amongst his greatest achievements in Hong
Kong.

As early as 1884, Stewart Lockhart was actively promoting the
cause of the Po Leung Kuk within the Hong Kong Government.
As Acting Registrar General, he sent a memorandum to Gov-

ernor Bowen[35] elucidating the aims of the society and outlining its history. His praise of the organization was fulsome, and he concluded that 'the assistance it gives in detecting cases of kidnapping and brothel slavery cannot be too highly estimated', noting at the same time his satisfaction at the committee's wholehearted co-operation with his department.[36]

A year after he wrote the report, Stewart Lockhart worked with the Tung Wah Hospital Group on a major relief project. This was one of many he and the committee were to be involved in over the years. In 1885, he became Treasurer of the Guang-dong (Kwangtung) Inundation Fund which was organized to relieve hardship caused by severe flooding in parts of the Province. When the North River had burst its banks that sum-mer, thousands of people were made homeless in the Guang-zhou area, and a major appeal was organized for their relief. The Tung Wah helped distribute rice, money, and clothing to the destitute, a role they were to have to play far too many times over the next few decades. It is some indication of the influence of the Tung Wah Board that they succeeded in collecting dona-tions for the fund from around the world. The Chinese com-munities in San Francisco, Singapore, and Australia were par-ticularly generous though, of course, money from these far-flung parts took some time to reach the fund in Hong Kong. Because of this delay, the fund was left with HK$34,000 at the beginning of 1886, months after the main monies had been dispersed as relief. This caused problems which reflected the peculiar status of senior members of the Chinese community in Hong Kong, most of whom had close members of the family living on the Chinese mainland. The Government of Guang-dong Province obviously felt that all Chinese — whether Hong Kong residents or not — should ultimately submit to their rule. Thus, on discovering that a substantial sum remained in the fund's coffers, the Treasurer of Guangdong Province *commanded* that the Tung Wah Board forward the surplus to him, indicating that a refusal to do so would bring wrath on the Board's relatives living in the Province.[37]

Stewart Lockhart brought the matter to the Governor's atten-tion, pointing out that the Board had been of immense assist-ance to him in raising money for the relief of thousands of destitute people and that the Board had already set aside the surplus for future disaster relief.[38] The Colonial Office took

Stewart Lockhart's protests to heart. The Tung Wah Board kept their fund in Hong Kong and the British Minister in Beijing was sent to the Chinese Foreign Ministry, the Zongli (Tsungli) Yamen, to protest in the strongest terms about the treatment of the Board and to instruct Beijing that the Treasurer of Guangdong Province was never again 'to speak to the Tung Wah Hospital board in such a manner'.[39] One suspects, given the general tenor prevailing in the Colonial Office at the time, that the British were highly sensitive to the Chinese implication that mainland China, and not Britain, had jurisdiction over Hong Kong residents. Stewart Lockhart took a far less global view: his friends were being threatened and swift action was required to protect them.

In 1882, an Englishman, Osbert Chadwick, drew up a report on the appalling sanitary conditions in Hong Kong at the request of the Secretary of State.[40] He had arrived in the colony the previous year to begin his investigations as a Special Commissioner, and his extremely comprehensive report proposed, amongst other things, the establishment of a Sanitary Board. In July 1883, a Sanitary Board of three members[41] was established with 'wide powers of inspection and control'.[42] Chadwick's report had exposed a huge number of shortcomings in the sanitary and water arrangements of the colony, and despite all of Governor Bowen's good intentions, the board faced a herculean task to improve the existing situation: 'Its weakness was revealed almost immediately after its birth, for in the summer of 1883 the Colony suffered a serious outbreak of cholera.'[43] Appalling conditions of overcrowding were to be encountered in the colony, with dozens of families crammed into ramshackle hovels. Property owners were reluctant to alleviate the situation as this reduced the amount of rent they would be able to obtain, and the board made little or no headway during the first three years following its establishment. In 1886, the first unofficial members were appointed to the board and, two years later, a landmark in the history of Hong Kong was reached with the election by ratepayers of two unofficial members. Unfortunately, the ability to elect members to such an august foundation failed to excite the general population over-much, and the percentage of people who actually bothered to vote at any time was never very high.

In 1887, Stewart Lockhart joined this unhappy board in his

capacity as Registrar General. Opposition to improvements from property owners was as strong as ever. The Chinese, too, disliked the board's interference, and it was not until the calamitous plague of 1894 that people were finally prodded into action by the board, and that Chadwick's reforms began to be implemented. Stewart Lockhart's private views about this ineffective body are not known, but as a board member he worked as hard as he could to bring together opposing interests to find a consensus of opinion regarding improvements. He was singularly unsuccessful.

After he had been relieved of his duties as Acting Registrar General, a job which had resulted in a particularly trying time because of civil unrest, Stewart Lockhart once more threw himself wholeheartedly into the scholarly study of Chinese language and culture. Even as a cadet, he had contributed book reviews and short articles to the *China Review*,[44] and in 1884 he managed to undertake sufficient research to co-author an article on Taiwan which was published in it.[45] In 1885, when his administrative burdens had lessened somewhat, he founded a Chinese reading club which met each Wednesday at 5 p.m. in Stewart Lockhart's house, Stonehenge. The first meeting was held on 20 May 1885, and was attended by Stewart Lockhart, the Revd Dr Chalmers, the Revd Faber, a Mr Wright, a Mr Falconer, and a Mr Ball.[46] Stewart Lockhart seems to have initiated the whole idea of such a club at which Chinese texts were translated by everyone present and discussed. The club met on a regular basis throughout 1885 and 1886. The first signs of disbandment were heralded in the early part of 1887, when Stewart Lockhart wrote to Dr Chalmers: 'I very much regret that I have to sever my connection with the Reading Club, for the time at least, as I have applied for leave of absence and intend to proceed to England next month.'[47] The leave of absence was greatly overdue and, given the pressures of his work, doubtless needed. Stewart Lockhart had actually requested the leave a year earlier, but had had his request refused on the grounds that the administration was so short staffed that there was no one to replace him; an interesting reflection on the colony's resources at that time.[48] A few months after Stewart Lockhart began his leave, the club met for the last time, and Dr Chalmers wrote to Stewart Lockhart to tell him that as 'Mr Hartmann and I are the only remaining readers now; and Mr Hartmann goes to the country next week'[49] the club would cease thereafter. For two years the club had provided a small group of people with a degree of intellectual stimulation which must have been a refreshing change from the frenetic sociability of Hong Kong's sporting community. Stewart Lockhart was most unusual in enjoying both the sporting and academic life, a combination few others in Hong Kong shared. It is typical of him, however, that, having had the idea of bringing those interested in Chinese literature together, he felt compelled to form a club. For most of his life, he was a man who joined or formed clubs, revelling in the society created through such organizations.

Whilst he was a member of the reading club, he continued other language studies alone, making notes in a child's English-Chinese primer, underlining unfamiliar nouns, noting at every opportunity correct pronunciations, and generally refining his knowledge of the Chinese language. He also continued to maintain contact with intellectuals outside Hong Kong. Cheery letters passed regularly between him and E. H. Parker, who had given him Old Au, and who now addressed his quite eccentric letters to Stewart Lockhart as 'my dear Lokkiskvartio'.[50] He also continued to receive lengthy letters from Ku Hung-ming, from whom he had requested advice regarding the study and practice of Chinese. Ku Hung-ming told him: 'learn to read in Chinese with fluency ... without that you can never catch the spirit of the whole work that you read, much less understand the literature as one connected whole'.[51] Ku Hung-ming's reply was, one suspects, taken very much to heart by Stewart Lockhart, for he studied assiduously for the rest of his life.

Stewart Lockhart had also apparently asked Ku Hung-ming how best to further his studies of Confucianism. The Viceroy's Secretary was not very helpful. 'It is very difficult to recommend a course of studies that will lead you to understand Confucianism', he wrote.[52] The young Scot was evidently undeterred, making the subject a lifetime's study. Indeed, when his daughter Mary presented his collection to the Merchant Company Education Board, she did so with the following dedication:

I hope enough has been saved to reveal JHSL in the light of a Great Confucian. JHSL was a follower of Confucius. The sage was once asked: What is Knowledge? Confucius replied: Knowing People. What is Humanity? Confucius answered: Loving People. No man had Greater Knowledge and Humanity, in the Confucian sense, than James Haldane Stewart Lockhart, nor used them more devoutly and devotedly. This small collection will ever be the perfect illustration of his Faith.[53]

His faith in knowledge was to flower in the sweltering heat, dirt and noise of Hong Kong, inspired by his constant contact with the Chinese people.

There seems little Stewart Lockhart would not undertake to study in the 1880s, folk-lore being just one case in point. This subject was quite the fashion in the late nineteenth century. Throughout Europe, traditional fairy tales were being written down for the first time, and wherever a group of Europeans settled, a folk-lore society would almost inevitably be established. Hong Kong was no exception. Stewart Lockhart was a member of the Folk-lore Society, based in London, from 1883,[54] and in 1886, as the Hong Kong local secretary of the Folk-lore Society, he wrote an open letter in the *China Review*, setting out his objectives:

The only possible way of dealing effectively with the vast field of Folk-lore in China ... is to invite the co-operation of all Europeans and Americans resident in China ... What is now proposed is to endeavour to obtain as far as possible collections of the lore peculiar to different parts of China, and its dependencies.[55]

The letter closes with a request for people to contribute articles on the subject of folk-lore in China to either the *China Review* or the *Folk-Lore Journal*, and, in addition, to submit any other information to him. To ensure his letter reached the maximum audience possible, he asked his colleague Addis to make arrangements for its translation into French.[56] The response to his plea was heartening, and for the next two years he corresponded with dozens of people throughout the East who had replied to his original open letter. His own researches culminated in 1890 in a lengthy article published in the review, *Folk-Lore Journal*, concerning Chinese folk-lore.[57] He was to remain fascinated by the subject for many years more, and continued to make notes about it until at least 1914.[58]

Despite the prodigious amount of research he was undertaking personally, Stewart Lockhart also found time to pursue his love of numismatics and art, whilst still managing to fit in a full social life. He rowed regularly, weighing in at 12 stone 4 pounds for the 1884 Victoria Regatta,[59] and in 1887 his non-official achievements were sufficiently newsworthy to merit a mention in the *Hongkong Telegraph*:

Mr Stewart-Lockhart, who made his debut on the concert-room platform, created a most favourable impression in Pinsuti's 'Queen of the Earth' and at once took a front place amongst local baritones. This gentleman has a rich and fairly powerful voice, and he has acquired the somewhat difficult art of knowing how to use it effectively.[60]

On the sporting field, he also continued to make his mark. Still Honorary Secretary of the Victoria Recreation Club, he added to the jollity of the Hong Kong sporting scene by founding the Hong Kong Football Club on 12 February 1886.[61] A report of the first game played by the new club concludes that 'Lockhart was very much on the alert the greater part of the time; in fact it was only his vigorous play which staved off a number of goals'.[62]

These myriad activities were, even more astonishingly, taking place against a background of an increasing workload in the Registrar General's office. In 1887, Stewart Lockhart quantified the growth of the office under his direction in a report.[63] Since 1883, the number of girls placed under the protection of the Registrar General had risen from 41 to 287 and paperwork had increased by fifty per cent. He concluded:

The staff are much harder worked than they have ever been before; translations from and into Chinese have become more numerous; the correspondence with . . . other Departments more extensive; the interviews with deputations and individual members of the Chinese Community more frequent . . . and the Chinese are becoming to know more and more that the Protector of Chinese is an Officer who can listen to their complaints in their own tongue.[64]

Stewart Lockhart, as Registrar General, was in many ways the victim of his own success. His knowledge and understanding of the Chinese and their language, and his sympathetic support for their Hong Kong institutions inevitably led to his services being called upon more frequently. His stamina must have been exceedingly good. The colony did not provide a good climate in which to work at the best of times — Governors Bowen and Des Voeux both found it extremely trying — and one can only wonder at Stewart Lockhart's immense strength and propensity for hard work which enabled him to continue such a punishingly energetic schedule for so many years.

Chapter 4

A FAMILY MAN
(1889–1895)

1889 was a momentous year for Stewart Lockhart. On 12 January he became a member of the Legislative Council and, barely six weeks later, the *Hongkong Telegraph* announced his marriage: 'on the 25th inst. at St John's Cathedral, by the Rev. W. Jennings, Colonial Chaplain, James Haldane Stewart Lockhart, M. L. C., Registrar General, to Edith Louise Rider, second daughter of Alfred Hancock, Hongkong.'[1] Alfred Hancock, a Hong Kong bullion broker,[2] lived in a house on the Peak with his Sheffield-born wife, Harriet.[3] She bore him eight children, of which the first two, Cecil and Reggie, died in 1887. Their fourth child, Edith, was born in Hong Kong on 14 June 1870. Although Edith married at the young age of eighteen, she must have known Stewart Lockhart for some time. Mr and Mrs Hancock were well known in Hong Kong society, and Stewart Lockhart met them and their family frequently at social functions. Despite the age gap of twelve years, the marriage was to be a long and happy one. Edith was recognized, particularly in Weihaiwei, as an excellent hostess, and at no time can one find a harsh word spoken or written about her. Charming and sociable, she was, in many ways, the perfect partner for her fun-loving and energetic husband. Quite non-academic in her outlook, however, she did not share her husband's love of scholarship and seems to have been left quite cold by his enthusiasm for all things Chinese.

Shortly after their marriage, the happy couple left for long leave in Britain. Numerous letters of congratulation were sent to them before their departure, including greetings from the Chinese traders and the people of Hong Kong.[4] One of the most superficially tantalizing letters of congratulation came from Stewart Lockhart's old friend, Sir John Jordan, then working at the British Legation in Beijing who added a special request in his letter about an unspecified article:

In all probability *that* article — the joint production of our youthful enthusiasm — has perished long ago, but should it by any chance have escaped the wastepaper basket, don't on any account try to rescue it from its deserved oblivion. Its publication in any shape could not fail to do me much harm. Our present Chief strongly and as I now think rightly objects to public utterances of any sort on the part of his subordinates.[5]

Research has revealed that the article concerned was a manuscript called 'China in Transition', which traces the history of foreign incursions in China, and discusses the Chinese view of foreigners. As the up and coming official in Beijing, Jordan's career would doubtless have suffered had the article ever reached publication, noting, as it did 'the over-whelming [*sic*] arrogance and proud self-complacency' of the Manchu court.[6] Such sentiments would hardly have endeared any official in the British Legation to the Chinese Government of the day. Stewart Lockhart with his usual magpie instinct, had not in fact consigned this small piece of history to the wastepaper basket, and the article which was causing Jordan so much anxiety survives today amongst the piles of papers in the Stewart Lockhart collection. It has remained unnoticed until now and casts some interesting light on the views of these two young officials at the start of their careers, showing how strong their feelings for the Chinese nation were, even at this relatively early stage. While decrying the incursions of foreign powers in China, and damning the backward-looking rule of the Manchus, Jordan and Stewart Lockhart also stated in the strongest terms their belief that the Chinese were people like any others, and should be treated as such. For neither man was racial discrimination a creed to be countenanced.

It was at the time of his marriage that Stewart Lockhart formally adopted the double surname he had been using informally since his arrival in Hong Kong. He introduced his wife to the history of the Stewarts gradually, and it was not until her twentieth birthday that Edith was presented with objects of profound historical significance by her new family. On that birthday, Stewart Lockhart's father, Miles, sent his daughter-in-law a Jacobite snuff box which had been passed down through the Stewart line of the family.[7] James gave his wife a ring, an even more important treasure from the Stewarts, and enclosed the following short history with his gift.

This ring was given by Prince Charles Edward to Alexander Stewart of Invernahyle, who was one of the old Highland warriors to whom Sir Walter Scott refers in his preface to *Waverly* ... [it then passed] as a 'precious relic' to my maternal grandmother, Annette Stewart ... I now present it to my wife ... Long may she be spared to wear it and may it always remain in our family.[8]

Known as 'Prince Charlie's Ring', it was one of the few relics of his heritage which Stewart Lockhart had to give to his wife.

Quite what the Hong Kong born Edith, with her English parents, thought of the strange Scottish clan she had married into, we do not know. Certainly the Hancock family, being resident in the colony, kept in much closer contact with the married couple than did the Lockharts, who had seen their son only twice since 1879. Stewart Lockhart greeted his new family with gusto, and had numerous pictures taken of himself with Edith and her sisters, Hettie, Gertie, and Beattie at the races and during picnics at Deepwater Bay. Other photographs show him sharing his love of sport with Edith's brothers, Dick and Harry.[9]

In November 1889, nine months after their marriage, their son, Charles, was born in England. Stewart Lockhart paid his old friend and colleague from Guangzhou days, Charles Addis, the compliment of naming his first born son after him, a gesture which touched Addis deeply.[10] Mindful that he now had a baby's welfare to consider when returning to the rigours of the Hong Kong climate, Stewart Lockhart asked for, and was given, an extension of leave for a further six months. The family returned to Hong Kong in the middle of 1890, ready to start life in a new house which was being built for them in Plantation Road. Named Ardsheal, after his childhood home, the imposing building was designed by the Hong Kong civil engineers, Danby and Leigh. The house reflected Stewart Lockhart's status within the community, and while it was not on the scale of some of the wealthy merchants' mansions, it was, nevertheless, a home designed for grand entertaining. The rooms were thirteen feet high, the drawing and dining rooms being the most spacious of all. A verandah running round three sides of the building completed the house.[11]

Edith enjoyed her role as hostess of Ardsheal and the couple frequently entertained leading members of the British Hong Kong society there. The Keswicks, a major force in the firm Jardine Matheson, and distantly related to the Stewarts of

Appin, often dined with the Stewart Lockharts. Stewart Lockhart's friends also crossed all racial boundaries and he invited Chinese friends to the house as well. This was unusual, given the prejudices of the period. Swires' compradore, Mok Man Cheung, Sir Poshan Wei Yuk, and Sir Robert Ho Tung, were all close Chinese friends who visited Ardsheal regularly. Like many Europeans in Hong Kong, Stewart Lockhart had daily dealings with people from other races, but unlike many Europeans, he took this process one stage further with people he liked, and became their friend, whatever their racial origins.

Racial prejudice amongst Europeans in the colony was not directed solely against the Chinese. The Sassoons, for example, close friends of the Stewart Lockharts, and also friends of Edward VII when he was still the playboy Prince of Wales,[12] were never admitted to the Hong Kong Club, because of their Bombay Jewish origins even though Frederick Sassoon was a member of the Legislative Council. By comparison with the open social snobbery of Hong Kong, Ardsheal appears a haven of racial harmony.

Frederick Sassoon and Stewart Lockhart were particularly close friends, the Scot calling Sassoon 'Little Sass'.[13] Sassoon had a vibrant sense of humour, which he used to good effect in describing Stewart Lockhart at his home in Plantation Road:

He first *dilates* on the beauties of the Peak, where he has his palatial abode, with the hope that at the first convenient opportunity after 2 years (he is engaged till then) you will pay him a visit there ... There is only one drawback to existence on the Hills, he will tell you in confidence, and that is the difficulty of transporting suitable materials for a warm breakfast on a cold day.[14]

The acquisition of wife and child, and the social pressures of entertaining Hong Kong society at the new house, did not hamper Stewart Lockhart's ability to work with his customary enthusiasm and efficiency. Life as Registrar General was filled with problems; a situation which did not ease with a change of Governors when Robinson replaced Des Voeux in 1891. To some extent, Stewart Lockhart seems to have thrived on these, though he was steadfast in his support for the Chinese bases of power in Hong Kong and in his loathing of the ignorance and bias shown by one race to another. The following extract from a paper on which he made several notes illustrates his critical view of the prejudices of many British who came out to Hong Kong:

... both missionaries and officials arrive in China fully imbued with the notion that their views of men and things, of religion and morals, are the only correct ones, and that there is nothing to be learned from an old fossil like China. They regard themselves from first to last as teachers, not learners, and the attitude they assume with regard to China is entirely onesided.[15]

In complete contrast, Stewart Lockhart sought constantly to learn from the Chinese people and their culture. He particularly admired the symbolism which plays so great a part in Chinese art and philosophy, and in one notebook jotted down the virtues and strengths of the bamboo.

To start with the bamboo has *seven* virtues of its very own: it is clean and unspotted in itself: a sheath covers the stem as it pierces the dark earth so the bamboo has protection from the world: being hollow it is symbolical ... of a pure heart: it is strong and unyielding: the stem being divided into segments is orderly: the stalk is pure green without blemish: and is lastly eternal and enduring.[16]

He bought many black and white Chinese paintings of this plant, is known to have admired them greatly, and seems to have aspired to developing these virtues in his own working life, although he could never realistically think of himself as being without blemish. He was, for example, extremely ambitious. No sooner had he become Registrar General, than he was pushing for the post of Colonial Secretary, a post he first applied for in 1889 when Dr Stewart died suddenly. The Colonial Office, however, decided to make an appointment from outside Hong Kong; and Fleming, Colonial Secretary of Mauritius, was given the job.[17] Stewart Lockhart submitted a second application when Fleming was appointed to Sierra Leone as Governor in 1892, but once more the Colonial Office decided to bring someone into the colony, and this time selected O'Brien from Cyprus. On neither occasion did London feel that Stewart Lockhart was unsuitable for the job. Indeed, during his second application, Governor Robinson had been full of support, telling the Colonial Office 'that there is no one in the Service here better qualified than he is to fill the office',[18] and London was itself aware that Stewart Lockhart was 'invariably spoken of in the highest terms and should be borne prominently in mind for promotion'.[19] He was passed over on these two occasions because of the Colonial Office preference at the time for introducing 'new blood' into the colonies, thereby increasing promotion prospects for officers from a wide geographic area. Obviously, where posts necessitated a specific language qualification, as it did in the instance of Hong Kong's Registrar General, this policy could not be applied, but in other instances this very policy was to stifle Stewart Lockhart's own opportunities for advancement.

Stewart Lockhart found the lack of swift movement in his career extremely frustrating, and often wrote privately to his colleague, Charles Lucas, whom he had first met when Stewart Lockhart was a cadet attached to Whitehall, urging his case. Lucas was forced, in return, to point out on several occasions that there were men with greater experience than that of Hong Kong's Registrar General awaiting promotion, and that Stewart Lockhart would have to bide his time.[20] The constant striving for promotion resulted in Stewart Lockhart taking on what was, at times, a punishing workload. In 1891, in addition to his duties as a member of the Legislative Council, he was appointed a member of the Executive Council. A year later, he was appointed Chairman of the Board of Examiners in Chinese, and also joined the committee set up to administer the Bokhara Fund. By 1894, when he became Acting Colonial Secretary, he was also on the governing body of Queen's College. In addition to all these responsibilities, he carried out his salaried public duties to the full. What is even more remarkable is that the early 1890s were also a period when he produced some of his finest academic research. He was surely a man of prodigious energy!

Hong Kong was not the easiest place in the world in which to function as a government official — 'The Hongkong public man is nothing if not severely critical'.[21] The traders of the colony constantly demanded value for money from their local officials, and disagreed on any official policy which affected trade. The Registrar General, being Protector of the Chinese, was not an official who might expect to have the full confidence or support of the European trading community, and yet, whether because of family ties or because of the Scottish background he shared with so many of Hong Kong's brightest businessmen, Stewart Lockhart survived and held the respect of most of them. Considering the rough treatment Pope Hennessy received at the hands of the business community who wanted free enterprise at any cost, Stewart Lockhart remained relatively unscathed. This was a remarkable achievement, and was in no small measure due to his innate ability to communicate successfully with groups as disparate as the British traders and senior members of the Chinese community on equal terms. Even the *Overland China Mail* — no lover of officialdom — had kind words to say about him following the first report he wrote about the Registrar General's department. It praised Stewart Lockhart's revival of the department 'after a period of sorry languishment during the stormy and tortuous regin of Sir John Pope Hennessy'[22] and noted with satisfaction that the cost of running the department was only two-sevenths of the total revenue collected by it. There, perhaps, lies the key to Stewart Lockhart's success as Registrar General· he managed to maintain a department which efficiently and loyally served Chinese interests while at the same time was sufficiently cost-effective to make no demands on the public purse.

The Hong Kong merchants were not, however, a group to rest on their laurels over-long, and by 1894 felt their grievances to be sufficiently strong to warrant sending a petition to the House of Commons.[23] The problems had begun in 1892 when the Hong Kong dollar dropped 20 per cent of its value against the pound. A further 16 per cent drop occurred the following year and because the government's spending was in sterling, Hong Kong had to raise a £200,000 loan from the home government to cover expenditure on essential schemes such as upgrading the water supply and improving the sewage system. Government loans, however essential, cost money, and the merchant community felt not unjustifiably that they, as ratepayers, would be penalized financially for the administration's decisions in the face of falling currency. Officials held the majority on the Legislative Council, and were in sole command of the Executive Council, leaving the merchants with no effective elected representation and no power to challenge government decisions. From 1892, the merchants argued vociferously for some control over finance, as well as a voice in other areas. Their only weapon was the unofficial members of the Legislative Council who voted in 1892 to reduce the salaries of officials to 1890 levels. The motion was, naturally, thrown out by the official majority, hence the resulting petition to London and letters to the Colonial Office. Rather wearily, Lucas observed to Stewart Lockhart that 'Hong Kong has been giving us a deal of trouble lately, what with the gaol, the Unofficial members and the finances.'[24] The merchants, for their part, continued to seek concessions from the government, complaining: 'the Executive Council sits and deliberates in secret. The Legislative Council sits with open doors . . . but there is virtually no true freedom of debate.'[25] They demanded elected representatives for the eight hundred or so British adult males living in the colony at the time. This demand was flatly refused by the British Government on the grounds that representation for such a small portion of the population would in itself be unrepresentative and also unfair to the Chinese community.

It is indeed ironic that, almost a century later, the British Government, still in trouble over elected representation in Hong Kong, should continue to maintain that democracy remains an unsuitable system for the colony.[26] One gets the impression that London continues to find the democratic aspirations of Hong Kong rather tiresome: Lucas certainly felt that about the merchants in 1892.[27] His analysis of the leading members of the group was less than edifying, noting that 'the unofficial members are practically led by Mr Whitehead, whose strings are pulled by a Mr Francis, a barrister in the colony, who has for many years been a factious member of the community.'[28] These words could as easily have been written by Stewart Lockhart as by Lucas, and it is quite possible that Hong Kong's Registrar General provided Lucas with the information to write this minute. The two men wrote informally to one another on a regular basis and, occasionally, Lucas would include all or part of such letters in official correspondence. More usually, however, he would digest the background information sent to him and incorporate it into his official minutes without necessarily giving his sources. The association between Lucas and Stewart Lockhart was to continue throughout their careers. Generally supportive of his Hong Kong colleague, Lucas was nevertheless aware of Stewart Lockhart's faults and prejudices — particularly his high ambitions — but found him an invaluable source of well-informed 'unofficial' information about the colony. This rapport between the two men was to be particularly significant during the acquisition of the New Territories when Lucas and Stewart Lockhart worked closely together to achieve their objectives.

Mindful of the Hong Kong Government's official and unofficial assessment of the 'factious' unofficial members, the Colonial Office did little to support the merchants' position. Moves were made, however, to pacify the merchants by satisfying some of their more vocal demands, and in 1896 the first two unofficial members took their seats on the Executive Council. The noise which the merchant community had made over the representation issue served to make the colony's officials, Stewart Lockhart included, more mindful of the vociferous minority with whom they shared council space, particularly as some of the reforms which were a direct result of the unofficial members' complaints caused posts to be amalgamated and financial restraints to be imposed within departments.

Governor Robinson did not have a particularly easy passage in Hong Kong. He was well enough liked, but events seemed to conspire against him. Falling currency, disgruntled unofficial members, and a succession of natural disasters made his Governorship, and the task of his officials, a difficult one. One tragedy which struck the small European community in Hong Kong particularly hard was the sinking of the S. S. *Bokhara* in October 1892. Travelling from Shanghai to Hong Kong, the full ship ran aground at P'eng-hu Lieh-tao (the Pescadores). Only two passengers survived and, to the increased distress of the bereaved families, a large number of the bodies of those who perished were never recovered. Everyone lost family or friends in the tragedy and the colony was plunged into deep mourning.[29] A relief fund was immediately established to help those made destitute through the loss of their families, with the residue being used to erect a memorial to the victims.[30] Characteristically, Stewart Lockhart flung himself into the administration of the fund. Like other Hong Kong residents he had lost close friends in the accident, for almost all of his colleagues in the Hong Kong cricket team had perished in the *Bokhara*.

1894 was another particularly bad year for the colony. First, severe typhoons struck the area, and then bubonic plague broke out. The latter appeared in May, introduced apparently from Guangzhou where it had been claiming between four and five hundred victims a day. Given the confined living spaces in

Hong Kong, the plague must have been a nightmare for all concerned, particularly as the mortality rate of those afflicted was almost one hundred per cent.[31] By the end of May, 700 people had died, and the plague had spread to the British garrison. Panic swept the colony, and 600,000 fled Hong Kong.[32] Despite a huge medical relief operation, 2,500 people died in three dreadful months, and not until the advent of the summer rains did the plague abate. Stewart Lockhart's family had less to fear than most as the Peak escaped the plague's ravages, but he and his wife must have feared for their children; particularly as their second child, Mary, was born at Ardsheal when the plague was at its height in June 1894. Mary's imminent arrival precluded Stewart Lockhart from sending his family away from Hong Kong, as so many others had done. Instead, he had to watch his family remain in splendid isolation on the Peak whilst he coped with the crisis at a senior level, combining the posts of Registrar General and Acting Colonial Secretary during the plague months.

Much of the tragedy of the plague must be laid at the door of the colony's totally inefficient sewage system and the ineffectiveness of the Sanitary Board. Overcrowding of horrendous proportions, with as many as 1,500 people crammed into an acre of living space in Taipingshan, aided the plague's dreadful spread. Over half of all the 2,500 plague deaths originated from this single area in Victoria, the scene of some of the colony's worst slums.[33] But even in Taipingshan conditions were never as serious as in Guangzhou where an estimated 35,000 people perished.[34] In Hong Kong, medical officers, Stewart Lockhart, and the Governor were unanimous that drastic measures were required to eradicate the plague from the colony, and the decision was made to flatten Taipingshan[35] which contained the equivalent of one-tenth of the total housing in Victoria. The Shropshire Light Infantry demolished the slums, but in doing so did not succeed in eradicating the disease from the colony. Despite stringent new regulations issued by the Sanitary Board, which included the banning of any excavation work between May and October, the plague made its deathly annual visitation for many more years. Over a decade later, bubonic plague still claimed about three hundred deaths each summer, and in 1906 — a particularly bad year — over nine hundred people died.[36] It was simply a case of far too little done far too late.

Stewart Lockhart was at the forefront of the troubles caused by the plague and knew better than probably anyone else in the administration that the demolition of Taipingshan would cause further problems, however necessary the action was. The backbone of the colony's workforce, the coolies, lived in many of the slums, and he was aware that their landlords would be most unwilling to lose their lucrative multiple rents in the cause of better housing conditions. Two sections of the Chinese community therefore felt under threat from the demolition of Taipingshan: the coolies, who were losing their low rent houses, and the landlords who were losing their high profits. The resulting problem was to dog Stewart Lockhart for the next two years.

The great plague of 1894 also caused problems for the worthy Tung Wah Hospital:

Being the link between the Government and the people, the Tung Wah Hospital authority had to observe Government regulations on the one hand and to take heed of the traditions and general opinion of the public on the other. During the crisis of the great epidemic, therefore, misunderstandings arose as to the manner in which the hospital served the patients and the hospital authority became the target of criticisms.[37]

The criticisms were so strong that in 1896 a Commission of Enquiry was established, with Stewart Lockhart as its chairman, to investigate the running of the hospital. In the meantime, the Registrar General had more than enough to cope with as both the epidemic and the typhoons hit the Chinese population far harder than the European, compounding the department's problems and workload. Despite the problems which beset his office, Stewart Lockhart still found time to relax with friends. One of them, Frederick Sassoon, gave the following vivid and humorous description of Hong Kong's Registrar General in his kingdom:

The atmosphere of the official precincts is redolent with Red Tape as you approach the Celestial servitor who enacts the role of Janitor ... On enquiry he will tell you, with a smile that is indelibly fixed on his countenance, that 'Mr Lockhart, he inside, but velly busy' ... you hastily inscribe your name on a well-worn slate which is presented by the aforesaid domestic to you ... the surroundings are not luxurious, and it was only quite recently that the ravages of white ants were discovered to have assumed such dimensions that the life of the

Registrar General was in considerable jeopardy from the proximity of rotten beams, etc. — The building is just recovering from a lengthened ordeal at the hands of innumerable painters and workmen ... On receiving a favourable intimation you open the door and are ushered into the apartment where Mr Lockhart with an engaging smile, rises with outstretched arms to greet you, the cordiality of his manner fixing you with indignation at the suggested abolition of him and his office 'in toto'. — Waving you to a comfortable easy-chair, without any arms or cushions, placed near a fire-place (there is no fire, Mr Lockhart being a hardy Norseman, finds it difficult to keep cool, even in the coldest day of the severe winter) the Registrar General of Hong Kong, hastily concealing a yellow-backed novel — one of Braddon's latest — seats himself in his well-worn seat and suavely enquires your wishes.[38]

Sassoon gives a marvellous impression of Stewart Lockhart's musty office and the good humoured geniality which so endeared him to his contemporaries. The description of the working conditions, albeit humorous, was not totally off the mark. One visitor to the colony noted that 'the Hong Kong Post-Office and Supreme Court are housed in the most wretched building ever dignified with the name of a Government office ... the Colonial Secretary's department ... and the Registrar General's office are little better off'.[39]

In his capacity as Registrar General in the early 1890s, Stewart Lockhart was responsible for major projects which were to consolidate the power base the Chinese community had formed as their informal administration within the governmental organization proper. The development of the District Watch Committee and of the Po Leung Kuk has already been outlined, and by 1890, the District Watch Committee was well established in Hong Kong. However, the committee appears to have been run on fairly informal lines until this date.[40] In order to strengthen the links between the committee and his department, Stewart Lockhart proposed in 1891 that the committee be given official recognition, thereby placing it on a far more formal footing. He recommended that twelve, well respected Chinese should sit on the reformed committee, including an unofficial member of the Legislative Council, Wei Yuk. One of the most enthusiastic supporters of the scheme, Wei Yuk had been educated in Scotland and was a good friend to Stewart Lockhart. He and his wife were frequent visitors to Ardsheal, and the links between the two families were further reinforced when Stewart Lockhart became godfather to Wei Yuk's son, Lock.[41] The combined enthusiasm of the two men ensured that, by 1892, a newly constituted District Watch Committee, nominated by the Governor on the advice of the Registrar General, had been established. Working closely with the Registrar General, the new body gave the Chinese members status and power, while continuing to give the government an equally important asset: the ear of the Chinese community.[42]

Anything which improved the dialogue between the British administration and the Chinese community could only assist Hong Kong to prosper. Stewart Lockhart was more cognizant of this than most, appreciating that Hong Kong's future prosperity lay as much in the hands of the Chinese as the Europeans. He constantly underlined the fact that the Chinese were a race from whom the British could learn a great deal — a view which did not accord with contemporary popular opinion which looked on China as a festering giant, ripe for conquest. The fact that so many of his close friends were Chinese undoubtedly made him more receptive to the Chinese view of Hong Kong than might otherwise have been the case; but a lesser man might have shied away from the radical moves Stewart Lockhart made as Registrar General to give upper class Chinese a positive voice in the running of their own affairs. A decade earlier, Pope Hennessy had tried to improve the lot of the Chinese to a far less radical extent and had caused uproar in the colony. Stewart Lockhart's way was more subtle and diplomatic, although it earned him the enmity of some of his countrymen, and resulted in a lasting base of power and commitment for the Chinese within the framework of the British administration in Hong Kong.

The clever diplomacy of the Registrar General could turn attack, and even potential defeat, into victory. The most striking instance of this happened with the Po Leung Kuk in the 1890s. The first years of that decade were not particularly happy ones for the society. It had few financial resources, and without the assistance of the Tung Wah, would not have been able to survive.[43] The society did not even have permanent premises, and instead had to function in a space situated above the Tung Wah Hospital wards. The society appealed to Stewart Lockhart for assistance, and he in turn prepared a draft ordinance which would have given the Po Leung Kuk legal status. By April 1892, the ordinance had still not been passed by the Legislative

Council, some of whose members had grave reservations about the society and the function it performed. One unofficial member, T. H. Whitehead — a prime mover in putting forward the merchants' complaints against the government between 1892 and 1896 — accused the Po Leung Kuk of being a secret society, and was not alone in expressing such concerns.[44] Governor Robinson wisely decided that a special committee should be set up to report on the society and make recommendations as to whether, as Stewart Lockhart proposed, the society should be governed by legal statute. The committee was also instructed to investigate Whitehead's allegations and the financial and other problems the society faced. The committee was chaired by Stewart Lockhart who, as Registrar General, was the obvious candidate for the post, though his appointment was strongly resisted by Whitehead. The four other committee members were Whitehead, C. P. Chater (a second dissenting voice from the Legislative Council), May, the Acting Colonial Treasurer, and Ho Kai.[45] In Ho Kai, May, and Stewart Lockhart, the committee had a majority voice sympathetic to the society; and the Registrar General, certain from the outset that Whitehead's allegations would be firmly refuted, saw the committee as a golden opportunity to reorganize the Po Leung Kuk on a basis which would benefit the Chinese community and further the Registrar General's ties with it. It was to be a consolidation of the work already begun with the reorganization of the District Watch Committee, and would ensure the society's stability.

Whitehead withdrew his original allegations before the committee had even finalized the procedures it intended to adopt; this is made clear in the following account:

when he called the Po Leung Kuk a Chinese Secret Society, he had not meant that it was a Secret Society such as is liable to be dealt with by the Ordinance against Secret Societies, and . . . he had never brought any charge against the Po Leung Kuk Society of obtaining subscriptions improperly by 'pressure' and 'order' but had meant to refer to the influence of the Registrar General.

Not a complete *volte face* by Whitehead, his statement was merely a realignment of the battle lines drawn between himself and Stewart Lockhart.

The Committee's meetings took place amidst a great deal of acrimony from both sides.[47] From May 1892 until February 1893, the meetings produced snide remarks from Whitehead, and exasperation and anger from Stewart Lockhart. The Registrar General, however, won the day, and the committee of the Po Leung Kuk was legally formalized, with the Registrar General as chairman. Eitel, in his evidence to the committee of enquiry, gave a most lucid explanation of the Registrar General's importance in this matter:

The Registrar General is the one Officer in the Government service who not only knows the Chinese language but is supposed to be in perfect sympathy with the Chinese. The Chinese look to the Registrar General not merely as their protector but as their friend.[48]

Stewart Lockhart's achievement in establishing this confidence cannot be overestimated.

Two years later, when the foundation stone for the new Po Leung Kuk building was being laid, Stewart Lockhart's efforts could be seen to have succeeded. Even the press now backed the society, noting: 'of the Po Leung Kuk . . . nothing but what is favourable can be said. It has lived down suspicion and now enjoys the good will of everyone.'[49] Even the irascible Whitehead was present at the ceremony to show his support. Once again, Stewart Lockhart had succeeded in reconciling his positive support for the Chinese with the potentially more ambivalent attitude that his position as an official of the British Government seemed to demand. It was indeed a tricky political balancing act to be seen on the one hand to be bringing Chinese organizations under some sort of government control while bringing no additional costs to bear on the public purse; and on the other to imbue confidence in the Chinese community that he was giving them support, not additional governmental interference. He succeeded only by convincing the government that they were being given direct involvement in Chinese affairs, and by convincing the Chinese that they were getting a responsible, semi-official and prestigious structure of their own. Thus Stewart Lockhart managed to satisfy both sides of the equation while at the same time consolidating his own position as Registrar General.

In June 1893, having concluded the Po Leung Kuk investigation, Stewart Lockhart left Hong Kong on the *Empress of India* to travel to London to confer with the Colonial Office regarding proposed Chinese emigration to Brazil. His friends gave him a send-off in true Hong Kong style with a lavish fifteen course meal. Reflecting the racial variety of the company, the meal was an intriguing mixture of Chinese and British fare, bird's nest soup contrasting with crab rissoles, and fried shark's fin with roast sucking pig.[50] The business trip was combined with long leave, and so Edith and Charles accompanied him. The long sea journey home gave Stewart Lockhart ample time to relax, during which he helped produce the on-board magazine, *The Growler*. Once business at the Colonial Office was successfully concluded, Stewart Lockhart travelled to Southport to stay with his mother, and during his visit he permitted the exhibition of a scroll which had been presented to him by the Chinese community before his departure from Hong Kong. The exotic scroll was displayed in Southport Art Gallery, where it caused a degree of interest amongst local people.[51]

The Stewart Lockharts returned to Hong Kong at the beginning of 1894, again travelling across the Pacific on the *Empress of India*. The on-board magazine, to which Stewart Lockhart once more contributed, was the grandly titled *Pitch and Toss, or The Kurile Intelligencer*. Included in the publication was an article about 'The Hong Kong Man'; a humorous description of Stewart Lockhart which provides a little more information about him, whilst underlining his love of games.

He is a polyglot and speaks the language of Dante and of Confucius equally fluently. He is an ardent admirer of the Chinese, and we believe the Chinese have a weakness for him ... He is good at sport, plays cricket, baseball, football and made a good fight against the Marshall with the Maritime Bonnet for the sea cricket championship. He belongs to the Morning and Evening Whist Clubs, and seems to like winning.[52]

Considering everything else Stewart Lockhart achieved in the years 1889 to 1895, it is remarkable that he had any time at all for scholarly research. He fitted in his academic work early in the morning, prior to his official duties, and at the end of the working day. Long holidays provided further opportunities for research, and during the leave in Britain following his marriage, he had collected notes, which filled three notebooks, on Roman law, some of which was researched at Edinburgh University.[53] At the same time, he was involved in an intensive study of the history of Christianity in China, using the facilities of the British Museum Library for this research at the beginning of 1890.[54] It was a prodigious project, ranging from the Jesuits and Dominicans in China to the Christianity of the Portuguese in Macao. Books on the subject in French and Italian, as well as those in English, were carefully read. The results were never published: the case with so many of his studies. He did read extensively for his own enjoyment and knowledge, rather than for the education of others, and he certainly had an enormous personal appetite for knowledge, but his writings were not always converted into material suitable for publication. For example, the great survey of Chinese folklore on which he amassed so much information culminated in only one article and a few specialist papers. Sometimes his official workload undoubtedly held him back from the final leap into publication, but on many other occasions he leapt into one subject with ferocious enthusiasm, only to discard it a year or so later for another new project. The topic of Christianity in China was certainly one on which he intended to have material published, for he wrote to a Jesuit priest that he wanted 'to make as complete a study as possible of all that has been published regarding the labours of your Order in China before I commit myself to print.'[55] Some research continued to be of direct relevance to his work in the Hong Kong administration. The study, for example, of British enterprise and trade in the Far East, which he undertook in the early 1890s, appears to have been made purely to assist his understanding of the current situation in Hong Kong.[56]

The period to 1895 is marked, however, by two particularly important publications from his hand. The first, *A Manual of Chinese Quotations*, was greeted with considerable controversy when it appeared in 1893, while the second, *The Currency of the Farther East*, remains a standard text in its field to this day. *A Manual of Chinese Quotations* is a translation of a compilation of Chinese phrases which were commonly used by Chinese intellectuals in their writings. As Stewart Lockhart explains in his introduction to the manual:

One of the chief characteristics of the written language of China is its love of quotation . . . This frequent use of quotation is one of the great stumbling blocks to the foreign student of Chinese, even before he has advanced very far in his study of the written language.

Ouyang Hui, Stewart Lockhart's Cantonese teacher, had introduced the manual to him, and the translation published in 1893 was the result of these initial studies during the early 1880s. The translation can have been no easy task: finding equivalent meanings in English for often obscure Chinese phrases required a great deal of linguistic fluency and a sensitivity to the original work. Indeed, Stewart Lockhart continued to refine his translations, and his own copy of the manual in the Stewart Lockhart Collection is covered with notes and amendments, some of which, judging by the handwriting, were made over several years. Eitel appreciated the complexities of Stewart Lockhart's task and noted in his review of the book: 'it is evident that the English translation which was intrinsically very difficult work, is the result of much labour. To find for such pithy sayings, equally pithy yet idiomatic equivalents was no easy undertaking'.[57]

The book received favourable responses from some of the most highly respected sinologues of the day. Dr Chalmers, who had advised Stewart Lockhart on some parts of the translation and who had recommended its publication, was no less supportive than Eitel had been of the finished work. Chalmers' views are, perhaps, not unexpected, as the manual was dedicated to him, but less biased critics were no less pleased with the publication. Watters, Acting Consul in Guangzhou, found the manual to be of such excellent scholarship that he proposed: 'the H Kong and Singapore Governments ought to subsidize you by taking a certain number of copies. It is very likely that all the Consulates will be supplied with copies.'[58] One of the foremost authorities of the day, Professor James Legge, likewise believed the manual to be a 'great credit to the author's Chinese scholarship and general ability.'[59]

Having been given such fulsome praise from so many eminent quarters, it must have come as a shattering blow for Stewart Lockhart to read a lengthy, damning review by Herbert Giles in the *China Review*. He defended himself vigorously and the controversy raged within the journal's pages for two years,[60] with the editor concluding that 'in most important points Mr Lockhart has not come off second best'.[61] Stewart Lockhart brought his friends Ho Kai and E. H. Parker to his defence in the review's pages, and drew up a ten page reply to Giles' attack on his scholarly reputation. But perhaps the most comforting words of support came from Eitel who wrote:

Poor Giles, he seems to breathe and live in nought but controversy and so he takes the China Review's need for lively papers as an excuse for renewing his attacks. It seems now that what provoked his ire in the first instance was my having had the baldness of including in the sacred circle of 'sinologues' any one but himself.[62]

Stewart Lockhart emerged from the battle bruised but not broken. Nevertheless, it must have required considerable courage and personal confidence on his part to send a copy of the second edition of the book to Giles in 1903. Giles, by now Professor of Chinese at Cambridge, praised Stewart Lockhart 'for the friendly spirit you manifest towards a hostile critic'[63] and told him 'you may now congratulate youself on having produced a work for which the student of Chinese will be deeply grateful'.[64] Despite Giles' criticisms of the first edition, Stewart Lockhart had established a firm foothold in the field of Chinese scholarship with the publication of the manual. This book provided him with the impetus to publish again, and in 1895 his second work, the first two volumes of *The Currency of the Farther East*, went on sale to the public. This publication was to be completed by a third volume, published in 1898.

Numismatics were a lifelong passion for Stewart Lockhart. He may, in common with so many schoolboys, have collected coins as a child; he certainly collected Chinese coins with enormous enthusiasm from his earliest days in China, sharing his interest with E. H. Parker. Always one to throw himself into any pursuit with wholehearted enthusiasm, with his coin collection Stewart Lockhart was to surpass even his own normal level of involvement. By the end of his life, it had become one of the most comprehensive collections of Chinese currency in private ownership. His collecting began on a small scale when he started amassing copper cash during his Guangzhou cadet days, and a wider interest may have been fostered by his research into Chinese culture. By the early 1890s, Chinese numismatics had become no less than an obsession with him, and he bought from any source he could find. Friends, colleagues, and casual acquaintances alike were asked to keep a look out for any unusual coins, with the Colonial Office network providing a particularly rich source of contact.

From the early 1880s, Parker corresponded on numismatic matters with Stephen Bushells, physician at the British Legation in Beijing,[65] and it is likely that it was Parker who introduced

Bushells to Stewart Lockhart. Bushells was particularly know-ledgeable about Chinese ceramics and metalwork, and wrote an important book on oriental ceramic art after he retired in 1899. As a collector of art himself, and being based in Beijing, Bushells had good sources of supply from the Chinese treasure hunters of the north, and Stewart Lockhart tapped into these sources to good effect, and at some considerable cost. In 1896, Bushells sent a statement of account, pointing out that the Chinese coin hunter he had employed on Stewart Lockhart's behalf had cost HK$300 for six months' work, and suggesting that the spending spree should be halted, at least in the short term. This was a large sum of money to spend, although Bushells assured him: 'you will find some of the coins of considerable rarity and I don't think the cost was more than I paid for my own specimens'.[66] The $300, the equivalent of more than two weeks' salary, is put in perspective by another coin collector from Shanghai, H. P. Wadman, who was worried that, having acquired twenty-three coins for Stewart Lockhart, the cost of HK$3.20 might be too much.[67] Stewart Lockhart eased Wadman's mind on that point.

Bushells is acknowledged in *The Currency of the Farther East* for his help in deciphering some inscriptions,[68] and he had also given Stewart Lockhart a great deal of encouragement whilst the latter was working on the project. The numismatic publication, dedicated to Stewart Lockhart's parents, was begun by Stewart Lockhart virtually as soon as *A Manual of Chinese Quotations* was published. Not a textual exploration of the subject, the first two volumes of *The Currency of the Farther East* are an illustrated catalogue of G. B. Glover's collection of Chinese, Japanese, Korean, and Annamese coins. A member of the Chinese Im-perial Maritime Customs, Glover had woodblock prints of his coin collection made. When he died, Mrs Glover gave the wood-blocks to Stewart Lockhart in order that he might under-take a written description of the collection, a task Glover left uncompleted on his death.

Following the publication of *The Currency of the Farther East*, suggestions about other material suitable for publication were not slow in coming forth. Dr Chalmers put forward the idea that Stewart Lockhart should work on an index to the *Zuo Zhuan* (*Tso Chuan*), the commentary on the Confucian *Spring and Autumn Annals*,[69] an idea which was not to reach fruition until 1930.

Stewart Lockhart was also continuing his research into the folklore and language of China in addition to his work on Christian missions. His ability to work simultaneously on several different subjects is impressive, and at the same time slightly alien to modern minds, accustomed to in-depth specialization in a narrow field. But Stewart Lockhart's wide-ranging interests were by no means unusual amongst his contemporaries in China. Many of his colleagues and friends had what must be seen as the peculiarly Victorian attribute of carrying out wide-ranging and comprehensive research into a huge variety of topics, covering a multitude of academic disciplines. Addis, writing from his Shanghai home, describes a life which was equally devoted to the twin gods of scholarship and service: 'The furniture is scanty but I am a little proud now of the dimensions my library has assumed. Perhaps only 250 books, but then they *are* books and not novels in toto. The great secret is, I think, to weed it.'[70]

The desire of Stewart Lockhart and others to investigate seemingly any and every aspect relating to China is due, to no small extent, to the paucity of research in this field prior to 1880. Some works about China by continental authors exist from earlier decades, but little had been written about China in English. In most of their work they were tilling virgin soil, and in certain areas -- notably language and the arts — were discovering treasures hitherto unknown to scholars. The excitement of preparing the first complete translation of a Chinese text, as Stewart Lockhart had done, must have been exhilarating despite Giles' criticisms. Likewise, the catalogue of the Glover Collection provided information which had, until publication, been available to none but the Chinese-speaking specialist. The personal sense of achievement Stewart Lockhart received from such fundamental studies must have been an immense stimulus to producing other work. It was an exciting period for all scholars in China, though not one without pitfalls and dangers. Stewart Lockhart was himself aware, through personal experience, of the hazards awaiting those who studied Chinese art and culture, noting that collectors of Chinese art 'are at best raw recruits, whose knowledge of the subject is only sufficient to make it dangerous.'[71] The collector-turned-scholar faced equal perils.

Stewart Lockhart was more fortunate than many in his research, being ably assisted by numerous Chinese friends. In Hong Kong, his work brought him into daily contact with men who were willing to lend a hand to help with thorny Chinese translations. These men, however, were primarily merchants and not scholars, and it was thus that Stewart Lockhart looked outside the colony for intellectual companions of Chinese birth. Ku Hung-ming, whose lengthy epistles have already been mentioned, was one such contact outside the colony, and Stewart Lockhart was to rely many times during the 1890s on Ku's scholarly, if verbose, advice. Throughout this decade, the Scot was to extend his scholarly contacts further with men of the same persuasion as the Viceroy's secretary.

The five years following his marriage had been fruitful in every sense. Stewart Lockhart had become both husband and father, had established himself centre stage in the theatre of Chinese scholarship; and in addition — almost, it would seem in his spare time — had continued to pursue his career in the Colonial Service with considerable credit. Further merits and prizes awaited him, the first of these being his appointment as Colonial Secretary. At long last, Stewart Lockhart was approaching the summit of power.

Chapter 5

TRIUMPHS AND TRIBULATIONS
(1895–1898)

ON 26 March 1895, Stewart Lockhart was finally appointed to the post he had first applied for six years earlier. At the relatively young age of thirty-seven, he had become Colonial Secretary, and the Governor of Hong Kong's most senior official. The promotion was accompanied by an attendant rise in salary, and henceforth he received an annual salary of HK$9,720, the equivalent of a handsome £2,000 at the rate of exchange then prevailing. Stewart Lockhart's power within the colony was immense, for, as an economy measure, the posts of Colonial Secretary and Registrar General had been combined into a single appointment. With an eye to financial stringency which was to become increasingly marked over the next two decades, the Colonial Office set his salary at the level of a Colonial Secretaryship, with no additional allowance made for Stewart Lockhart's extra workload in combining the two posts. Overnight, he became the official to whom both the Chinese and non-Chinese looked for governmental guidance and protection. It was an enormous workload, and one which quickly took its toll, but his onerous responsibilities did not go unnoticed. From the Colonial Office, Lucas sent words of encouragement and sympathy:

I am not likely to forget that you were my pupil because you have done such great credit to the teacher. Mrs Rodger who met you in Hong Kong thinks that you are overworked, and I fear that you must find the combination of colonial secretary and registrar general very heavy.[1]

It is difficult to appreciate the enormous variety of problems, both major and minor, which Stewart Lockhart was called upon to solve on a daily basis. One moment he would be working in an international context as the Governor's assistant, and the next on some trivial domestic disagreement. It is to his credit that he survived this political commando course at all, and even more commendable that he generally acquitted himself so proficiently in his multifarious official tasks. Occasionally, however, his patience snapped, and from a man considered in the main to be warm-hearted and genial — though he had never suffered fools gladly — he became angry and stubborn. Whitehead, Manager of the Chartered Bank, had frequently succeeded in raising Stewart Lockhart's temperature with his petitions and memoranda during the Po Leung Kuk enquiry, as the official papers so eloquently testify. In 1896, Stewart Lockhart's temper was once more raised to boiling point by a petition. He enclosed both petition — now sadly lost — and reply to Addis in Hangu (Hankow) and received in return a rebuke of the kind which none but the oldest friends can serve in such a situation, pleading for a measure of Christian charity from the Colonial Secretary and concluding:

It strikes one at this distance as if the pummelling of your opponents carried a certain amount of zest with it and to a man in your position such an impression is undesirable . . . No doubt you were expressing a very natural indignation and they deserved no better at your hands, but — well, all things are lawful to a Colonial Secretary but all things are not expedient.[2]

Stewart Lockhart was too intelligent to ignore such advice, and he usually managed to keep a clear head, although he retained a quite definite flashpoint of which all who knew him well were keenly aware.[3]

When he assumed the office of Colonial Secretary in March 1895, Hong Kong was just beginning to recover from the disastrous effects of the great plague of 1894. Numerous sanitary ordinances had been introduced as a result of this epidemic including the inspection of lodging houses. Conditions in the Chinese slum areas of Hong Kong were terrible, with many areas no less overcrowded than doomed Taipingshan had been. Inspection of flea-ridden lodging houses was not a process guaranteed to please either the inhabitants or their landlords. The slum dwellers had nowhere else to live, and when Taipingshan was levelled, landlords elsewhere realized that any measures the Government undertook to improve slum properties in Hong Kong would threaten the quantity of dwellings available and cost them money. The resultant civil unrest led finally to a strike by coolies, in March 1895,[4] protesting over the demolitions at Taipingshan. The strike quickly paralysed the colony's trade and ensured that Stewart Lockhart was put under pressure to solve the crisis from all the parties whose diverse interests he was nominated to serve.

As Registrar General in 1894, he had already had experience of trouble from the coolies, when in March that year, rival feuding clans had sparked off riots.[5] Then, Stewart Lockhart had marshalled senior members of the Chinese community to his aid. The District Watch Committee met with him and the coolie leaders at the Tung Wah Hospital: a move which ensured that Stewart Lockhart spoke to the coolies with the full backing of the Chinese community behind him. Ringleaders were immediately banished, and the coolie leaders made to understand in no uncertain terms that the Registrar General would brook no more violence. To preclude further riots, a Riot Committee was established; with Stewart Lockhart as chairman. Unfortunately, its work was postponed in June 1894 because the severity of the plague meant officials had no time to cope with anything but that particular emergency.[6]

When plague prevention ordinances were issued in the autumn of 1894, 'considerable trouble was anticipated by the Registrar General in getting the coolie masters to comply with the provisions of the law'.[7] Again, Stewart Lockhart called on the District Watch Committee to help him try to avoid further unrest, but the coolies felt their very habitation was being threatened and realized that increased rents — the inevitable consequence of better housing conditions — were the same for them as a cut in wages. The coolies loaded and unloaded every piece of cargo going through Hong Kong and their strike, hitting trade as it did, brought the colony to its knees within a matter of days. As Colonial Secretary, Stewart Lockhart was charged with resolving this situation; one which he viewed with distaste. He had no sympathy whatsoever for the coolies. In his view, he had given the coolie leaders every opportunity to negotiate months earlier, and the striking coolies were no less than law breakers: a breed beyond contempt in Stewart Lockhart's code. He summarised his feelings at a meeting of the Legislative Council: 'To my mind this is one of the most extraordinary disputes in the history of labour ... here we have a large number of coolies without any actual grievance and without being able to formulate any grievance.'[8] His stubborn stance, refusing to budge an inch, finally worked. By early April the strike had collapsed without the coolies wresting a single concession from the government. Further government action was taken the following July when the Riots Committee was reactivated under Stewart Lockhart's chairmanship to investigate the possible requirement of additional governmental powers for the prevention of riots.

During this time the administration seemed to lurch from coping with one disaster to another. Plague and strikes were barely out of people's minds when drought hit the Colony. By June 1895, the Governor had to report that Hong Kong had just one week's supply of water remaining as a result of only a third of the normal rainfall levels arriving that summer.[9] Despite the unseasonably dry heat (rain did not arrive in quantity for another month), the sanitary measures seemed to have been worth the trouble caused by the coolie strike, for only nineteen cases of plague were reported that June.[10]

Stewart Lockhart's reverence for the statute of law and his abhorrence of those who broke it crossed all boundaries of race, creed and social status. It was one area in which he did not compromise, and although one may applaud his moral stance generally, he sometimes showed a lack of humanity as a result; as in the case of the extradition of criminals to China. When it came to dealing with one of China's most popular revolutionaries, Sun Zhongshan (Sun Yat-sen), his resolve was no less strong. Sun Zhongshan's belief that the Manchu dynasty should be overthrown and replaced by a socialist republic was an anathema to Stewart Lockhart: it would be the end of an existing order and break the laws of the Empire. Stewart Lockhart knew the Manchu Empire was rotten to the core, but he looked for change by means of a slow, democratic process, rather than by revolution. Between 1894 and 1896, Sun Zhongshan organized his anti-Manchu revolutionary society, and their first attempted uprising took place in Guangzhou in 1895; a revolt which resulted in Sun's banishment from Hong Kong. For the next year, Sun fought Stewart Lockhart's ban, a contest which resulted in one of the best known letters written by Stewart Lockhart, a letter which, as with his treatment of the coolies, brooked no argument.

I am directed to inform you that this Government has no intention of allowing the British Colony of Hong Kong to be used as an Asylum for persons engaged in plots and dangerous conspiracies against a friendly and neighbouring Empire, and that, in view of the part taken by you in such transactions, which you euphemistically term in your letter 'emancipating your miserable countrymen from the Tartar Yoke' you will be arrested if you land in this Colony under an order of Banishment issued against you in 1896.[11]

No quarter given, no exceptions made. For Stewart Lockhart, the law was stated in black and white, and was there to be followed rigidly. Had this rigid approach encroached into other aspects of his life, he would, in fact, have been a dismal failure as Registrar General, where compromise and common sense were essential. Indeed, it is difficult to equate the man who supported so enthusiastically the Po Leung Kuk when suggestions of irregularities were mooted, with the uncompromising official who broke the coolie strike and banished Sun Zhongshan. Of course, Stewart Lockhart knew that the Po Leung Kuk was a responsible law-abiding organization, whereas the coolies and Sun Zhongshan's revolutionaries were not. This obviously made an enormous difference to his attitude, but another reason may have been that, between 1895 and 1898, he was under a great deal of pressure in his daily work. This is certainly reflected in the terseness and tension of his official papers and actions during these years. He was never less relaxed than at this time, and it shows, for he was personally less able to compromise whilst fulfilling the joint position of Colonial Secretary and Registrar General than at any other time in his career. He was indeed fortunate that no major disasters blew up in his face, the saving grace being that, while his judgement sometimes became clouded during these years, it was never completely misdirected.

Civil upheavals and natural disasters were not the only problems he had to tackle in 1895. There was also an external threat, for rumours were rife in the colony that Japan might try to annex Hong Kong as a result of the Sino-Japanese war, and it was not a peaceful time for anyone living in the Far East. This conflict was to have the most adverse effect on Stewart Lockhart's career, dealing him a shattering blow from which, it can be argued, his career never really recovered.

This blow came in 1896 when Stewart Lockhart received bad tidings from the most unexpected quarter: the home government. By then he was not quite half-way through his potential career of forty years in the Colonial Service. At thirty-seven, because of swift and steady promotion, he stood second in command in one of Britain's most important trading colonies. Hong Kong did not have the historical cachet of the West Indies, or the high status of India, but despite being one of the smallest colonies in the British Empire, it was recognized as a crucial area of wealth creation and of great strategic importance. As Hong Kong's young Colonial Secretary, and combining that post as he did with that of Registrar General, Stewart Lockhart would understandably have been confident that nothing less than a glittering career and further promotions awaited him within the Colonial Service. At no point, until 1896, was he led to believe anything to the contrary. Numerous Colonial Office minutes had already testified to his skills: he was an extremely able administrator who was intensely ambitious and competitive, and his future career seemed promising.

Hong Kong followed the usual Colonial Office practice of appointing an Acting Governor during any gubernatorial absence from the Colony, and in Hong Kong the acting position was normally filled by the Colonial Secretary. An eminently sensible arrangement, it ensured an easy transfer of power to the official whose everyday work covered all aspects of the colony's control. In addition, it gave Colonial Secretaries an opportunity to assume the reins of government for a probationary period and availed the home government of the opportunity to study the effectiveness of a potential gubernatorial candidate in a position of assumed control. As Registrar General and Colonial Secretary, Stewart Lockhart had a greater knowledge of the myriad aspects of Hong Kong's Government than any of his predecessors. He controlled both European and Chinese affairs and was, no doubt with typical far-sightedness, preparing to assume the cloak of Acting Governor the moment Governor Robinson left the colony. What Stewart Lockhart did not know until the beginning of 1896 was that in October of the previous year the Secretary of State for the Colonies, Joseph Chamberlain, had initiated moves to remove any possibility of Stewart Lockhart becoming Acting Governor of Hong Kong. The situation in the Far East was unsettled with France, Japan, Germany, and Russia jostling for power. Governor Robinson was due to retire in 1897, and because of the uneasy truce between the powers in China, it was felt that, should an Acting Governor be required in the immediate future, a military man might be the most sensible choice. Colonial Office officials suggested to Chamberlain that a firm decision, one way or the other, had to be made well in advance of Robinson's retirement. Stewart Lockhart's old ally, Lucas, was just one of many who felt this way.[12] Chamberlain wrote to Robinson, seeking his advice on the position, and suggesting that the General commanding the troops in Hong Kong might be the best choice as Acting Governor,[13] a view with which Robinson wholeheartedly agreed. Chamberlain also consulted the colony's Chief Justice, who likewise concurred.[14] The senior parties in agreement, it was left to the Governor to pass on the Secretary of State's decision to Stewart Lockhart. In a letter to Stewart Lockhart Robinson explained that Hong Kong 'is to be the Gibraltar and Malta of the East in more ways than one' adding that 'I may be the last Civil (in every sense) Governor.'[15]

Stewart Lockhart was understandably furious when informed of the Government's decision. His lengthy reply to the Governor underlined his unhappiness and made clear the problems he felt he would face as a result of the decision:

The community of Hong Kong and especially the Chinese portion of it — for in China a Military official always ranks below a civil official — will not unnaturally consider that the reason for depriving the present C. S. of the privilege of administering during the absence of the Governor is of a personal and not a political nature.[16]

There was some sympathy at the Colonial Office for Stewart Lockhart's predicament, but the main body of opinion was that he had taken the decision too personally. Even Lucas felt this: 'he has reason to be sore but in my opinion he cannot be promoted to another colony — at least for some time to come'.[17] Lucas was, to some extent, playing the devil's advocate. Within the Colonial Office he was stating that as far as future promotion went, there were 'others with stronger claims, and he has got his present position through his knowledge of Chinese',[18] whilst he was writing to Stewart Lockhart at the same time, blaming the decision (which he, Lucas, had supported from the start) on Chamberlain's desire to have his own appointees promoted.[19] Despite these slightly two-faced dealings, Lucas undoubtedly supported Stewart Lockhart more than the other officials in the Colonial Office, some of whom felt the young Colonial Secretary's rise already too rapid, leaving behind more deserving men.[20] Chamberlain believed Stewart Lockhart protested too much, not considering that the facts of the case were such 'as to justify so serious a view as he has taken of the matter'.[21] Lucas was less sure of this than Chamberlain, and certainly felt that something should be done by way of consolation, suggesting that Stewart Lockhart 'might be given a CMG rather earlier than might have been',[22] but Chamberlain declined to find space for a further Commander of the Order of St Michael and St George that year.

In Hong Kong, Stewart Lockhart was unaware of these diplomatic machinations. Given his own high opinion of his abilities, it would have been easy for him, in distant Hong Kong, to blame this career setback on the Secretary of State. Chamberlain had a reputation for being somewhat dictatorial, and certainly for placing his own, chosen appointees in positions of power. Thus when Robinson put forward Stewart Lockhart's name for promotion a year later, Chamberlain's terse reply was that he could not hold out any immediate prospect of promoting Stewart Lockhart.[23] The lack of progress must have made the Colonial Secretary despair, for he could not know, in 1897, that his name had been forwarded for a CMG in the next available honours list.[24] However, at no time did Stewart Lockhart look to the Colonial Office as the scapegoat for the setback. Once his original anger and disappointment was gone, he could look on the episode as one in which historical circumstances had conspired against him, finally believing that Chamberlain was the best Secretary of State under whom he served, being 'imaginative, progressive and keen'.[25]

If Stewart Lockhart did not believe himself to be personally slighted at this point, the time was shortly to come when he was firmly convinced that a personal vendetta was halting his career. In later years, when the Governorship of Hong Kong eluded him, he was to look back on the period before Robinson's retirement as one when he became a 'marked man', forever more to be passed over in the Hong Kong hierarchy. According to his family, Stewart Lockhart blamed Governor Robinson and Major General Black, who became Acting Governor following Robinson's departure, personally for his lack of promotion. The reason was related to his daughter, Mary, by her mother after Stewart Lockhart's death and written down in Mary's notebook. It bears all the hallmarks of a Victorian melodrama:

Miss Black was the General's daughter. JHSL at this time was the Registrar of Births, Deaths and Marriages. Miss Black became secretly engaged to an A. D. C. to the Governor and wished to marry him in secret. Her parents were not to be told anything. JHSL warned the girl that the marriage was quite unsuitable and refused to marry her whereupon she went to the Governor who sent for JHSL and ordered him to perform the marriage. When the General heard what had happened he vowed he would ruin JHSL's career somehow or other ... the reason the governor interfered was becos [sic] he himself was having an affair at the time with Miss Black, and found the ADC a good cover.[26]

It is impossible to contradict or verify this tale, but Stewart Lockhart's family believed, with their father, that this incident blotted his career, and they were not alone in thinking this. Apart from his daughter's recollection, the incident is referred to, briefly, by Sir Henry Blake, a Governor of Hong Kong.[27] Otherwise, however, the incident remains a shrouded mystery, further confused by the fact that Governor Robinson was at pains to write very highly of Stewart Lockhart in government correspondence, and no hint of animosity appeared in Black's correspondence when he was Acting Governor. Whatever the truth, the unalienable fact is that, before too many years more, Stewart Lockhart's glittering career was to be halted in its tracks, and for no tangibly apparent reason.

Stewart Lockhart was not alone, of course, in being denied promotion when he felt it was deserved. The Colonial Office had, at the turn of the century, a surfeit of equally experienced, equally deserving administrators awaiting promotion. This point was amply illustrated in 1902 when the Colonial Office was debating the appointment of a new Colonial Secretary in Hong Kong. The Hong Kong cadets were, it was felt, getting disproportionately more promotional opportunities than men in the Straits Settlements or in Ceylon, and the Colonial Office felt that a change of policy was due. Lucas wrote a minute regarding the possibility of promoting May, another former Hong Kong cadet.

We appointed Mr Lockhart from the inside for a particular reason — because he was registrar general and we wished to combine the registrar generalship with the colonial secretaryship. Having appointed from the inside last time is a real reason for not doing so now. If Mr May is appointed there is a charge [sic] that the post may be looked on as belonging to the Hong Kong service. And though Mr Lockhart and Mr May are capable men and have a qualification of knowing Chinese, I am not prepared to say that they are as capable as several others who have had much longer service but not had the same chances.[28]

The days of endless opportunities were being limited by a shift away from internal promotions to ones which broadened the horizons of the Colonial Service as a whole. Colonial Office policy had changed, and this would probably have affected Stewart Lockhart's own fortunes, even without Black's vendetta.

Despite the heavy work-load and the disappointment at Chamberlain's decision, Stewart Lockhart continued to be meticulous in his attention to every duty, large or small. Numerous examples of his daily work-load remain in his collections of papers, including one letter which illustrates his ability to care for the small man and his problems, despite the continuing stress of the dual appointment. In this, the compradore of Gaude, Price and Company, P'ang Shau-chun, remembered how, when Stewart Lockhart was Colonial Secretary, 'he rendered me valuable assistance by bringing some robbers to book in connection with a robbery at my house in the interior of China, for which I am so grateful to him that I can never forget'.[29]

Weihaiwei, shortly to figure so prominently in his life, also involved him in official work during this part of his career, when Admiral Cai Tinggan (Ts'ai T'ing-kan), then a senior Chinese naval officer, was captured by the Japanese there. The Admiral escaped from his captors and wrote to Stewart Lockhart, applying for British citizenship in Hong Kong.[30] Stewart Lockhart presumably retained the letter in his personal files because of its possible historical significance — the Admiral describes the battle and capture at length — little realizing the personal significance Weihaiwei was soon to play in his life.

In addition to his daily duties, Stewart Lockhart was constantly being called upon to chair committees. 1896 was the year of the committee which examined the condition of British trade in Hong Kong, whilst 1897 saw him appointed Honorary Secretary of the Jubilee Committee to celebrate sixty years of rule by Queen Victoria, a duty which earned him a gold medal from the Queen.[31] Some official duties were naturally more pleasant than others, and one which must have given Stewart Lockhart particular satisfaction was his attendance at the ceremony to lay the foundation stone of the new building for the Po Leung Kuk. The proceedings were good natured, with even Whitehead present and exuding bonhomie while watching the Governor lay the foundation stone. A contemporary account of the ceremony, however, illustrated some of the underlying prejudices still held by many of the British against the Chinese. This was a newspaper article in the ever contentious *Hongkong Weekly Press* which documented the Governor's regret 'that after fifty years of British rule the Chinese community should remain so little Anglicized'.[32] The Governor's comment was used by the newspaper to support its objection to the Chinese Chamber of Commerce who continued to practise 'the fengshui superstition, one of the chief barriers to progress in the neighbouring empire'[33] during the opening of their new building. Such prejudices could surely only underline for Stewart Lockhart the importance of gaining Chinese support for the Hong Kong Government by giving them a base of power sufficiently substantial to withstand European ignorance. 1897 gave him just such an opportunity, when he chaired the commission enquiring into the work and organization of the Tung Wah Hospital. Whitehead, Stewart Lockhart's old adversary, spearheaded the allegations against the hospital, which was criticized for being inefficient and anti-government. In addition, some Chinese felt the hospital had been too supportive of government measures during the 1894 plague.

The commission of enquiry was virtually the same as that set up to study the Po Leung Kuk, its members being Stewart Lockhart, Chater, Whitehead, Ho Kai and in addition, the Assistant Colonial Secretary, A. M. Thomson. The commission sat nine times over a five-month period.[34] Of the fourteen witnesses, several European medical officers called for the introduction of Western-style medicine into the hospital, a move which the hospital authorities were later to adopt.[35] Despite fulsome backing from Stewart Lockhart and Ho Kai, the commission's hearings were, at times, as strident as those during the Po Leung Kuk enquiry; and 'the contention became centred on the continued existence or abolition of the Tung Wah Hospital and led to heated arguments on which the Board of Directors defended the hospital as best they could'.[36] Despite a minority dissenting report by Whitehead, Stewart Lockhart once more won the day; the hospital was absolved of any alleged misdemeanours, and its supportive community care applauded.

One has only to glance at the rules laid down by the board to appreciate how straightforward the people running this organization were. With great common sense, the board declared:

Medical treatment will be offered to the helpless free of charge, but medical expenses will be recovered from employees who have friends to support them. This is to make a distinction between what is serious and what is not, and not to confound pearls with fish-eyes.[37]

Unfortunately, Whitehead and the medical officers were blinded to the basic soundness of the Tung Wah's motives, seeing only the 'antiquated quackery'[38] of a medical system which did not 'bleed, or leech, or blister'[39] in the course of medical treatment, as was the custom in Western hospitals. Stewart Lockhart, absorbed as he was with the Chinese way of life, had no such misgivings, and his service to the Tung Wah during the commission's proceedings was later praised by the Chinese of Hong Kong as showing 'plainly the desire which has always actuated you that fairplay should be shewn to us in our efforts to do good, however faulty and insufficient they may appear to Europeans'.[40]

In return for the endless hours he had endured in committee rooms, the years of wading through official papers, and the trials and tribulations which accompanied his life as a colonial officer, Stewart Lockhart was awarded the CMG on 21 May 1898, four days before his fortieth birthday. He was given it slightly earlier than might have been expected, as a consolation for being deprived of the Acting Governorship. The award was for public service, and in recognition of his work in Hong Kong. He received the medal from Queen Victoria herself in December that year at a ceremony in Windsor Castle. He must have felt that he was, at last, receiving just recognition for his labours. The desire for further advancement was, nevertheless, to remain as strong as ever.

1898 was a year of immense importance not only for Stewart Lockhart, but for the colony of Hong Kong as well. One must look back some years, however, to find the source of certain momentous events which were to lead to the expansion of Hong Kong. Less than a week after Stewart Lockhart was appointed to the joint responsibilities of Registrar General and Colonial Secretary, Japan and China signed the Treaty of Shimonoseki, concluding the Sino-Japanese war begun in 1894. Japan's forces had decimated those of China during the conflict and she claimed the Liaodong (Liaotung) Peninsula in north China as the prize for her victory. The Japanese encroachment into China was to result in a scramble for territory and concessions from China by the European powers, each eager to protect, as they viewed it, their own interests. The situation was akin to a global chess game. The balance of power in Europe was at that point fairly evenly matched: Germany and Russia stalemated one another militarily, whilst Britain's power — her navy — matched those of France and Russia combined.[41] The players, therefore, finding the European game to have reached a standstill, promptly switched boards to the rest of the world and proceeded to jostle for power in this new arena. China, during the scramble for concessions, was a major victim; though not the only one in the world. In the final sixteen years of the century, Britain alone added three and a half million square miles of territory to her Empire, with most of that coming from Africa.[42] Not one of the participating aggressors was to emerge with a single ounce of moral vindication for their actions, though each power tried hard to justify what they were doing and had strong mercantile or territorial reasons for behaving as they did.[43] The Sino-Japanese war had caused a great deal of anxiety in Hong Kong, with the scale of the Japanese victory itself being a cause for concern. One historian summed up the prevailing reaction to Japan's overwhelming victory, declaring that 'no one realised how rotten the state of China had become and very few people in the West had any knowledge of Japan at all'.[44]

Britain, long the foreign power of primary influence in China, initially held back from major interference in Japan's aggression. Russia, France, and Germany, however, had fewer scruples and immediately formed a triple intervention, forcing Japan to return the Liaodong Peninsula to China in return for a cash indemnity which Russia, France, and Germany were only too delighted to lend to China in return for land leases and commercial concessions. Britain did little but observe the grasping of the other nations for the two years following the Treaty of Shimonoseki, believing that to do otherwise might tear China apart. As one writer put it, 'the maintenance of the Chinese Empire is essential to the honour as well as the interests of the Anglo-Saxon race'.[45] British non-intervention at this period was also due to Prime Minister Salisbury's attitude to China, described by one Member of Parliament who noted that 'Lord Salisbury does not seem to know that there is such a place as China, and some one should point out the place where it is to him'.[46] Circumstances were, by 1898, to force Britain to indulge in some territorial leasing from China, the alternative being to sit back and lose all hope of exerting a major influence within the country. The MP, George Curzon, put the British case for protection of her interests in no uncertain terms:

It is only in the East, and especially in the Far East, that we may still hope to keep and to create open markets for British manufactures. Every port, every town, and every village that passes into French or Russian hands, is an outlet lost to Manchester, Bradford or Bombay.[47]

The commercial and political pressures were finally irresistible to Britain and, as a result of political and diplomatic manoeuvring, she had, by the end of 1898, acquired two pieces of Chinese territory which were to provide Stewart Lockhart with employment in the Colonial Service until his retirement in 1921: the New Territories of Hong Kong, and Weihaiwei. Because Britain continues to occupy the New Territories until her lease expires in 1997, the area has received a certain amount of recognition among the general public. Weihaiwei, on the other hand, has faded into obscurity, a forgotten part of Britain's imperial past. Both places were to play equally significant parts in Stewart Lockhart's career, however, and he in turn was to play a formative role in the shaping and organization of each of these territories.

Even before the Sino-Japanese war, a body of opinion in Hong Kong favoured the further acquisition of land on the Chinese mainland. The hills on the Kowloon Peninsula overlooking

Hong Kong provided the colony with its one major defensive weakness, and in November 1894 Governor Robinson pointed out those weaknesses at length to the Secretary of State, Lord Ripon.[48] In addition, the commercial community wanted more space in order to enable industry to expand and develop, and to make land available for agricultural enterprises. A third group, which included both the military and the traders, saw expansion as a move which would help eradicate certain Chinese criminal elements which were infiltrating the colony, by making it more difficult for criminals to slip across the border into city settlements. These various groups all had their own particular reasons for wanting more territory, but another, more general, reason was also pertinent. In 1898, Hong Kong's population reached a quarter of a million, and British Kowloon was bulging at the seams. In the simplest terms, the colony was running out of space. Stewart Lockhart 'had no strong bias towards extension except in the immediate vicinity of British Kowloon',[49] an opinion which accorded most closely to that which believed military considerations to be of primary importance.

Towards the end of 1897, events in China were moving at such a pace, with Germany and Russia vying for leases in northern Chinese ports, that Britain could not fail but involve herself in territorial acquisition in north China. Simultaneously, France sought a broader base of power in southern China and in 1898 gained a ninety-nine year lease on the bay of Guangzhou (Kwangchou). Although Britain had been relatively reluctant to obtain a lease for Weihaiwei in north China,[50] no such reluctance was apparent in the case of south China when her commercial supremacy there was under threat. In the final analysis, though military considerations were important in pushing the British Government towards obtaining an extension to the colony, commercial interests and considerations provided the final catalyst which led to the demand for further concessions from the Chinese Government.[51]

In April 1898, Britain requested an extension to her territory in Hong Kong[52] and, two months later, under the Convention of Beijing, China leased to Britain over three hundred and fifty square miles of Guangdong Province which have been known ever since as the New Territories. Until the signing of the convention, Stewart Lockhart played no part in the leasing.

Indeed, at the beginning of 1898, he had taken six months' leave.[53] Whilst in Britain, however, he kept abreast of the news from China through Lucas in the Colonial Office who, as Assistant Under-Secretary in the department, was heavily involved in the leasing of both Weihaiwei and the New Territories. Lucas and Stewart Lockhart maintained close contact: indeed, it was Lucas who informed him that his leave was to be cut short because Chamberlain desired him 'to visit and report upon the territory on the mainland adjacent to Hong Kong about to be leased by the Chinese Government to her Majesty the Queen'.[54] For the ten months following June 1898, Stewart Lockhart was projected into a flurry of activity.

Stewart Lockhart was at his mother's house in Southport when Lucas' note arrived, and he set off immediately for London. There, he received specific instructions as to how he should ascertain 'by what means revenue can in the first instance be best raised from the new territory, without exciting the suspicions or irritating the feelings and prejudices of the Chinese inhabitants'.[55] He was therefore going to have to display a deal of tact during his survey. Certainly, he was not going to be able to enter the territory in the guise of a victorious conqueror. Financial, not military, considerations were by now uppermost in the mind of the British Government, and their official on the spot was directed to act accordingly.

Given the spirit of enterprise which exists in Hong Kong to this day, one should not be surprised that financial considerations featured so strongly, and not just in the mind of the Colonial Office. The Viceroy of Guangdong Province had himself to issue a warning against land speculation within a month of the signing of the convention. In a leased area where 'the conditions have not been settled nor the boundaries marked',[56] the Viceroy warned of the dangers of speculatively purchasing land which might, or might not, remain Chinese territory, and the attendant loss of money which was liable to occur as a result of such speculation. It should be noted that his proclamation did little to prevent the speculative acquisition of land in the New Territories.

Stewart Lockhart was to become completely immersed in the leasing and organization of the New Territories. During 1898 and 1899 this work ruled his life to the virtual exclusion of everything else, and the decisions he made were to be as crucial to the colony of Hong Kong as his support of the Chinese had been at earlier points in his career. As Special Commissioner, Stewart Lockhart was to mould the form of the extension to the colony, working with a treaty which has remained controversially enforced to the present day.

Chapter 6

NEW TERRITORIES, NEW HORIZONS
(1898–1902)

FOR the two weeks prior to his departure for Hong Kong, Stewart Lockhart had a series of meetings at the Colonial Office about the New Territories.[1] The specific brief sent to him by Chamberlain[2] was privately expanded by him during these meetings, the Colonial Office being of the opinion that Stewart Lockhart 'will be the best judge of what is necessary'.[3] In fact, a number of decisions regarding the New Territories were delayed until Stewart Lockhart had had the opportunity to visit the area. The settlement of the boundaries and the question of Chinese jurisdiction in the walled city were two of the most important points awaiting resolution.[4]

He left England on 25 June 1898, sailing via Vancouver to arrive in Hong Kong on 2 August. Meetings with Chamberlain's military appointee as Acting Governor, Major-General Black, followed, before Stewart Lockhart set off by gunboat to commence his survey of the New Territories. He was to spend less than a month in the area before leaving Hong Kong at the end of August to make the long journey back to London to report his findings personally to the Colonial Office. During the humid weeks of August 1898, he covered as much of the newly leased area as possible, his research finally resulting in a thirty-one page report on the territory.[5] The report was a comprehensive social and economic survey of an area containing approximately 100,000 people. Complete in every detail, it even contained a list of villages close to, but not included in, the leased territory.[6] Because the boundaries had yet to be firmly fixed, Stewart Lockhart cast his geographical net as wide as possible, in case the British Government required negotiation of additional territory. In addition to an analysis of the social and geographical features, the report also included his proposals for the future government of the territory. It was a mammoth task to gather the requisite information in the time given and the report itself was written during the sea journey back to Britain.

Throughout his tour of inspection, Stewart Lockhart kept a daily journal which, while it included many of the aspects covered in the published report on the extension, had a generally more informal tone and often demonstrates another side of him: the romantic highlander with a love of the country. Some of the passages in the journal are, as a result, quite poetic:

The country westward is exceedingly beautiful, being diversified by hills and pretty valleys resembling the interior of Ceylon or parts of Japan. The hills are forest clad and silver streams gurgled down over the mountain sides or tumbled down in graceful falls. The crops along the way is [sic] rice, sweet potatoes, tarro, indigo and beans. Oxen and cows can be seen grazing in the hill sides or along the banks that divide the paddy fields.[7]

As Stewart Lockhart and his party made their progress through the territory, villagers set off fire crackers in welcome. Photographs were taken of the inhabitants and their surroundings, and the survey, at times, resembled a gentleman's holiday, with Stewart Lockhart visiting 'a large pawn shop from which a very old gun of the Ming dynasty was bought'.[8] On Stewart Lockhart's instructions, the party introduced some informality into the proceedings whenever possible. Sedan chairs were abandoned at villages and towns so that the observers could walk round built-up areas, and Stewart Lockhart accepted invitations to visit houses large and small. The confidence of the local children was won by Mr Ormsby, Director of Public Works, who scattered some Chinese coins for the children to pick up. The scrambling 'proved to be highly appreciated by the village boys'.[9] The keynote of the visit was generally one of amiable informality with Stewart Lockhart discovering as much as he could by talking to the people themselves. During the second week of his two week sojourn in the territory he felt sufficiently at ease to send the rest of the party back to the base launch, HMS *Plover*, whilst he remained with a single interpreter for the night in a small town west of Ping Shan to find out the customs and local organization of the villages: 'Much valuable information was gathered during the evening.'[10]

That same evening, some village boys showed Stewart Lockhart crickets fighting, and it is vignettes like these which illustrate the Colonial Secretary's ability to inspire confidence in the most wary of people. Such a simple demonstration by local children would never have happened had Stewart Lockhart made himself unapproachable or condescending. He was doubtless aware of the value of information which could be gathered from the people in the New Territories, but he also seems genuinely to have enjoyed his first visit there. Indeed, on the day following his overnight stay, Stewart Lockhart decided to explore further, arranging to go overland to Sham Chun rather than by sea in HMS *Plover* with the rest of his party; quite an adventure, given the lack of roads in the area, the terrible summer heat and the heavy rain.[11]

At the end of the fortnight's journey, Stewart Lockhart had gathered the mass of information required by the British Government and had done so with sufficient tact and courtesy to have been, on the whole, well received by the inhabitants of the New Territories. He had ruffled few feathers and had won the approval of the Chinese who had been impressed by small, but significant matters, such as these: 'His escort made exceedingly few demands upon us for assistance, and in going over our fields there was no molestation even to the extent of frightening the domestic animals.'[12] Stewart Lockhart's sensitivity to detail had carried him through with great merit. Life in the New Territories was not, however, to remain peaceful, and even during the idyllic August journey trouble had reared its ugly head at Kam Tin, where Stewart Lockhart's party was refused entry to the village. Kam Tin was to be a trouble spot in the New Territories for many months to come, and this single episode has been greatly over-emphasized by some writers, as it certainly did not mar the pleasure or the success of the visit as a whole.[13]

Stewart Lockhart barely had time to pack his belongings before he was once more embarking on the long sea journey back to Britain. His notes and journal accompanied him, enabling him to write his official report on the territory whilst aboard ship. One immediate result of this was that the Colonial Office saw the report before the Hong Kong administration who, until October, had to content themselves with Ormsby's survey of the territory, presented to them at the beginning of September.

Stewart Lockhart's report established the approximate geographic area of the lease, the territory's social structure and its economic potential. In addition, he put forward proposals for the administration, suggesting that 'the organization at present in existence should be as far as possible utilized'.[14] He therefore recommended that although a colonial police force should be introduced, existing village constables should be retained; although a British system of justice should be employed via District Officers, existing village tribunals should be retained; and although the study of English should be introduced, existing village schools should be retained. In other words, Stewart Lockhart proposed that the status quo of old China should be upheld as far as possible under British rule. His position was a strong one. The Colonial Office had given him the task of reporting on the New Territories believing him to be the best qualified man to judge the situation. In view of this it seemed likely that Stewart Lockhart's recommendations for the administration of the New Territories would be accepted without too many amendments.

At that point, Hong Kong was headed by the Acting Governor, who was due to relinquish his post in November. The Colonial Office therefore requested Stewart Lockhart's swift return following his visit to the New Territory not only to report to them as quickly as possible, but also in order to give him the opportunity to brief the new Governor, Sir Henry Blake, before Blake travelled to the colony to begin his duties in November.[15]

In his recommendations, which advocated so vigorously the maintenance of the existing order, Stewart Lockhart was accepting that the acquisition of the New Territories, being in the form of a lease, was historically temporary, and was therefore a quite different situation from that pertaining in the rest of Hong Kong. This distinction was clear in both his mind and his acts. Had the New Territories reverted to China when the other 1898 leases reverted, the transition for those living in the territory would hardly have been traumatic, for life under the British at the beginning of the twentieth century provided few alterations to a village life which had been in existence for generations.[16] This desire to retain existing modes of life and social habits also manifested itself in his administration of Weihaiwei.

Having tried to promote a Chinese base of power within Hong Kong, where it was difficult to maintain more than the merest flavour of traditional Chinese society, Stewart Lockhart's report on the New Territories gave him the opportunity to consolidate his ideas about minimizing British control. Hong

Kong before British rule was little more than barren terrain, whereas the New Territories had an existing social structure which Stewart Lockhart did not wish to see dismantled. His belief in upholding the Chinese pattern of life was not an altruistic one. He simply believed it to be common sense that people worked more peacefully and effectively given minimal official interference. In his report he had every opportunity to propose radical change for the area and took no advantage of this, preferring instead to maintain existing values. Had the initial acquisition of the area taken a more overtly British aspect, turning the New Territories into a copy of Hong Kong as it then existed, and submerging its identity under the cloak of British habit, the People's Republic of China might have found it far more difficult than they ultimately have done to have Hong Kong returned to them. A colony of entirely British complexion, such as one finds in the Falkland Islands, would have been a far harder nut to crack than one which includes the thoroughly Chinese complexion of the New Territories. In maintaining such an overtly Chinese way of life in the territories, Stewart Lockhart was excluding the possibility of mass British colonization of the area. Had he instead introduced a system thoroughly British in style, proposing the abandonment of the village system, one suspects that the British Government would have been less compliant about returning Hong Kong to China than they have been in the 1980s; and the lease might still today be the subject of dispute between the two nations.

On his return to London, Stewart Lockhart had an enormous number of points to discuss with the Colonial Office. The first of these was how the administration of the area should be organized. Even as he was leaving Hong Kong, Chinese in the colony were pressing the Acting Governor to have the Scot appointed as resident 'in sole charge of the territory'.[17] This was the option, understandably, which Stewart Lockhart himself favoured, suggesting that 'the head of the Administration should be a Commissioner, subordinate to the Governor of Hong Kong, but in all other respects independent'.[18] Such an arrangement would have preserved the identity of the New Territories in toto; an option to which the Colonial Office could not agree on either political or financial grounds. For one thing, a Commissioner's appointment would cost more money, and they were loathe to incur additional expense when they could arrange, at no extra cost, for Stewart Lockhart, as Colonial Secretary, to be 'in special charge' of the territory.[19] Also, although the convention clearly stated that the New Territories were only leased, the British Government had decided that it was in Britain's interests to join the territory as closely as possible to Hong Kong proper[20] in order that the leased area could, from the outset, be regarded as being incorporated into the rest of the Colony.[21]

The final decision regarding the New Territories was therefore a compromise between Stewart Lockhart's proposals and the political wishes of the Colonial Office. Existing systems of village life were retained whenever practicable, but the territory as a whole was joined to Hong Kong as closely as possible, thus giving the territories their unique social identity whilst binding them tightly to a larger whole. Because of his appointment in the territory, Stewart Lockhart was to abandon his role as Registrar General, enabling him to work as Colonial Secretary with the dual responsibility of the administration of the New Territories. Although the Colonial Office wished to relieve him of his duties as Registrar General immediately, Stewart Lockhart advised against such action until the territory had been fully assimilated into the administration of Hong Kong,[22] and on this point the Colonial Office finally concurred. In reality, an Acting Colonial Secretary worked on his behalf in Hong Kong until the administration of the territory was operational, and he did not relinquish the Registrar General's post until the middle of 1899.

Having completed his briefings with the Colonial Office, Stewart Lockhart took the remainder of the leave which had been disrupted earlier in the year because of the new British acquisition. Staying long enough in Scotland to visit Edinburgh to attend the farewell dinner held by the Watsonian Club on 7 December for his former headmaster, George Ogilvie, he then returned to the south of England to receive his CMG from Queen Victoria before departing for Hong Kong on 29 December, returning to the colony in time for the official handing over ceremony. By the time he returned to Hong Kong the new Governor had arrived. Little else, however, had changed, and Britain seemed no closer to taking formal possession of the new area. Delays had been caused, in part, by the Chinese insistence that their officials remain in the walled city of Kowloon. British officials (Stewart Lockhart included) were unhappy with this arrangement, foreseeing future conflict as an inevitability between the officials of the two countries. From the Chinese point of view, removing their officials was tantamount to total secession, and they adamantly refused to alter their position. Thus in the two leased territories of Weihaiwei and the New Territories Chinese officials remained in the two principal walled cities on the understanding that their position was not inconsistent with British military requirements.[23] The Chinese magistrates and their troops, of course, did not survive for long in Hong Kong. Following the troubles which were to appear at Tai Po, Britain used the disturbances as a pretext to remove all trace of Chinese governmental power in the walled city.

The delineation of the boundaries caused further delay. The original convention was surprisingly vague on the matter: indeed, many of the delays in Britain taking over the territory were caused by the lack of detail in the convention, a fact which was noted by a number of contemporary observers. The China Association had written at length to the Acting Colonial Secretary on this very subject, remarking that 'the Agreement is couched ... in general terms which leave much to be subsequently defined'; a situation they found alarming.[24] When the convention was signed, it was stated that the boundaries would be fixed following surveys of the area by both sides. As a result, the Governor of Hong Kong appointed Stewart Lockhart as Britain's representative 'for the purpose of fixing the exact boundaries of the extension of Hongkong in accordance with the terms of the Convention'.[25] The Chinese appointed the Viceroy of Guangdong's Foreign Secretary, Wong Ts'un-shin, as their commissioner, and within eight days of their first meeting, the two men had fixed the boundary of the leased territory, signing a detailed memorandum defining the northern boundary on 19 March.[26] They appear to have worked swiftly and amicably. Time was obviously of the essence, and both were under pressure from their respective masters to resolve the question of the boundaries as quickly as possible. At the end of the negotiations they were on sufficiently good terms for Wong Ts'un-shin to present Stewart Lockhart with two scroll paintings of landscapes in a gesture of friendship.[27]

The boundaries defined, Monday, 17 April, was designated as the day when the British flag was to be hoisted over the territory and a public holiday was declared for that date. But even the best laid plans can falter, and no one in the British administration was prepared for the uprising which preceded the ceremony of raising the flag. Trouble began almost as soon as the boundaries were fixed, when Captain May, the Inspector of Police, selected a site for the matshed, a temporary police station, at Tai Po Hui which was to be the police headquarters.[28] Villagers had protested that the siting upset the *feng shui* of the area and, in order to keep the peace, May eventually had the matshed moved to another site approved by the local population. A week later, on 1 April, workmen erecting this matshed were threatened by local people who seemed to be using *feng shui* as an excuse to thwart British jurisdiction in the area. At the same time, placards denouncing the British began appearing in the territory, and Governor Blake was sufficiently concerned at the situation to meet the Viceroy to protest about the behaviour of the local population.[29] Two days later, May and his party were attacked while inspecting the newly built matshed. The elders at Tai Po again introduced the excuse that the offending building was interfering with the *feng shui* of the area, and when an exasperated May refused to demolish the matshed, the locals attacked his party with bricks, May replying with a bayonet charge. That night, further trouble ensued, the matshed was set alight, and May withdrew to Hong Kong. Fierce activity and late night memos between officials in the colony followed May's withdrawal and by midnight the Governor had decided that Stewart Lockhart, with a force of 200 men, should go directly to Tai Po to resolve the crisis. Blake had every confidence in Stewart Lockhart's ability to handle the situation, as the man 'whose knowledge of the people is great, and who has means of obtaining special information.'[30] The British situation, however, was a difficult one. They had yet to cede the territory formally to British jurisdiction and in the meantime decided to retain nominal Chinese control, using the Viceroy's own troops as far as possible. Chinese troops were therefore sent to protect the offending matshed, now rebuilt, at Tai Po. For a week, the situation appeared settled, but when May went to inspect the buildings three days before the British flag was to be hoisted, he discovered that the building had again been burnt down, despite the 'protection' of the Viceroy's troops. May returned to Hong Kong, collected a company of the Hong Kong

Regiment, and was back at Tai Po by the following day, 15 April. There, he was met by about 1,200 Chinese who opened fire before being seen off by May's troops. The following day, Stewart Lockhart arrived with more troops and the British flag was hoisted at 3 p.m. in front of May and 500 men from the Hong Kong Regiment. Meanwhile, the Governor's proclamation of British rule was hastily posted throughout the territory.

The unseemly haste to hoist the flag and proclaim British rule did not deter the rebels. The day the flag was hoisted, one of the men appointed by Stewart Lockhart to post the Governor's proclamation, Tang Cheung-hing, was siezed at Kap Shui Mun. On the following day, several thousand Chinese attacked the British camp at Tai Po. They were repulsed by British troops and suffered heavy casualties, but in the interim gave the British authorities a few unsettling moments. On the same day as the attack, Tang Cheung-hing was brutally murdered at Ha Tsuen. His body was not discovered for another three days, but when it was, Stewart Lockhart acted swiftly and had the houses of Tang's murderers burnt to the ground, the criminals having already fled the territory. In addition, the villages from whence the criminals had come were ordered to compensate Tang's widow, whilst at Ha Tsuen the villagers were ordered to support her thereafter. The justice meted out by Stewart Lockhart was not of a kind to be found in any British criminal code, and Blake did not approve of his deputy acting like a Chinese Magistrate. He censured Stewart Lockhart, albeit mildly, for his 'unfortunate' actions, but Stewart Lockhart remained stubbornly convinced that he had followed the only proper course:

I have not the least hesitation in saying that had we acted otherwise than we did and sat still doing nothing until we had tried to obtain strictly legal proof, which may never be forthcoming, a most unfavourable impression of British justice would have been created among the people.[31]

He was equally thorough in his diffusion of the Tai Po crisis. In the week following the battle, Stewart Lockhart, with a party of troops, had meeting houses searched for incriminating documents, villagers interviewed, evidence collected, and arms confiscated. A week after the flag was hoisted, he could report that 'all the villages along the route received us with crackers and in most cases had the white flag of submission flying'.[32] Stewart Lockhart was all for the banishment of the rebels, something which Blake could not sanction, as it was prohibited under the 1898 convention. However, whilst curbing Stewart Lockhart's desire for revenge, Blake was taking equally stern measures on his own. While Stewart Lockhart was commencing his inter-rogations at village level, another party, of Hong Kong Police, were pursuing the Tai Po rebels, many of whom had fled to the safety of the rebel village of Kam Tin. The village was walled, and had large iron gates which the villagers securely fastened against the police; the rebels therefore believed themselves to be safe. However, Blake gave the order to have the gates removed 'as a punishment for the resistance offered by the natives', and carried to Hong Kong.[33] Blake, often depicted as the person who tempered Stewart Lockhart's actions,[34] was so pleased with the capture of Kam Tin's gates, and the resulting defeat of the rebels, that he later removed these same gates when he left Hong Kong, and eventually used them to adorn his house in Eire.[35]

Work in the New Territories kept Stewart Lockhart away from Hong Kong and his family for months on end. In May 1899, the disturbances in the New Territories finally quelled, he was appointed Special Commissioner for the area, a post he was to hold until he left Hong Kong three years later. Despite the fact that the New Territories were a rural area, lacking even the most rudimentary road network to facilitate communication (a basic road system was not established from Kowloon until 1908), Stewart Lockhart quickly set up a British method of rule closely in line with the traditional Chinese one. In the villages, elders continued to hold sway. However, instead of a Chinese Magis-trate ruling over them, British District Officers based in the countryside now fulfilled that function. The only additional layer of power which immediately affected the populace was the police force, stationed at strategic points throughout the ter-ritory to maintain law and order. One suspects that, after the initial disturbances in April, the inhabitants of the New Territ-ories were aware of little noticeable change in their lives follow-ing the assumption of British rule. Stewart Lockhart's approach was to tread gently, looking to Chinese custom for a model whenever possible. Even his aggressive pursuit of wrongdoers after the troubles was followed through in a most Chinese manner, with him behaving exactly like an outraged Chinese Magistrate. In that sense, he was right to have defended his actions against Blake's criticisms: the villagers would have found his behaviour far less understandable at that juncture had he resorted to the strict rule of British law which was, at that point, an alien concept to them. Later, he wrote to the Governor to explain his attitude to law in the New Territories, when advocating the gradual introduction of laws and ordinances to the area.

Although the new territory is to be incorporated as part of the Colony of Hongkong, this incorporation will not for some time affect the great difference existing between the Chinese inhabitants of Hongkong and of the new territory. The former have been accustomed to British rule for a period of more than fifty years; the latter have hitherto had no experience of it. At first everything will be strange to them, and it will require much tact and discretion to administer their affairs in such a manner as to allay that suspicion and alarm for which the Chinese as a race are so notorious.[36]

The administration and organization of the New Territories took several months of feverish activity and a flurry of ordinances. Stewart Lockhart spent weeks on end in the area, supervising the smallest detail, making it 'his' territory. From April to July 1899, he spent less than a week in Hong Kong, and the rest of the time worked from a countryside camp. Knowing his love of hunting and riding, and the sheer enjoyment he felt from being in open spaces, he must have found the experience exhilarating, despite the arduous nature of his work. Conditions, even for a hardy Scot, were hardly luxurious, however, and it was not until late June that the Hong Kong administration found time to send their Special Commissioner a bed on which to sleep.

The April disturbances had cast a shadow over the acquisition of the area and it was some time before the Governor deemed it politic to make an appearance in the territory. When he finally arrived to meet the village elders, Blake did so amidst elaborate preparations. Disembarking from HMS *Pigmy*, with a guard of honour from the Hong Kong Regiment, he was greeted with firecrackers and clanging gongs. His speech to the elders, translated by Stewart Lockhart, emphasised the need for law and order and promised as little interference as possible with existing local customs.[37]

The pressure of all this work was undoubtedly great and academic studies were postponed during Stewart Lockhart's stay in the New Territories for the first time since his arrival in Hong Kong. Even so, he somehow managed to see the third volume of *The Currency of the Farther East* published in 1898, and the scholar in him was not to be suppressed for too long. In the midst of dealing with the delineation of the boundaries, he still found time to draw a sketch plan of the ancestral hall of the Tang family in San On, complete with translations of the scrolls found there.[38]

The Tang hall scrolls would have been of particular interest to Stewart Lockhart who was, by that time, the owner of a growing collection of Chinese paintings. A number of the first scrolls he acquired had been presented to him by Chinese friends.[39] Perhaps such gifts encouraged him to forage further into the world of Chinese art. Certainly, by the mid-1890s, he was commissioning paintings directly from artists of the thriving Cantonese and Shanghai schools. Many foreigners living in late nineteenth-century China bought Chinese paintings pre-dating the Qing dynasty. Indeed, many European public collections of oriental art in existence today owe their artistic strength to the enthusiasm of such men. As we shall see later, Stewart Lockhart purchased pre-Qing paintings during his tenure in Weihaiwei, but he was also unusual in supporting work by living Chinese artists. Lively and colourful works by Cantonese masters such as Zhu Cheng (Chu Ch'eng, 1826–1900), were purchased by Stewart Lockhart as they became available on the open market, and by the late 1890s he was commissioning works by living Cantonese artists for his own pleasure. As a result, bird and flower, and figurative paintings from the Cantonese school comprise the majority of his collection at this time. His support for contemporary Chinese art was to continue during his years in Weihaiwei, making his collection of art to this day one of the best holdings of nineteenth-century Cantonese and Shanghai school paintings in existence in Britain. Stewart Lockhart's enthusiasm for 'things Chinese' is typified by this interest, not only in the ancient, but in the modern too. To him, China was not the degenerate fossil lampooned by so many contemporary observers, but a country with a living culture and a glorious past.

The leasing of the New Territories had disrupted Stewart Lockhart's leave in 1898, and, after eighteen months of intensive work in the territory, he must have anticipated with some eagerness his next leave. By 1900, the administration of the New Territories was running smoothly. District Officers were in place to oversee the administration at local level and the transfer of power from China to Britain was absolute. With the territory organized to his satisfaction, Stewart Lockhart began a nine-month leave of absence from the colony in February 1900. He and his family spent much of their time with family and friends in Scotland, and it was during a visit to friends in Dumfriesshire in south-west Scotland that the Colonial Office requested his immediate return to Hong Kong.[40] Although it was early August and Stewart Lockhart therefore only had six weeks of his leave remaining, his masters deemed the situation in south China sufficiently alarming for them to require the Colonial Secretary's immediate return. Accordingly, Stewart Lockhart set sail for Hong Kong at the end of August, leaving his wife, Edith, and their two children to return at a later date. The situation which was causing such panic at the Colonial Office and in Guangzhou, from which cadets had been removed for their own safety,[41] was the Boxer Rising. The rising, particularly that part which resulted in the siege at Beijing, is well documented by contemporary accounts,[42] and merits little discussion within these pages. The Boxers, bands of Chinese peasants with a fervent bias against foreigners, had been active in China since 1898 when the scramble for concessions had reached its zenith. From a series of peasant uprisings in Shandong Province, the Boxers' rebellion had spread throughout China until, by 1900, they turned on foreign — and particularly missionary — settlements, burning, murdering, and looting. Spurred by a hatred of foreigners and their religious and commercial encroachment in China, and covertly supported by the Dowager Empress, who saw the peasant armies as a means to eradicate foreign influence in her country, the Boxers gained a menacing strength. Finally, the unthinkable happened, and the Boxers laid siege to the Legations in Beijing: the centre of foreign governments in China. In June 1900, Britain feared that her subjects living in the Legation quarter were dead, and what little news was filtering out of China was not optimistic. Although holidaying in Britain at the time, Stewart Lockhart was certainly aware of the Legations' troubles in Beijing and a fellow officer, Alex Michie, who had studied Cantonese with Stewart Lockhart, and was likewise on holiday in Britain at the time, wrote tersely: 'Awful news from China. Situation unprecedented and unimaginable'.[43]

It was not until August that the Legations were relieved and the victorious European forces extracted their revenge by sacking the Summer Palace, looting imperial treasures. By that time, Stewart Lockhart was on board ship, sailing back to Hong Kong. He arrived in time to see the Boxer troubles over and the European powers extracting a huge indemnity from the Chinese Government in reparation for the rebellion. It seems likely that Hong Kong's Colonial Secretary was less than happy at having his leave abruptly terminated unnecessarily.

He arrived to find the colony once more smitten with plague which had spread its deathly virus even to Hong Kong's Peak. Sir Henry Blake had lent his summer house on the Peak to the Director of Public Works, and one of the Director's coolies had died there.[44] The occurrence of plague in Hong Kong's most prestigious European quarter brought home to the inhabitants the risks inherent in living in the Far East, where mortality rates for all races were high. After almost twenty years in the Far East, Stewart Lockhart had proved to be of remarkably robust health, not once succumbing to the diseases which commonly afflicted one in Hong Kong. However, his luck ran out in 1900 when, shortly after he returned to the colony, he was struck down by typhoid. This debilitating illness was of such severity that he was not back on his feet until the beginning of 1901 when he resumed duties briefly before retiring from the colony for a two-month holiday. Two months were not long enough to visit Britain, so he instead journeyed to north China leaving Hong Kong at the end of April and stopping off first at Shanghai before travelling on to Weihaiwei. His stay in Britain's recently acquired territory was a brief one, being merely a point of transition between Shanghai and Yantai (Chefoo), before moving on to Beijing to spend a week in the great city. Shortly before his holiday, Stewart Lockhart had acquired his newest 'toy' — a Kodak camera — and from then on became, in his own words, an inveterate 'snapshotter'. The camera was taken with him on his Beijing visit where he photographed the Forbidden City, abruptly vacated by the Dowager Empress following the Boxer Rising. The great palace complex looks forlorn and deserted, though one photograph captures a painter redecorating the exterior of the Empress Dowager's apartments in readiness for her imminent return.[45] The looted Summer Palace was likewise captured on film, recording for posterity its shameful desecration at the hands of the foreign troops.

By the summer of 1901, Stewart Lockhart had recovered his zest for life as if he had suffered no illness at all. The administration of the New Territories, in tandem with the Colonial Secretaryship, continued to keep him fully occupied, though time was found to take Edith to see the sights of the mainland countryside. Together they visited Tai Po, taking photographs of the countryside and its inhabitants as they went. The rural flavour of the territory was likewise captured; farmers ploughing their fields, and wayside pottery stalls contrasted with walled villages. Stewart Lockhart also used his Kodak to capture more serious subjects which touched his official duties, including the queues of anxious workers lining up for their daily water ration during the water shortage of 1901 when the taps were turned on each day for only an hour.[46] Photographs like these, showing the distress of the ordinary man, say more than any words can about the awful conditions produced by Hong Kong's annual drought.[47]

Upon his return, the administration of the New Territories now settled, Stewart Lockhart once more began to turn to his duties as Colonial Secretary more fully. A photograph taken in his office in 1902 shows him at his desk, surrounded by books.[48] The desk itself, piled high with papers of all kinds is a most illuminating testament to his daily workload. One senses that a highly organized form of chaos reigned in this sanctum.

By 1901, Stewart Lockhart had been Hong Kong's Colonial Secretary for six years, and his restless, competitive spirit was seeking new challenges. Within the administration of Hong Kong, he had a breadth of experience which was unrivalled and no other official could equal his knowledge of and dealings with the Chinese community there. Cantonese was, of course, the dialect in which he worked, but no amount of fluency in Cantonese would fit him for an administrative post elsewhere in China. Therefore, with one eye on future prospects and another on the expansion of his academic studies, he had also mastered the Mandarin dialect over the years. Perhaps his visit to north China in 1901 gave him the impetus to seek a new posting within the Colonial Office, or perhaps it was merely his own ambition that made this quest inevitable. For whatever reason, by August 1901, Stewart Lockhart was suggesting that he might be 'employed in China outside Hongkong, should occasion arise'.[49] His suggestion that a post outside Hong Kong might be found was made with one specific job in mind. When, in 1898, Britain had leased the New Territories, she had also leased an equivalently sized area of north China, at Weihaiwei. Since then, Weihaiwei had been governed by a military commander but now, three years on, a civil administration was under consideration. Aware of these moves, Stewart Lockhart was indicating that he would like to be considered as the man to set up the civil administration of Weihaiwei. His experience in the New Territories made him superbly well equipped for such an appointment, sufficiently so for it to be noted at the Colonial Office that he might 'be *very* useful in connection with Wei-haiwei'.[50] It took a few months more before a final decision was made, but in January 1902, Stewart Lockhart was informed that his appointment as first civil Commissioner of Weihaiwei was confirmed,[51] and that his duties in Hong Kong would cease on 22 April that year. The Stewart Lockharts had only three short months in which to pack up home and family and move to the other end of China.

Whilst Stewart Lockhart was undoubtedly delighted to be faced with a new challenge, one senses that Edith viewed the prospect of life in Weihaiwei with slightly less enthusiasm. Hong Kong and Hong Kong society had, until then, been her life. Not an academic, and with little interest in the Chinese, Shandong Province, in which Weihaiwei was situated, held no excitement for her. Close friends of the couple made light of conditions in Weihaiwei, whilst extolling the district's few virtues: 'The climate, I fancy, will be a great improvement even on the atmosphere of the Peak and the want of Society which may be a little suspicious at first will be I fancy a drawback very soon righted.'[52] It is unlikely that Stewart Lockhart and Edith had any opportunity to analyse their feelings about the move to Weihaiwei until after the fact. The final weeks in Hong Kong passed in a flurry of festivities and farewells, with most of April occupied by dinners and presentations of parting gifts. Every organization Stewart Lockhart had ever been involved in gave him a farewell address,[53] all praising his good qualities and, naturally, ignoring his shortcomings. The inhabitants of the New Territories spoke of his kindness,[54] the Chinese community of Hong Kong of his friendship,[55] the Po Leung Kuk of his unstinting support,[56] and the Executive and Legislative Councils of his administrative efficiency.[57] Such addresses are, by their very nature, flattering, but beneath all the traditional courtesies, the admiration and affection which many in Hong Kong felt for him is clearly apparent. This is particularly obvious amongst senior members of the Chinese community who looked upon him as 'a good friend' who, over the years, had 'completely won their respect and confidence'.[58] It would appear that many people in Hong Kong were genuinely sad to see their Colonial Secretary leave the colony and crowds came to bid the Stewart Lockharts farewell when they departed. Years later, Hong Kong newspapers were to recall that 'he was an exceedingly courteous and popular official and earned the respect of all with whom he was brought in contact'.[59] Both the administration and the society of the colony were to feel his loss, yet all congratulated him on his new posting, confident that Weihaiwei would thrive under his care.

Chapter 7

BREAKING DOWN THE BARRIERS
(1902-1904)

WHEN the British Government leased the New Territories it had
— in Britain's view — sound mercantile and military grounds
for doing so. By comparison, the lease of Weihaiwei was signed
for a variety of confusing reasons. The British Government's
views on the territory were muddled from the start and the
development of Weihaiwei was to suffer accordingly.

The leasing of Weihaiwei was a product of the scramble for
concessions by all the European powers in the late 1890s.
Germany, in addition to mining and railway concessions in
Shandong Province, had leased the town of Jiao Xian (Kiao-
chow) in the province in 1898. Meanwhile, Russia had occupied
Lüshun (Port Arthur), which almost faced Weihaiwei and was
opposite Korea's western coast. Britain therefore felt the need to
maintain the balance of power in north China and demanded a
base in the area.[1] Weihaiwei was, in many ways, the obvious
choice. Britain, in an effort to protect her world-wide trading
interests, greatly increased her naval expenditure between 1898
and 1900, and the acquisition of Weihaiwei, however reluctant,
was not out of line with the general naval strategy of the day
which was to support Britain's influence abroad. Set on the tip
of the Shandong Peninsula, the territory was held by the
Japanese until June 1898 as part of the agreement formulated
under the Treaty of Shimonoseki. The leases in north China
were little more than the product of arbitrary bartering by the
European powers to retain an equal footing with one another,
and neither Germany, Russia, nor Britain seemed to have been
particularly enthusiastic about their acquisitions.[2] Germany had
wanted a more southerly port as a coaling station, dependant as
she was on Britain's goodwill in Hong Kong to coal her ships,
and had favoured Amoy which, because it was a treaty port,
was unavailable for her exclusive use. Russia, on the other
hand, really wanted a port in Korea as a counterweight to
Japanese influence in the area and, by comparison, Lüshun was

second best. Britain, one may believe, only took a lease of Weihaiwei to maintain her 'face' amongst the other nations, and never realized the territory's full potential. Even during the first discussions at cabinet level, there was disquiet about acquiring a territory of such dubious value: 'The naval experts present were all against it, but on someone mentioning that the Germans would seize it if the English did not, the cabinet changed its mind and decided to secure a lease upon it.'[3] Almost from the start, Britain failed Weihaiwei; Britain's attitude was summed up in one parliamentary debate by Lord Charles Beresford who spoke of his being told by a German admiral that, 'the Russians are working with very great activity to fortify their fort, the Germans are working with very great industry in making a parade ground, and you are employed with great industry in making a cricket ground.'[4]

Even the lease under which Britain held Weihaiwei was imbued with uncertainty, Britain's terms being that she keep the territory 'for so long a period as Port Arthur shall remain in the occupation of Russia'.[5] When, in 1905, Lüshun was transferred to Japanese hands, the lease was immediately under threat, though Britain kept Weihaiwei at that point by maintaining that Lüshun was still being leased from China. Almost from the first, rendition of the territory was a subject which was discussed frequently. When, for example, Stewart Lockhart paid an official visit to Jinan (Chinan) in 1906, the press reported rumours that he was going to discuss the rendition of Weihaiwei with the Governor of Shandong.[6] Such rumours, however groundless, did little to aid Weihaiwei's prosperity. The uncertainty over Weihaiwei's future contrasts sharply with the optimism shown when the lease was first announced. More than one newspaper hailed the lease as more significant than that of the New Territories and *The Graphic* summed up the opinion of the day: 'Wei-hai-wei affords an excellent and secure anchorage for our fleet in the China Seas, including ships of the largest size ... This fact cannot but greatly improve our position in the Far East as a naval power.'[7] Beresford, who had lamented Britain's lack of support for Weihaiwei in parliament, also noted shortly after the lease had been executed that it was 'an immense acquisition to our naval strength in the China Seas, as with but a comparatively small expenditure of money it could be made a most efficient and powerful naval base'.[8] Not everyone had

Beresford's enthusiasm, however. The editor of *The Times* wrote that he was 'not much smitten by the idea', believing Britain's position in north China would gain little from the lease of Weihaiwei.[9]

Early reports on Weihaiwei suggested it might be an excellent naval base, offering a relatively healthy climate. Further, some dredging between the island of Liugong Dao (Liu-kung Tao) and the mainland would have enabled the entire China Squadron to undertake a variety of naval exercises without being observed.[10] The mild summer climate made Weihaiwei greatly preferred to Hong Kong, and the China Squadron was undoubtedly keen to expand the base.[11] Other reports on the area upon which Colonial Office policy was formed were less enthusiastic. Sir Frank Swettenham made his independent report on the territory in 1900 at the request of the Colonial Office; a report which was accepted without any particular reservations, although 'the tradition is that he had to satisfy himself by viewing the lovely shores of Weihaiwei from the deck of HMS *Terrible* being unable to land on account of an attack of fever which no doubt accounts for his having described the place as a colder Aden!'[12]

Plans for turning Weihaiwei into a major naval base, however, never materialized. The territory was never to become Britain's Asian Gibraltar, for, within three years of leasing the area, Britain had decided that major military and naval fortifications were too costly to build and maintain.[13] Britain could not afford to turn Weihaiwei into a major defensive station, as to make any base there impregnable would have been extraordinarily expensive;[14] neither could she return it to China whilst Germany and Russia held territory in the area. It was useful as a summer naval base, even though it could only 'be used as a coaling station . . . during the summer in times of peace'.[15] There was, Colonial Office logic followed, only one solution and that was to try and make the territory a commercial success, or at least self-supporting, under a civil administration. For this task there was only one obvious candidate, James Stewart Lockhart. His administrative handling of the New Territories provided him with the ideal experience for setting up a civil administration and — equally important — his strong contacts with the Hong Kong Chinese gave the Colonial Office hope that his influence might encourage them to bring their commercial flair to north China. There was just a chance that, under his guidance, Weihaiwei might become Britain's next commercial success in Asia. With this in mind, and brimming with enthusiasm, Stewart Lockhart arrived in Weihaiwei.

He was going to face an uphill task in this project. Weihaiwei was so poorly equipped prior to his arrival that the officer commanding had included requests in his supplementary estimates for some legal reference books, a boat and crew to provide transport, and a typewriter to replace the one which the administration 'loaned occasionally'.[16] The lack of the most basic office equipment reflected the attitude of the Government in London — Weihaiwei was to cost as little money as possible. Even defence was to be kept at a minimal level unless the territory itself could afford otherwise: 'We do not want a garrison at Wei hai wei ... we particularly want to run the place entirely as a non-protected trading station. If the trade comes we will begin protecting.'[17]

Stewart Lockhart cannot have been unaware that life was not going to be easy. Even in distant Selangor, one of his friends had heard that the government 'expected to obtain a large revenue from the place under your able administration' and likened the decision to switch from naval to mercantile objectives as making 'Wei Hai Wei a local Margate, instead of a Portsmouth'.[18] Perhaps, in later years, Stewart Lockhart was to wish he had been posted to Margate rather than to Weihaiwei.

From the day of his arrival on 3 May 1902, the omens were not good. Stewart Lockhart and his family had given up the spacious comfort of their house on Hong Kong's Peak to move into what they expected to be commodious quarters provided by the government. Unfortunately, there had been neither time nor money to build a Government House and the Stewart Lockharts had instead to settle for second best: the house intended for the Secretary to Government. Set on a hill overlooking the bay, 'Government House' could not be described as imposing. The largest room in the house, the dining room, measured only fifteen feet by twenty-two feet, whilst the smallest of the four bedrooms was a meagre ten by twelve feet. Comprising seven rooms in all, the house hardly conjured up an image of the power and magnificence of the British Empire.[19] Built without internal sanitation or running water, heated by coal fires, and lit by oil lamps, the Stewart Lockharts were to live in these conditions (ones they would never have tolerated in Hong Kong) for more than eight years before the home government sanctioned money for improvements. This lack of funding was apparent in other areas, too. Stewart Lockhart had to fight hard before he had even set foot in Weihaiwei to have his salary conserved at Hong Kong levels, with the Treasury at one point actually suggesting he take a cut in salary to move to the territory.[20] Financial constraints were to become no less stringent as time went on.

Enthusiasm, however, was the keynote of Stewart Lockart's work on his arrival, and whilst Edith did her best to make their new home comfortable, Stewart Lockhart turned one of the three public rooms into an office, there being no other accommodation available, and settled down to the organization of government. His task was to formulate the administration of a territory which in size (394 square miles) and population (150,000) was roughly comparable to Hong Kong's New Territories. Stewart Lockhart was starting, as far as the administration was concerned, on virgin territory. Everything, from a mail service to the registration of births, had to be organized from scratch.[21]

An Order in Council gave him powers to make and proclaim ordinances using Hong Kong's laws as a model.[22] He was head of the justiciary and chief administrator rolled into one, running a sizeable area of north China with the aid of a tiny staff. The parallels between Weihaiwei and the New Territories were many, for both contained a predominantly rural Chinese population, and were economic and social backwaters at the time they were leased. The major difference, of course, was that Hong Kong gave the New Territories every possible trading advantage whereas Weihaiwei was too far from anywhere to be immediately promoted. Before Stewart Lockhart could establish a trading base in the territory, however, he had first to impose a Western administration upon a non-Western population without disharmony.

Because of the naval base, Weihaiwei was well served with sporting facilities. In addition to hunting and riding, shooting and skating could be had on the mainland in winter, while on the island of Liugong, tennis, cricket, hockey, football, and athletics were available all summer. Arriving in May, Stewart Lockhart, although busy setting up the administration, must

1 Government House, Weihaiwei, 1918.

2 Queues for water during the water famine of 1901, Hong Kong.

3   James Stewart Lockhart in the Temple of Confucius, Qufu, 1903.

4 James Stewart Lockhart with Duke Kong and Chinese officials outside the Kong Mansion at the Temple of Confucius, Qufu, 1903

5 James Stewart Lockhart visiting the Governor of Shandong Province at Jinan, 1903.

6   The captain of the *Jing Hai* with his family, 1903.

7 The city of Boshan, seen by Stewart Lockhart and his party during the visit to the Governor of Shandong, 1903.

8   Reginald Johnston with the portrait of King Edward VII before its presentation to Duke Kong in 1904.

9 The bund and shore, Port Edward, *c.*1908–1910.

10 New roads in Weihai City, *c.*1920.

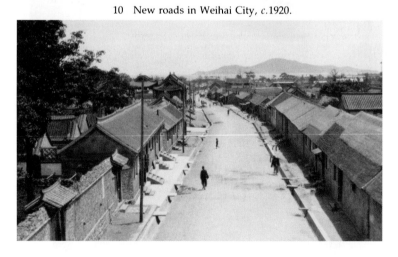

11   A family in a shenzi, Weihaiwei, 1909.

12   The Commissioner's picnic at Weihaiwei, 1913.

13   The 21st and 22nd contingents of the Chinese Labour Corps preparing for embarkation from Weihaiwei, 14 May 1917. Although early summer the men are wearing their winter kit, their contracts and identity disks pinned to the front of their uniforms.

14 James and Mary Stewart Lockhart in Weihaiwei, *c.*1916.

15 Reginald Johnston in the sable cloak given to him by the last Emperor of China in the Forbidden City, Beijing, 1922.

16 Yao Baoshu, A Solitary among the Hills. Ink on paper, 1911. Yao Baoshu was Magistrate of Wendeng District and painted this work for Stewart Lockhart.

17 Yao Yi, Tigers and Pine Tree. Ink and colour on paper. Bought in Weihaiwei, March 1914.

18 Lan Fou Nong, Bamboo. Ink on
paper. Nineteeth century. One of
Stewart Lockhart's most highly
prized paintings of bamboo.

19 Lin Xi Tang, Moon Rising above
Bamboo. Ink on paper, 1837. One
of a set of four scrolls by an artist from Wendeng District which
Stewart Lockhart purchased in
1913.

have found the sport available a most congenial diversion. In summer, Weihaiwei was a fashionable watering hole for Hong Kong society escaping from the heat of the south and, in addition, a sanatorium provided excellent conditions for sick or convalescing Europeans.[23] Thus, during the summer months the Stewart Lockharts could, to some extent, enjoy a social scene which reflected their Hong Kong days. Colleagues from government service in Beijing and Hong Kong would visit at that time of year, and the British and Japanese navies also paid frequent visits during these months. Friends from Hong Kong would also descend from May to September.[24] Winter in Weihaiwei, however, provided a stark contrast. Apart from the occasional visitor from Shanghai or Tianjin, winter was a time for creating one's own amusements. The weather was bitterly cold, making it 'absolutely necessary to keep fires burning both during the day and the night'[25] in Government House. The winters proved to be particularly hard for Edith to bear and, as the years went by, she spent increasingly larger parts of these months with family and friends in Shanghai and Hong Kong.

Stewart Lockhart was destined to spend nineteen years in Weihaiwei: nineteen years running a territory less than four hundred square miles in area and tucked into one of the most remote areas of Shandong Province. To a couple used to the noise of Hong Kong, arriving in the sleepy hollow of the British Empire and moving into Government House at Matou (Ma-t'ou) must have been quite a shock. Low hills rose behind their new residence and rolled as far as the eye could see into Shandong Province. In front lay the centre of naval activity, the island of Liugong, presenting a barren profile across the harbour. Looking along the mainland coastline at Matou, the Commissioner could survey a broad sweep of land from the verandah of Government House and view Queen's Hotel on the bluff edge in the distance in addition to the peppering of houses mainly used by summer visitors. The verandah was also a place to sit and view the activities of the British fleet and the daily round of ferries shuttling to and from the island.[26]

Barely half a mile away from Government House lay the walled city of Weihai, where its two thousand inhabitants lived under the same lease terms as those originally applied to the walled city in Kowloon, with Chinese officials retaining jurisdiction within its walls. However, unlike Kowloon, Weihai was to retain its Chinese status. Sleepy coalescence with the British seems to have been the order of the day, and Stewart Lockhart's assistant was later to note that because of the faultless attitude of the officials within Weihai city, 'it has never been found necessary to raise any question as to the status of the little walled town'.[27] The rest of the territory was to prove as faultless to administer.

Moving away from the main centre of activity round Government House and the island, one entered a land where it was easy to believe that time had stood still.[28] Three hundred villages and hamlets were spread across the ten mile strip of land which Britain held. Roads were virtually non-existent,[29] and assisted travel was generally undertaken by mule, pony, or by shenzi (shentzu), a wheelless covered wagon supported on poles by a pair of ponies. When Stewart Lockhart first rode through the territory, he saw a countryside which, with its bare hills, little streams, and patches of scrub oak, must have reminded him of parts of his native Scotland. The climate, likewise, was close to that of his homeland, though summer temperatures were more welcomingly hot. The people around him were mainly farmers, as their ancestors had been for centuries, and they lived in this picturesque and often beautiful environment with little interference from the outside world.[30]

Social life was likewise quite different from that in Hong Kong. In Weihaiwei there would be no round of balls, no large circle of friends on whom to call. True, the Stewart Lockharts were to be kept busy in summer, and within two days of their moving into Government House, they hosted a reception for officers of the Chinese Regiment and various naval officers in port.[31] From May to September each year, Government House would welcome large numbers of visitors. In June, 1902, twelve naval vessels were stationed at Weihaiwei, and nightly receptions for more than twenty officers at a time were *de rigueur* for the Commissioner and his wife. The navy would appear in strength at Weihaiwei throughout the summer, their numbers swollen with visitors from Hong Kong and Shanghai in July and August.[32] During these two months, Edith lost the sense of novelty associated with being the sole female representative at receptions, a situation she faced all too frequently in Weihaiwei where, normally, she had difficulty in mustering together sufficient women to take afternoon tea on the verandah at

Government House.[33] Summer was also the time to take full advantage of the splendid coastline, and the Commissioner delighted in taking photographs of the informal picnics they held each year.[34]

However, come October, the winter chill had begun to set in and the visitors had departed. The naval strength shrank from a dozen ships to three and, by November, to one. Weekly, rather than daily, visits became the pattern at Government House, and from December 1902 until the following February, no visitors from outside the territory were received.[35] Despite their two children and small staff, the lack of invigorating society, even the lack of news and gossip, made the house less than inviting. Winter was a time of bitter cold, but unless the snow and frost prevented them, Stewart Lockhart and his family would take every opportunity to ride in the territory. He, his wife, and two children were all good riders and although he was the Commissioner, he was never too proud to risk taking a tumble in front of the villagers thereby providing them with no small amount of amusement.[36]

Stewart Lockhart's year did not alternate solely between social receptions and riding. There was a territory to be administered and work to be done. An immediate target was the raising of revenue in the territory, and a land tax was charged on the people. To the peasant farmers of Weihaiwei, such a tax differed little from that which had been levied by the Chinese Government a decade before. British officials, however, were more tax-efficient than their Chinese colleagues who always required a percentage of any takings for their own pockets, and the rate of exchange used by the British likewise benefited the locals. The lower rate of tax and the fact that, under British rule, they were not liable to salt tax, meant that the people of Weihaiwei had more money for themselves and little difficulty was ever encountered by the British in collecting land tax.[37] The method of collection devised by Stewart Lockhart was highly efficient and at the same time complemented the existing village structures. No funding was available for a full survey of the territory, so the land tax had to be based on existing land registers which Stewart Lockhart received from the Chinese Magistrates.[38] These were, at best, unreliable, resulting in a situation where the relations between land under cultivation and the land subject to taxation were 'extremely indefinite'.[39] Stewart Lockhart faced a dilemma:

he had to raise some form of tax, and yet he did not have the resources to compile a register which would ensure an equitable levy for all. In a decision which would have done justice to Solomon, he created a system which confirmed existing village structures, gave authority to existing village leaders, and was simplicity itself. Each village, by tradition, had a senior figure living within the community to whom all looked for guidance. This village headman was designated by Stewart Lockhart as the person responsible for the collection of tax. Each village was told annually what amount of tax it had to raise and the villagers themselves, led by their headman, apportioned the tax accordingly. It was the duty of all village headmen to collect the tax and bring it to the government office once a year. Thus a tax which raised almost £2,000 annually, cost virtually nothing to administer or collect.[40]

The existing headman system was finally used by Stewart Lockhart not only to collect tax, but also to post government proclamations, keep the peace, and issue deed forms for the sale and purchase of land. A small gratuity was given monthly to each headman in recognition of his government services, and eventually medals were also issued for exemplary service.[41] Stewart Lockhart could easily have left the headman system to founder and decay when he arrived in Weihaiwei. Instead, he chose to support it, just as he had chosen to support the existing administration of the New Territories. His continuation and strengthening of the headman system ensured that the Chinese had their own internal organization of responsibility. It was a mirror, on a smaller scale, of what Stewart Lockhart had achieved in his support of the Po Leung Kuk and Tung Wah Hospital in Hong Kong. In neither territory had his motives been altruistic. True, he believed firmly in retaining existing values and systems in China; and he did not consider it the task of British imperialism to turn Chinese peasants into British subjects with foreign dogma forcing an end to attitudes and customs refined over the centuries. On the other hand, he was well aware that by using the headman system in Weihaiwei he was gaining a cheap government service which distributed information and collected revenue.[42] It was also a system which, rather conveniently, ensured a certain amount of loyalty to the British administration, for the headmen were aware that what the government could give in the way of gratuities and medals, the government could just as easily remove if displeased with an individual's actions. For the headmen themselves, Stewart Lockhart's system must have seemed quite novel. Prior to British rule, they had had little direct contact with the Provincial Government of Shandong, based 450 miles away in Jinan.[43] Now, they were faced with a stranger who spoke their language, but was not of their race, and who fell off horses in a most undignified manner in their midst!

Stewart Lockhart, in fact, needed all the support he could get from the headmen, for he had to administer the territory with the aid of a tiny staff. Two officers were there to assist him, one of them, Walter, being a Passed Cadet with some six years experience in the Colonial Service. In addition, he had the support of two medical officers and five police inspectors and assistants, but that was the sum total of the European governmental staff at Weihaiwei in 1902.[44] Indeed, the paucity of staffing at Weihaiwei was something which Stewart Lockhart was quick to point out to the Colonial Office, contrasting this situation rather ruefully with that in German held Jiao Xian which had so many staff that some had trouble finding work to do.[45]

In addition to revenue raising, Stewart Lockhart had to try and bring some commerce into the territory. G. T. Hare had observed in 1901 that 'Wei-hai-wei and the leased territories have absolutely no commercial resources, and . . . the surrounding districts are of some of the poorest in China.'[46] Despite this depressing situation, the new Commissioner was full of enthusiasm and confident he would be able to turn Weihaiwei into a thriving trading centre. He arrived in the territory in the knowledge that his Chinese business friends in Hong Kong were keen to 'see what they could make of Wei hai Wei', despite the drawback of having to change ships at Shanghai.[47] Very quickly, however, Stewart Lockhart was to realize how difficult his task was to be, and how reluctant Hong Kong merchants were to invest until certain fundamental problems were resolved.[48]

First of all, potential traders needed some assurance of stability in the region and a commitment from Britain that the lease would continue. Only a year after his arrival in Weihaiwei, Stewart Lockhart was suggesting that the Colonial Office issue a statement confirming its resolution to retain the lease:[49] it never came. Although Weihaiwei had free port status, with its attendant lack of duties, the port derived little benefit from this without the ability to process goods from the interior of Shandong through the port. Two things were required before this could be done: a rail link and a decent road system. Stewart Lockhart commenced a road-building programme almost straight away, building forty miles of roads in the first eighteen months of his administration.[50] Good roads, however, stopped at the edge of the territory. Despite indications to the contrary, successive Governors of Shandong were not ready to create roads which would result in goods being exported through duty-free Weihaiwei in preference to their own port at Yantai.[51] Likewise, a rail link was an impossible dream. Britain's original agreement with China excluded the building of a British rail link because Germany had already snatched that concession and was not going to let Weihaiwei flourish by means of rail at the expense of German held Jiao Xian.[52] Stewart Lockhart was literally powerless to improve the situation and it is to his credit that by 1908, he had created a situation in which Weihaiwei had a surprisingly large sea-borne trade.[53]

Geographical remoteness and a lack of facilities, however, mitigated against large-scale commercial expansion, and the overbearing German presence in the area did little to help this situation. The Germans were seen as a threat to the whole of Shandong Province in the first few years of the century. Stewart Lockhart visited Jiao Xian before his first year in office was over,[54] and was to observe that 'there is bound to be trouble in Shantung someday on account of the high handed acts of the Germans.'[55] One of the problems was that Germany had a virtual monopoly on mining rights in the Province[56] and when, in 1903, China secretly gave Germany the concession to mine in the British sphere of influence, there was uproar in the British camp. The sphere of influence was a thousand square miles of the Province bordering the territory of Weihaiwei in which Britain had the right to erect fortifications and station troops but had no civil jurisdiction.[57] Stewart Lockhart managed, somehow, to lay his hands on a copy of the Chinese text, before which nothing 'had ever been known to the Legation of the terms of this concession'.[58]

Satow, British Minister in Beijing, had visited Stewart Lockhart in Weihaiwei in 1902, and the two men kept in close contact with the help, from 1903, of Morrison, *The Times*' correspondent in Beijing. Morrison visited Weihaiwei in August 1903,[59] and thereafter Satow was sufficiently *au fait* with the situation to protest to the German authorities in Beijing.[60] The British Government, likewise, took the opportunity to use the information Stewart Lockhart had uncovered to protest to the Germans. It was to no avail: the Germans believed their position in Shandong to be invincible and were unperturbed by the collapse of any plans to mine coal in Weihaiwei. The situation with Germany was one which Stewart Lockhart was to continue to monitor closely, being of the opinion, which he shared with the Colonial Office, that there was a real threat that, unchallenged, Germany was capable of turning Shandong into a German Province 'and the dismemberment of China will begin'.[61] The German stranglehold on Shandong was to kill off one of Stewart Lockhart's more promising commercial prospects for the territory; the Weihaiwei Gold Mining Company, which was floated in 1902.[62] Situated in Tiger Hill, on the boundary between Shandong Province and Weihaiwei, the Germans objected to the opening of the mine because of their exclusive rights.[63] Undeterred, Stewart Lockhart gave the project his full support, and the working mine was viewed in action by one author who reported seeing the local miners breaking the ore into small chunks before crushing it in a converted bean mill.[64] Years of wrangling over the rights and poor results, however, doomed the project almost before it started and the company finally went into liquidation in 1907.

In December 1902, the Governor of Shandong Province, Zhou Fu (Chou Fu), paid a brief official visit to meet Stewart Lockhart in Weihaiwei, inviting the Commissioner for a reciprocal visit the following year. Governor Zhou Fu stood at the head of an administration which governed thirty million people.[65] In line with the other Chinese provinces, the Governor stood at the top of a multi-layered civil service. Directly responsible to him were the heads of the Foreign Affairs Department, the Provincial Treasury, the Salt Tax Commissioners, the Literary Chancellor, and the Senior Judge of the Province. Beneath this, the Province was divided into three circuits, each with a Daodai (Tao Tai) at its head. The circuits were further divided into thirteen Prefectures which were, in turn, subdivided into ninety-six Districts, each run by a Magistrate. Weihaiwei itself was roughly the size of a small Shandong District, which should be borne in mind when one examines the extraordinary courtesy extended to Stewart Lockhart by successive Governors during official visits.

Governor Zhou Fu, a native of Anhui (Anhwei), was a senior government official who had served his country long and faithfully. Having met Stewart Lockhart in 1902, Zhou Fu laid elaborate plans to host the Commissioner's visit, ensuring that Stewart Lockhart had ample opportunity to visit the great cultural site of the Province, the birthplace of Confucius. Stewart Lockhart left Weihaiwei on 20 April 1903, accompanied by Captain Barnes of the Chinese Regiment who was to make full use of the visit to compile a secret military report of the areas they toured.[66] The Commissioner's small party was completed by a Chinese Secretary, four soldiers from the Chinese Regiment, three boys, a cook, and a photographer with an assistant. HMS *Eclipse* took the party north and west to Yantai where the Governor had set aside a cruiser, the *Jing Hai* (*Ching Hai*), to convey them to the entrance of the canal to Jinan, at Yangjiaoguo (Yang Ch'iao-k'ou). There, they were met in an impressive ceremony by government officials and a troop of cavalry. From a single cruiser the party now became a flotilla of ten boats which covered the canal trip of one hundred and sixty miles in four days. The Governor had taken elaborate steps to ensure Stewart Lockhart's comfort. This included the provision of an English speaking captain, educated at Hong Kong's Central School, to man the *Jing Hai*. If Stewart Lockhart felt his reception to be a generous one at this point, he must have been overwhelmed on his arrival at Jinan where a thirteen gun salute awaited him and 1,500 troops lined the streets as he and his party, accompanied by guards and cavalry, set out in sedan chairs to meet the Governor. Dinner that night was 'the most sumptuous feast Chinan could produce'[67] and heralded the start of a week's extraordinary hospitality.

Although Stewart Lockhart was the representative of a great foreign power, the relative size of the territory of which he was in charge was totally insignificant compared to the power wielded by the Governor and his deputies. Yet these men treated Stewart Lockhart as an honoured equal, going out of their way to make his visit as pleasant as possible. Stewart Lockhart could never repay their lavish hospitality, and Weihaiwei was never going to wield any influence in the world. Perhaps Zhou Fu thought Weihaiwei's Commissioner might be a useful ally against German encroachment — Stewart Lockhart was certainly keen that the Chinese 'differentiate ... between our acts and "the Huns"'.[68] Even so, any influence he could exert to divert German influence in Shandong was likely to be negligible. It would appear, therefore, that the strikingly cordial relations between Governors of Shandong and the Commissioner of Weihaiwei had their foundations in other than political motives. Stewart Lockhart's fluency in the Chinese language was undoubtedly a contributory factor, and his thorough knowledge of Chinese culture also impressed the officials of Shandong. But, more than anything else, it seems that the lessons learned from Old Au so many years before in Hong Kong were the cause of Stewart Lockhart's repeatedly warm reception during his various visits to Jinan. Stewart Lockhart knew exactly how to behave. His manners, speech, and compliments when in the presence of senior Chinese officials were those of a mandarin, and thus he was accepted as an equal. The inequalities of power were brushed aside because of the equalities of manner and learning. On Stewart Lockhart's part, the first trip to Jinan was a triumph, and he was to return there as an honoured guest many more times. Apart from the visits, he corresponded regularly with senior Chinese officials. Indeed, he seems to have kept in contact more frequently with them than he did with his London masters.[69]

Shandong Province was the birthplace of Confucius, and on his first trip to the Province, Stewart Lockhart was extended the honour not only of visiting the site of Confucius' birth, Qufu (Ch'u Fou), but also of meeting Confucius' direct lineal descendant, Duke Kong (K'ung). It was indeed a great honour to be invited to make this visit, a fact of which the Scot was well aware. He was the first European Duke Kong had ever met, let alone entertained in his palace.[70] Stewart Lockhart was deeply influenced by Confucian ethics as an administrator, and the visit was one of the high points of the entire journey, carefully documented by numerous photographs which remain to this day in his collection.[71]

Apart from occasional visits to neighbouring leased territories or into Chinese controlled Shandong Province, Stewart Lockhart's life revolved around the daily running of Weihaiwei. During his first two years in the territory, a flurry of ordinances and despatches winged their way back to the Colonial Office in London. Initially, despite the lack of staff and poor living conditions, Stewart Lockhart was fired with a tremendous enthusiasm to get things done, and, sometimes, this enthusiasm was to annoy the London based officials. Shortly after his arrival in Weihaiwei, he asked for permission to rename Matou, Port Edward, to celebrate the King's Coronation.[72] Permission was granted, but when, a fortnight later, Stewart Lockhart sent a second telegram to the Colonial Office seeking permission to rename Liugong, Alexandra, after the Queen, senior officials felt he was being absurd: it was one thing to name the main town of the territory after a King, but to name an insignificant speck of rock surrounded by sea after a Queen was deemed inappropriate.[73]

Like everything else, the dissemination of local news was also organized by the government in Port Edward. Shortly before Stewart Lockhart had arrived a printing press had been purchased by the administration from the navy.[74] Given the shortage of staff in Weihaiwei, there was no one to man the machine, and Stewart Lockhart quickly lodged the press with the local protestant mission who printed government publications thereafter free of charge in return for the use of the press. A local broadsheet, called the *Weihaiwei Lyre*, had been published throughout 1900, becoming the daily *Weihaiwei Gazette* in 1901.[75] With the transfer to a civil administration, the daily news-sheet had been discontinued, and it was one of Stewart Lockhart's first tasks to restart the *Gazette*, priced ten cents a copy, on his arrival in Weihaiwei. A mixture of news and gossip, the *Gazette* published notices of meetings, the arrival of the mails, and even some international news. In 1903, its international section announced plans 'for a new suspension bridge 10,000 ft. long, between New York and Brooklyn',[76] though quite what the level of interest in Weihaiwei was on reading such information is uncertain. From 1902, the *Gazette* was a single page broadsheet, but by 1909 a far more professional version was being produced. Now published twice weekly, instead of daily, four pages of news could be purchased for the same cost as the original publication. The *Gazette* gave one gossip, and should not be confused with the *Government Gazette* which provided official notices and news for the entire territory. Published in English for the benefit of Europeans in Port Edward and the island, a

Chinese version of the *Government Gazette* was given to the headmen to post in the villages, and all the official news and ordinances were disseminated to the population through this publication.

Stewart Lockhart unwittingly managed to cause antagonism at the Colonial Office with his ordinances. Sometimes, the antagonism was minor: 'Mr Lockhart must really be told to send home separate Ordinances in separate desps.'.[77] It is clear from other Colonial Office minutes, however, that Stewart Lockhart was suddenly a less than favoured figure in London. Barring his old friend, Lucas, the officials in the Colonial Office did not, in the main, know him personally, were unaware of his talents, and seemed to dislike Stewart Lockhart and his administration from the start. To some extent, he was protected as long as Lucas was at the head of the section, but when Lucas was moved to head the Dominions Division in 1907, Stewart Lockhart was to be left defenceless against the daggers by then drawn in London.

Pressure to organize Weihaiwei was considerable in the first two years of his commissionership. With the help of his assistant, Walter, and the occasional assistance from officers of the Chinese Regiment, he had to administer a territory where even the finances and accounts were found to be in a state of confusion on his arrival.[78] The raising of revenue was a primary objective. The land tax was quickly organized, and three other government monopolies, of opium, native wines, and a government abattoir, were also contributing revenue by the end of his first year in Weihaiwei.[79] Whilst Stewart Lockhart was drafting laws and raising revenue, Walter was acting as Magistrate for the entire territory as well as carrying out the duties of Secretary to Government. Stewart Lockhart asked for additional staff in both 1902 and 1903, but no money was found by the Treasury, and, without the presence of the officers of the Chinese Regiment, the administration would not have coped with the quantity of work which had to be tackled on a daily basis. Thus, when Walter was given leave in the autumn of 1902, Captain Johnson from the Regiment acted in his place as Magistrate.

The Chinese Regiment, recruited from the Chinese of Shandong, was headed by British officers. Although the men were native Chinese, the Regiment had successfully taken part in the relief of the Legations during the Boxer Rising.[80] For the next few months, the British Government were quite content to maintain the Regiment as the main military force in Weihaiwei, but when, at the end of 1901, it was decided that the territory was to be run on civil, rather than on military, lines, the disbandment of the Regiment was begun.[81] The first stage of this disbandment was to reduce the numbers of soldiers from 1,200 to 500 men, retaining sixteen officers and six NCOs.[82] The strength was kept at this level until the Russo-Japanese war ended, when the Regiment was disbanded in its entirety. The disbandment was to be a loss keenly felt by Stewart Lockhart: not, characteristically, for military reasons, but because he had 'so many friends in it, whose presence here helps to make life more pleasant'.[83]

It is not surprising that he should be so aware of the loss of sociable company: the Regiment provided him with his sole male companionship throughout the winter months. The paucity of the social circle in Weihaiwei had another important effect on Stewart Lockhart; his family began to play an increasingly important part in his life. Sadly, his mother died in August 1902, and, having lost his father almost a decade earlier, he must have felt that a great era was over. Unable to go home because of his commitments in the territory, the bereavement must have been a double shock when he received a letter from her, two weeks after he had been informed of her death.[84] Mail took six weeks to arrive from Britain, hence the mistiming which could only have served to underline the sacrifices colonial officials had to make. The loss of his mother must have been tempered by his pleasure in having his family by his side. His young daughter, Mary, was a particular joy, having an uninhibited delight in life in 'High High', as she called the territory. Family joy further increased when, the day after Edith's thirty-third birthday, their daughter, Margaret, was born in Port Edward. Baby Margaret flourished in the gentle summer of 1903, the last summer the Stewart Lockharts were to be together for many years. Mary Stewart Lockhart signed her name in the Commissioner's visitors' book on Christmas Eve that year, something she would not return to do for another seven years. Shortly after, Edith set off for England with both girls. Charles was already in Britain, as, aged fourteen, he was about to enter the Royal Navy. Mary, at nine years old, was ready to receive formal schooling and her mother felt, quite naturally, obliged to accompany her. For more than two years, Stewart Lockhart was to lead a bachelor existence: an existence which might have been unbearably lonely without the companionship of one extra-ordinary man, Reginald Johnston.

Chapter 8

GOOD COMPANIONS
(1904–1906)

AT the end of 1903, Stewart Lockhart wrote to the Colonial
Office to inform them that one of his assistants, Walter, proposed to take home leave shortly and that a replacement for
him would therefore be required.[1] The Commissioner knew
exactly who he wanted for the post: Reginald Johnston, a young
official in the Hong Kong service whom he had befriended
before leaving to serve in Weihaiwei. The Colonial Office was
less sure about the suitability of Johnston for the post. Already,
there were murmurings from London that 'the services of an
officer of the position (and salary) of Mr Lockhart are rather
wasted at Wei Hai Wei, where the work could ... be done at
considerably less cost by a less experienced official'.[2] It was felt
that, rather than appoint an officer of Johnston's seniority, 'a
very junior officer will be quite good enough for the little work
at Weihaiwei'.[3] The statements do much to illustrate the tenor of
Colonial Office opinion at this stage. Less than two years after
assuming responsibility for the territory, Stewart Lockhart was
being given only minimal support by his London masters. As
it turned out, Walter, instead of taking home leave, was appointed on a temporary basis to the post of Emigration Agent at
Tianjin, supervising the emigration of Chinese coolies to the
Transvaal throughout 1904 to work in the gold mines.[4] Walter's
appointment was part of Britain's attempt to avoid the abuses
transporting contract labour had led to in the previous century.
This time, the emigrant labourers were permitted to take their
families with them, and Walter's task was to try and regulate
living standards and working conditions in liason with British
agents stationed in the Transvaal. At the time of Walter's
appointment, it was Lucas who suggested Johnston as the
replacement officer for Weihaiwei, ignoring all previous
discussion on the subject to push his choice through.[5] The
decision taken, Johnston arrived in May 1904 to work in

Weihaiwei,[6] a place with which he was to become associated for as long as Stewart Lockhart.

Born in Edinburgh in 1874, Reginald Johnston had an up-bringing and background typical of so many Hong Kong cadets. A lawyer's son, he was educated at the University of Edin-burgh where, in 1894, he displayed his scholarly abilities by gain-ing the prestigious Gray Prize for History in addition to first class certificates in English Literature, Modern History, and Constitutional Law. He continued his academic career at Magdalen College, Oxford, where he once more specialized in Modern History, being awarded his BA in 1898. He sat, and passed the examination for the India Service and Eastern Cadetships the same year, receiving his appointment as Hong Kong Cadet on 22 October, while in the middle of his degree exams. He sailed for Hong Kong less than a month later, arriving in the colony at the end of that year.[7] The Hong Kong administration was, of course, fully absorbed in the acquisition of the New Territories, and this may have been the reason why, instead of being sent to Guangzhou to learn Cantonese, Johnston remained in Hong Kong, combining his studies with the same post that Stewart Lockhart had first held as a cadet, that of Acting Clerk of Councils. Between 1900 and 1904, Johnston was Assistant Colonial Secretary, a post he combined, between 1900 and 1902, with the duties of Private Secretary to Governor Blake.[8] During Stewart Lockhart's final years in Hong Kong, Johnston and he were therefore close colleagues, and the two men quickly became staunch friends, despite the difference in their ages. They shared mutual bonds, not only in their Scottish background, but, far more importantly, in their love of scholarship. Even while Johnston was working in the Hong Kong administration, he found time to study for his MA, awarded by the University of Oxford in 1901, and he was eventually to become as eminent a scholar of Chinese as Stewart Lockhart.

When, with Lucas' help, Johnston was seconded to Weihai-wei as the Commissioner's assistant, Stewart Lockhart must have been delighted. Weihaiwei's Commissioner was already beginning to feel marooned in the territory, and, in an effort to disengage himself from the possibility of serving for decades in the area, was attempting to persuade the Colonial Office to give him a fixed term of tenure for four or six years.[9] Like the guarantee of tenure of lease, such assurances were never forthcoming from London, so it was just as well that at least Johnston arrived to provide stimulating company to leaven the long winters. Johnston moved into a house on the Bund in Port Edward, a stone's throw away from Government House where he spent many an evening sharing his interest in Chinese scholarship with his senior colleague.

When Johnston arrived in Weihaiwei, he spoke fluent Cantonese, but had yet to master Mandarin, let alone the peculiarities of that dialect as encountered in Weihaiwei.[10] Within three months of arriving in the territory, however, his knowledge of the northern dialect was sufficiently good for him to be entrusted with the task of taking an imposing, gilt-framed photograph of Edward VII to Qufu as a gift for Duke Kong; the result of a request from the Duke when he had met Stewart Lockhart the previous year. Having been sent from London, the portrait was transported from Weihaiwei with great ceremony in its own canopied chair to the Duke. The visit gave Stewart Lockhart the opportunity to use his emissary for the furtherance of Weihaiwei, and so Johnston also travelled to Jinan to see the Governor, having first delivered his gift to Duke Kong. Johnston sought permission from the Governor to handle Chinese emigration to the Transvaal through Weihaiwei, and was successful in receiving the Governor's approval.[11] The scheme would have brought both jobs and revenue to Weihaiwei but, like so many of Stewart Lockhart's attempts to bring prosperity to the territory, it foundered because of external opposition. The bulk of Chinese emigration to the South African gold mines was being handled through the Chinese port of Yantai. Despite the support of the Provincial Governor and the efforts of the British Minister in Beijing, Satow, the Chinese Government refused to give Weihaiwei the opportunity to handle the emigration at the expense of their own port.[12] In spite of such setbacks, and the Treasury's inexorable squeeze on Weihaiwei's grant-in-aid, halving it in three years,[13] Stewart Lockhart continued to try and improve the prosperity of the territory, but everything, it seemed, conspired against him. A visit to Hong Kong in 1904, which he had been planning for eighteen months with the intention of persuading his friends in the Chinese business community to invest in Weihaiwei, was cut short abruptly when Japan and Russia declared war.[14] Stewart Lockhart had to return immediately to Weihaiwei which, due to its proximity to the war zone, was formally declared to be neutral, despite Britain's alliance with Japan.[15]

Stewart Lockhart had hoped that the arrival of a capable officer of Johnston's calibre would give him the opportunity to leave Weihaiwei and return to Britain to spend Christmas 1904 with his family. The Russo-Japanese war instead stranded him in the territory, acting as host to a stream of journalists eager to be close to the battlefront. Illustrious figures such as Newell of *The Daily Telegraph* and Fraser and Morrison of *The Times* signified their presence by signing the Commissioner's Visitors' Book. Weihaiwei's stated neutrality was not easy to adhere to, as the sympathies of the British community in the Far East lay firmly with the Japanese. British naval activity in the area was pronounced, and the China Squadron stayed in Weihaiwei well into the winter of 1904, offering moral, though not physical, support to the Japanese; the Squadron was determined to remain in north China until Lüshun was captured by Japan.[16] Lady Blake, wife of Hong Kong's former Governor, was not alone when she declared she was 'heart and soul with the Japanese',[17] and even Stewart Lockhart, administering a neutral territory, was to confide that although he must appear not to favour either Russia or Japan, 'I really want Japan to win'.[18] It seems, however, that remaining neutral was little more than an inconvenience for Stewart Lockhart, forcing him to decline otherwise tempting invitations to events such as the party held in Weihaiwei's Japanese-run sulphur baths to celebrate Japan's taking of Lüshun.[19] Nevertheless, it remains likely that Stewart Lockhart raised a glass in celebration within the solitude of Government House that particular evening. The Japanese capture of Lüshun and, later, of Dalian (Dalny), may have been the cause for rejoicing in Weihaiwei, but within a matter of months the enormous cost in human life that these gains had caused became clear. The capture of Dalian alone resulted in 7,000 Japanese dead and 3,000 wounded, while the Russians lost 2,000 men and the numbers wounded were almost as many again.[20] Ten months after Japan and Russia agreed a peace which was, theoretically at least, acceptable to China, Stewart Lockhart and his wife visited Dalian and saw for themselves the devastation caused by the war. Mass graves held the dead, but

on the site of the battle books and bits of clothing remained
as a grim testament to the war. With their firmly pro-Japanese
views, it was not surprising that the Stewart Lockharts were
given lunch by the officer commanding Dalian, Admiral Mitzu,
during which the war was discussed in detail. As a result of that
lunchtime conversation, Edith Stewart Lockhart was to conclude that 'one never realised what a fearful fight the Japs had
... They may well be proud, they have much to be proud of.'[21]
For the Russian casualties, neither love nor tears were lost.

Whilst Edith was away with her daughters in Britain, Johnston became Stewart Lockhart's closest companion. It was a
relationship which was to continue to develop over the years
and remain a strong one for the rest of their lives; a friendship
which remained constant despite the comings and goings of
other officers in the territory. Stewart Lockhart, as sociable as
ever, had other friends who were colleagues at one time or
another, but a special bond developed between him and Johnston, a bond which is clearly reflected in more than six hundred
letters Johnston wrote to him.[22] A great deal about their early
friendship in Weihaiwei is narrated through Stewart Lockhart's
letters to his daughter in England. For example, Christmas 1904,
which should have been spent with the family in Britain, was
instead spent in the faintly eccentric manner so typical of
Johnston and Stewart Lockhart when left to their own devices.
Two shenzi were loaded up with provisions and, accompanied
by two boys and a cook, they set off to spend Christmas in a
temple in the territory. There, they sat down to a Christmas
dinner of turkey and plum pudding, which must have set a
strange scene in the middle of the Chinese countryside.

Amiable trips around the country were a light relief after the
tedium of daily work and Stewart Lockhart's continuing efforts
to put Weihaiwei on some sort of commercial footing. It is some
indication of the uphill task he faced that he had to begin this
process at the most basic of levels. When he first arrived,
travelling within the territory was confined to dirt tracks, and to
alleviate this problem and, hopefully, make commercial enterprise easier, the Commissioner commenced a road-building
programme, various stages of which he proudly photographed
throughout 1902.[23] Another improvement he introduced as
quickly as he possibly could was the reforestation of the countryside. Much of Shandong had been stripped bare of trees to

meet the fuel requirements of the population. The British saw
the improvements the Germans had made at Jiao Xian with their
reforestation programme and tried to emulate this progress in
Weihaiwei on a more modest scale.[24] Tree planting was begun
in a small way in 1903 and the project was to continue to expand
throughout Stewart Lockhart's tenure in the territory. Convicts
were used to plant trees on the mainland, and from the first
planting of a few hundred acacia, firs, and willows in 1903, more
than 40,000 trees were being planted annually a decade later.[25]
Within a few years, Stewart Lockhart had turned the island and
the roadsides of Weihaiwei into lush, green areas, an achievement of which he must have been extremely proud when he
finally left Weihaiwei. The verdant growth was to prove irresistible to the villagers, however, who, in their quest for kindling
were to strip the countryside once more of wood as the trees
matured in the 1920s. This pillage was sufficiently severe for one
official later to write of his disgust on returning to Weihaiwei in
1933 'to find hardly one willow along the Wench'uant'ang and
Lutaok'ou roads'.[26]

The reforestation programme begun, Stewart Lockhart cast
around for other projects to improve the physical and material
well-being of Weihaiwei. The mild climate held out the hope
that fruit trees might be grown commercially, a possibility
confirmed by a visit by the Superintendent of the Botanical
and Afforestation Department in Hong Kong in 1904.[27] Thus, in
January 1905, a Mr Gibbons, a fruit grower from England,
arrived to swell the ranks of the Weihaiwei staff.[28] Stewart
Lockhart had every hope that Mr Gibbons would succeed in
growing sufficient varieties of fruit to boost the economy and
entice local farmers into experimenting with fruit growing. A
test orchard with apples, pears, cherries, plums, peaches and
nectarines was planted beside Government House,[29] and by the
time Mr Gibbons left the territory in 1909, the first successful
crops had been harvested. Thereafter, Government House at
least was guaranteed supplies of fresh fruit, but fruit growing
on a commercial scale never developed. Few Weihaiwei farmers
could afford to set land aside for a crop which would take
several seasons to mature; a fact of which Stewart Lockhart,
despite his notes of optimism to the Colonial Office, was well
aware at an early stage.[30] The fruit growing, therefore, benefited
few but those at Government House in the short term. In the

longer term, however, fruit growing was to be a greater success than the reforestation programme, and visitors to Weihaiwei in the 1930s could report that Mr Gibbons' convictions that the area could produce first-rate apples and show a profit, were true, though one observer ruefully noted 'it is a pity that Mr Gibbons' effort did not result in showing the way earlier'.[31]

1904 had been a hard year for Stewart Lockhart. Isolated from his family because of the war between Russia and Japan, he and Johnston toiled to get Weihaiwei into some sort of serviceable shape. Some relief from the burden was at hand when, at the end of 1904, the Colonial Office finally submitted to eighteen months of requests and approved the appointment of a cadet for the territory.[32] The pressure Stewart Lockhart had, until that time, been under, was exposed a few months later, in January 1905, when he was forced to admit to a major administrative blunder. When he had arrived in Weihaiwei, the sulphur baths, built over hot-water springs, were in the state of disrepair they had fallen into during the Japanese occupation. Stewart Lockhart, ever with an eye to the development of Weihaiwei, saw these as a potential tourist attraction and therefore as something which would help boost the economy of the territory. He had obtained Japanese support for the refurbishment of the sulphur baths and had offered Government money in the form of a grant to aid the project. Unfortunately, in the chaos he had encountered on his arrival in Weihaiwei, he had omitted to seek Colonial Office approval for the expenditure which, by the time of completion in 1904, amounted to over HK$12,000: about £1,000. The Commissioner had no option but to own up and eat humble pie, which he did in a lengthy despatch to the Colonial Office.[33] His despatch caused an uproar amongst officials in London, underlining his lack of support there from anyone but Lucas. Fiddian, whose minutes suggest that he had never liked Stewart Lockhart, was particularly damning in his condemnation and concluded that 'Mr Lockhart has shown himself to be unfit for his post'.[34] Lucas disagreed strongly, citing the blunder as one of 'pure oversight', and declared that 'so far from thinking him unfit for his post, in spite of this slip, I know no one who would be fitter'.[35] Lucas' support went far, and Stewart Lockhart was served with no more than a severe reprimand which Lucas privately advised him to 'put ... in your pipe and smoke'.[36] The reprimand given, the matter was officially forgotten, but it remained in the minds of those at the Colonial Office who, unlike Lucas, did not know Stewart Lockhart personally. Younger officials such as Fiddian knew neither the man nor his background, and their animosity, when it later surfaced unchallenged, was to use episodes such as the sulphur baths reprimand, as just another nail in the coffin of Stewart Lockhart's career.

Johnston was to be tarred with a similar brush in 1905 when the Colonial Office announced that a senior military officer from the Chinese Regiment would assume the responsibilities of Government during any absence by the Commissioner.[37] Johnston, having been Acting Colonial Secretary at one time in Hong Kong, reacted with the same burst of outrage Stewart Lockhart had shown when deprived of the Acting Governorship of Hong Kong a decade earlier, and demanded that his rights to be Acting Commissioner be recognized. Harding, a like-minded colleague of Fiddian's in the Colonial Office, sarcastically noted that the territory could hardly be run by 'Mr Johnston, who is only 30 ... and has had only 9 months experience of Weihaiwei'.[38] Johnston's undoubted academic and administrative capabilities were to count for nought. Hong Kong's Governor, Nathan, did little to help matters by telling London that, although he did not know Johnston personally, he believed he was 'of sensitive character' and yearned 'for the contemplative life of a Buddhist priest'.[39] This observation was to damn Johnston as a crank for many years within the Colonial Office.

Adverse opinion in the Colonial Office amongst the 'young hawks' on the staff regarding the men in Weihaiwei seemed to be further strengthened with the arrival of the 1904 Annual Report for the territory. Stewart Lockhart's previous report had been hailed as 'cheerful and encouraging' in the press,[40] but he had bemoaned Weihaiwei's lack of resources at the same time. It was a charge he reiterated the following year, stressing the crucial importance of security of tenure if the territory was to have any chance of development. He concluded, somewhat petulantly, that 'Weihaiwei is by no means so unimportant a place as some seem to regard it.'[41] The Colonial Office was enraged, and cut the report savagely before it was printed. They felt that Stewart Lockhart was trying to force the Government's hand in a matter of policy and that 'his remarks about security of tenure are very improper in a report intended for publication'.[42]

Johnston's report, as Secretary to Government, was likewise condemned, and described as being, 'for the most part sheer twaddle'.[43] A censored version was finally published, depriving readers of the joy of some of Johnston's more irreverent moments. For example, in reporting the incidence of the first European marriages in the territory, Johnston could not resist noting that this meant that, at last, 'the reproach of celibacy has been for ever removed from this corner of the British Empire'.[44] Such lightness of touch caused no mirth in the Colonial Office.

In February 1905, Weihaiwei's cadet, Carpmael, arrived and was immediately sent off to Beijing to learn Mandarin.[45] Carpmael's stay in Beijing was brief, for he was brought back to Weihaiwei to assist Walter in May, and was to remain in the territory for many years to come. Often the subject of Johnston's scorn, Carpmael was, however, diligent enough in his work and his arrival brought some administrative relief to the other members of the government, releasing the Commissioner to the extent of, at last, allowing him some free time to himself. The cadet's arrival seemed to give Stewart Lockhart new impetus and, for once, events seemed to be conspiring for, rather than against, him. In July 1905, Governor Yang Shixiang (Yang Shih-hsiang) arrived for a short visit to Weihaiwei, giving Stewart Lockhart the opportunity once more to press Weihaiwei's claims as a port of emigration to the Transvaal. The close friendship which he cultivated so assiduously with a succession of Governors of Shandong now worked in his favour, and in August Weihaiwei finally achieved recognition as a port of departure for Chinese emigration to the Transvaal.[46] The decision came rather too late in the day, for the bulk of Chinese emigration was already over and Walter's secondment to Tianjin ended in 1905 without his being replaced. Weihaiwei's embarkation status therefore brought no great prosperity, but, from Stewart Lockhart's point of view, it was at least a start on the path to furthering Weihaiwei's trading prospects.

The long and severe winter of 1905–6 gave Stewart Lockhart ample time to plan a long overdue reorganization of the Weihaiwei administration. Until then, Weihaiwei's Government was based entirely in Port Edward, situated in the north of the territory. In an effort to increase communication with the community in the south, it was decided to split the territory into two districts and station a District Officer in the southern area. As the European community was concentrated in Port Edward and on the island, the officer sent to the southern district would have to be an extremely resilient soul, for he would be surrounded by non-English speaking people, and quite isolated from the European community. The duties of a District Officer were multifarious: 'judge, revenue collector, postmaster, police officer, government engineer and land officer',[47] and Stewart Lockhart made the conscious decision to create in the southern post an officer who would direct 'a village system of morality based on Chinese custom and Confucian teaching'.[48] In so doing, he was attempting to maintain a tradition of Chinese-style administration which had existed for centuries. Conscious as ever that, one day, Weihaiwei would be returned to Chinese rule, it was his desire that existing systems should be disturbed as little as possible. Weihaiwei was, in any case, a territory which seemed to be frozen in time. Johnston, in his book on the area, records practices in Weihaiwei which had disappeared a century earlier in less sheltered parts of China.[49] Both Johnston and Stewart Lockhart revered the system which dominated the lives of the people in Weihaiwei and had no desire to see it destroyed. For this reason, the headmen had been retained as important figures in the area's hierarchy and, with the same objective in mind, Stewart Lockhart took a British colonial post common throughout the Empire, that of District Officer, and turned it into one of a Chinese Magistrate.

District Magistrates were the nub of the Chinese system of administration. Known to the people whom they ruled as father-and-mother officials, *fumuguan* (*fu-mu-kuan*), 'it is they who are the direct rulers of the people, are supposed to know their wants, to be always ready to listen to their complaints and relieve their necessities.'[50] Being 'the living embodiment of imperial as well as merely patriarchal authority',[51] the Magistrate was viewed by officials further up the administrative ladder as being totally responsible for the thousands of people in his care. As Commissioner of Weihaiwei, Stewart Lockhart himself had powers roughly equivalent to those of a Provincial Governor, though, of course, the number of people over whom he administered was far smaller than that regulated by any Chinese Governor. Stewart Lockhart was responsible only to the home government and, unlike the Governor of Hong Kong, was not limited in the way in which he governed by the decisions of Executive and Legislative Councils. Given that he could, with the sanction of the Colonial Office, create ordinances as he saw fit, his belief in the existing order meant that 'the people are governed in accordance with their own immemorial customs, and it is only when the fact of British occupation introduces some new set of conditions for which local custom does not provide, that legislation becomes necessary.'[52] The Commissioner now desired to extend this system to District Officer level.

Stewart Lockhart's plans for the Weihaiwei administration were well formulated by the beginning of 1906, but with the Treasury squeeze on the territory as severe as ever, the problem of implementation arose. However, fate gave him a golden opportunity very quickly, when the Colonial Office notified him of their decision to disband the Chinese Regiment completely.[53] It is a measure of the preparedness of his plans that, within twenty-four hours of receiving this news, he could write to the Colonial Office to advise that the removal of a military presence in the territory would necessitate an increase in the local police force.[54] With a certain amount of cunning, and under the guise of the need to maintain law and order in the territory, he further advised of 'the necessity of having an officer resident in a central place in the Territory'[55] and, to mollify the Treasury, suggested the appointment of a District Officer in place of another Inspector of Police. His recommendation for this appointment was, of course, Johnston. Stewart Lockhart's plan had been carefully conceived and, with the disbandment of the Regiment, he was given an ideal opportunity to create a permanent post for Johnston in Weihaiwei. Johnston was at that point still on secondment from the Hong Kong service, and Stewart Lockhart's desire to retain his colleague in Weihaiwei was strong. The two men had established a good friendship and a first-rate working relationship, and Stewart Lockhart was also aware that Johnston had no desire to return to Hong Kong, preferring to work in a situation which allowed him 'some personal initiative and independence of action and ... intimate connection with native races'.[56] In these respects, the post of District Officer in Weihaiwei was tailor-made for him. The Colonial Office hawks, almost as a matter of course, objected to the proposals, with Fiddes describing Johnston as 'bumptious'[57] and other colleagues suggesting that the best policy would be to keep the existing administration as it was. Once more, it was Lucas who carried the day for Stewart Lockhart with the decision that the Colonial Office should work 'on the principle of letting Mr Lockhart have within reason what he wants to carry on the administration'.[58]

The territory was therefore split, for administrative purposes, into two divisions: north and south.[59] The headquarters of the north division, comprising nine districts, stayed at Port Edward where the North Division Magistrate was also Secretary to Government. The remaining seventeen districts were administered from a small village near the southern Weihaiwei–Shandong boundary line, called Wenchuantang (Wen-ch'uan-t'ang). This village was chosen for its proximity to other centres of population and for the District Officer's accommodation, available due to the liquidation of the Weihaiwei Gold Mining Company who owned a building there. It was to be some months before Johnston's appointment was confirmed, and the Wenchuantang site selected, for the new Southern District Magistrate at one point held out hopes of settling his officers within a temple near the village of Beikou (Pei K'ou), also in the south.[60] Indeed, the reorganization did not assume a complete form until Johnston returned from the leave which he had taken on Walter's return to the territory. The new arrangement seems to have delighted everyone in Weihaiwei. Walter, as Secretary to Government and Northern Division Magistrate, wrote to Stewart Lockhart of his delight 'to hear you have won the battle',[61] while Johnston made it clear that getting the Southern Division Magistrate's post had saved him from resignation.[62] On his return to Weihaiwei, Johnston was to settle into the division where, assisted by seven Chinese policemen and a small Chinese office staff, he directed control over 100,000 people.

The duties of Walter and Johnston, who presided over their own separate magistrate's courts, were extensive, combining as they did 'the duties of Registrar-General (Protector of Chinese), Puisne Judge, Police Magistrate and Captain-Superintendent of Police'.[63] Although the jail in Weihaiwei rarely held more than twenty prisoners, and serious crime was rare,[64] the magistrates adjudicated both civil and criminal cases, and a large amount of their time was consumed by civil court work. Johnston documents his frustration in this area of his work in numerous letters to Stewart Lockhart,[65] and one instance noted by another observer reflects the complications of Chinese attitudes to court procedure in Weihaiwei:

The principal witness, a poor coolie, had lied and lied and lied. The Judge finally got so angry when he ultimately came out with the truth that he was given a month's imprisonment for contempt of court ... asked why he had annoyed everyone by telling so many lies ... the coolie ... replied, 'The truth is very valuable, you can only use it once.'[66]

Neither Johnston nor Stewart Lockhart underestimated the problems of being a *fumuguan*.

At the time that Stewart Lockhart was presenting his plans for reorganization to the Colonial Office, Johnston was preparing for a long leave during which he intended to travel across China and down to Burma: an adventure he documented in his book *From Peking to Mandalay*. Stewart Lockhart could not hide his dismay at the loss of Johnston's company,[67] though he was greatly cheered by the return of Edith and his daughter Margaret in April 1906 following their two-year stay in Britain. The rooms of Government House were whitewashed in preparation for their arrival and a major reshuffle of the domestic staff took place. Aguai (A-Kwai), the senior houseboy who had been with the family since they first settled in Weihaiwei, was sacked. Although sorry to lose him, Stewart Lockhart found he had 'become so slovenly and disobedient' that he 'could not put up with him any longer',[68] and everything had to be in top form for Edith's long awaited return. Aguai would not be the last houseboy to cause Stewart Lockhart to despair, though Edith despaired equally of her husband's behaviour, writing to her daughter, 'I fear dads often swears at the boys ... It's very sad but they are so annoying and seem to me to get more and more stupid.'[69] Life at Government House was obviously not always as placid as might first appear.

Johnston's trip to Burma marks the first great period of letter-writing between the two men, a correspondence which was to continue for the rest of their lives. Varying in length from a few lines to several thousand words, the letters provide an amusing and informative chronicle of their lives in and out of China. The closeness of their relationship is reflected in the informal tone of the letters which are frequently peppered, in

the early days, with references to a series of imaginary characters which Johnston and Stewart Lockhart first invented to
amuse the Stewart Lockhart children. These characters were to
become part of the life of a close circle of friends in Weihaiwei:
the ultimate 'in' joke. In this imaginary world, the moon, given
female status, always wears trousers as a matter of propriety,
and Johnston reports on the state of her trousers throughout his
travels. The moon and her trousers were inspired by one of
Stewart Lockhart's party pieces, a song which he sang about the
moon,[70] whereas other characters developed from Johnston's
imagination. One of their favourite characters, who frequently
appears in the letters, is the Quork, an irrepressibly disreputable
lady with 'a bonnet box and a green umbrella'.[71] The summit of
Mount Macdonald, Weihaiwei's highest hill, was called Quork's
Peak,[72] and of all the characters it is she with whom Johnston
has most fun. The product of his childhood imagination,[73]
Johnston constantly threatens to send this unruly companion,
who accompanies him on all his travels, back to Weihaiwei.
Other characters are equally outrageous in their behaviour.
When the Quork was not causing trouble, Mrs Walkinshaw
was. Once, in the middle of the Chinese countryside, Johnston
reports the drastic action he was forced to take: 'I dropped Mrs
Walkinshaw into a rapid and hoped to have seen the last of her,
but she floated on a bandbox and reached land safely.'[74]

Reading Johnston's and Stewart Lockhart's letters, these
strange creatures adopt a quite positive reality. The Quork, one
learns, belongs to the race called the Elephantines, from whose
number also appears the Quork's great friend (and one of the
finest creations of Johnston's imagination), the Earl of Dumbarton. The Earl first appears in Johnston's letters in August 1908 as
a fully fledged character. A drunk who has been expelled from
all clubs, the Earl of Dumbarton spends much of his time in a
home for inebriates, although his permanent address is the
summit of Mount Everest.[75] As with so many of these characters, he behaves outrageously at every opportunity.

The banter about the Quork and company displays a refreshingly lively sense of humour in both men: a sense of fun
which doubtless helped relieve the tedium of life in forlorn
Weihaiwei. These characters also had their uses. When, in 1908,
Carpmael's wife became seriously ill, Johnston offered to curtail
his leave and return to Weihaiwei to relieve Carpmael of his

duties. Asking Stewart Lockhart to telegraph his reply, Johnston suggested the following code:

Quorks: You must return at once to Weihaiwei without going to P'u T'o and T'ient'ai.

Dumbarton: You must return to Weihaiwei but you may go first to P'u T'o and T'ient'ai.

Walkinshaw: It is not necessary to interfere with your leave. Proceed with your programme.

Hopedarg: You may go to Ningpo and await letters there.[76]

The crisis at Weihaiwei being over by the time he received Johnston's letter, Stewart Lockhart telegraphed 'Walkinshaw'.

Johnston's innate sense of humour shines through, even when he is not relying on imaginary characters. Frequently irreverent, particularly in matters of religion, he stays with missionaries whilst travelling to Burma, but admits, 'I have not told them I am a Buddhist!'[77] Politicians are treated with a similar lack of reverence, with Johnston once bemoaning the fact that in the twentieth century Prime Ministers were no longer burnt at the stake: 'otherwise Asquith might be a cinder in ten minutes'.[78] Reading Johnston's letters, it would be easy to believe that he and Stewart Lockhart are two minds out of synch with the rest of society in the Far East. Theirs were not the only eccentric minds in the vicinity, however. Lady Blake, the Hong Kong veteran, and a frequent correspondent to both men, displayed similar eccentricity. A Christian Scientist, but with Buddhistic leanings cultivated by Johnston, she caused him no small mirth with her assertion about a fellow Christian Scientist: 'Mrs Dunn, cured her cat. The cat is now dead.'[79]

Johnston made several trips to the interior of China as well as to countries on her borders. These journeys are narrated in his books *From Peking to Mandalay* and *Buddhist China*, and in numerous articles.[80] Throughout these visits, regular letters to Stewart Lockhart describe his travels in a narrative form far superior to that found in his published works. Marooned in Weihaiwei, these letters must have been like a breath of fresh air to the Commissioner, containing as they did vivid accounts of life on the road. Johnston revelled in the drama and danger of his solitary journeys, recounting them with skill:

Some of the passes were over 17,000 feet high, and are covered with eternal snow and ice. The population is naturally exceedingly scanty, and is entirely Tibetan in race, language, customs and everything else. After many days of toil, during which one or two of my mules died, I reached the Yalung which I crossed by a single bamboo rope, — hanging on to the pulley, with my feet dangling in the air. It is a curious sensation and I think most people would consider it required some nerve ... Sleeping out night after night without a tent and with no trees to shelter one ... is rather risky: but I did not get ill, nor did the panthers seize me. I sometimes found snow on my blanket when I woke up: and on the tops of the passes it was generally snowing more or less.[81]

While Johnston was journeying through the high passes of Tibet, Stewart Lockhart was making the shorter, and less dangerous, journey to Jinan to meet Governor Yang in what was becoming an annual event. His reception was predictably lavish, with the Governor ensuring that Stewart Lockhart would be seen to have an entourage appropriate to his station by placing at Stewart Lockhart's disposal no fewer than sixty-one people.[82] Every effort was made to extend courtesy to the small group from Weihaiwei, and the first official dinner held by the Governor was of European fashion, at which 'the choicest plates and wines have been served.'[83] During his visit, the Chinese-style banquets were no less lavish and Stewart Lockhart entered into the spirit of such occasions with undisguised pleasure, to the extent of composing, in the best traditions of Chinese scholarship, a series of verses in lieu of a speech at one banquet.[84] It is evident that both the Commissioner and the Governor enjoyed these celebrations, but such visits were not organized merely for pleasure: useful business could also be conducted in the interim.

A report on this part of the visit is illuminating in its description of Stewart Lockhart's conduct during such meetings.[85] The Scot is transformed into a true Chinese official, performing in this role with aplomb. With an eye to the correct form on such occasions, he compliments the Governor on his learning and his calligraphic skills, attributes which every senior Chinese official would wish to acquire. The compliment, graciously received by the Governor, leads gently into the main point of the meeting, as far as Stewart Lockhart is concerned, namely the question of Chinese education in Weihaiwei. The recent abolition of the centuries old official examinations in China deprived students in Weihaiwei of the opportunity of taking the lower grade degrees in Shandong Province. Stewart Lockhart was extremely keen that they should be permitted to sit the new, civil examinations in Weihaiwei, thereby giving them the opportunity to compete for higher civil posts on equal terms with their colleagues in Shandong Province. Delighted by Stewart Lockhart's genuine interest in promoting Chinese-style education within a British-held territory, the Governor quickly consented to the issue of a proclamation which declared that Weihaiwei students would be eligible for civil degrees. Stewart Lockhart's desire to ensure that the Chinese of Weihaiwei would not suffer educationally under British rule is typical of his belief in maintaining, whenever possible, a truly Chinese administration in the territory. This, and the way in which he conducted himself in the company of senior Chinese officials, was to ensure continued invitations and warm greetings from the Governors of Shandong Province until the fall of the monarchy.

Stewart Lockhart took the opportunity, during this visit, to see the Chinese educational system in operation, visiting a number of schools in the city.[86] His interest in Chinese educational systems was quite genuine. He himself had begun a free government school in Weihaiwei for Chinese pupils, which offered, in addition to the traditional teaching of the Classics, lessons in Arithmetic, History, Geography, and, in the higher forms, English.[87] With only three masters, and a roll of around 45 scholars, the school would never compete with the village schools dotted throughout Weihaiwei, but it did offer Weihaiwei's more able scholars the opportunity to have an education which offered real potential. Stewart Lockhart kept in close contact with the Anglo-Chinese school, attending prizegivings and distributing scholarships which were funded by a tax on theatricals in the territory.[88] His speeches on such occasions exhorted the students to study the Chinese classics for their own academic advancement.[89]

The visit, intended only to cement good relations between Britain and China, created a great deal of speculation in the press that Weihaiwei was about to be returned to China, and that Stewart Lockhart was visiting Jinan to discuss rendition. It was not the first time the question of rendition had been raised, nor was it to be the last, but the issue fuelled more speculation in 1906 than it had previously because one of the terms of the lease was no longer pertinent: Russia no longer held Lüshun, which she had lost to the Japanese. The British Foreign Office had done little to stop such speculation, refusing, despite Stewart Lockhart's repeated requests, to declare a fixed period of tenure for Britain. The London view was that Britain's position in north China was unaffected by Russia's loss of Lüshun and that as long as other foreign powers held territory in the area, and in particular, as long as Lüshun remained in non-Chinese hands, Weihaiwei would remain on lease to Britain.[90] However, within the Admiralty and Cabinet, Sir George Clarke and Admiral Fisher were against retaining Weihaiwei and wanted to see what they could get from the Chinese in return.[91] The British position was therefore only ever stated unofficially. Officially, there was no comment on any speculation. Stewart Lockhart was keenly aware that, without a guarantee of tenure for Weihaiwei, no business man would be prepared to invest in the territory. Since his arrival there, he had tried repeatedly to wring some firm commitment on tenure from the Colonial Office, but without success. In desperation, he suggested to Lucas that 'the best course with regard to Wei hai wei might be to attach it to Hong Kong'.[92] Unknown to Stewart Lockhart, it was an idea which had been considered when the Colonial Office had first acquired the administration, and at that time, Lucas had opposed the proposal 'thinking the place would have more chance if it was "on its own"'.[93] This time round, Lucas changed his mind, agreed with Stewart Lockhart, and, with the permission of the Secretary of State, Lord Elgin, wrote privately to Nathan, the Governor of Hong Kong, suggesting that he and Stewart Lockhart meet privately to discuss the matter in secret.[94]

At last, after eight years of indecision, it seemed that Weihaiwei was to be given a secure future. Unfortunately, like so many of the best laid plans for the territory, fate was not to smile on the scheme. Stewart Lockhart's hopes were dashed in the autumn of 1906 when he was given the news that China was demanding the restoration of Weihaiwei.[95] The British position remained unchanged — as long as Lüshun was leased to any foreign power, Britain intended to retain Weihaiwei. The damage, of course, was done. Wary of agitating the Chinese further, the secret plan for Weihaiwei was quietly dropped.[96]

Stewart Lockhart was devastated by the news. Not only was the decision to be the death knell for any hope of commercial development, it hit him personally. 'I try not to allow myself to be disheartened by the uncertainty which hangs over the administration but it requires an effort not to be dismayed.'[97] Weihaiwei's future could hardly have looked less promising.

One positive point did emerge from the whole question of tenure in 1906: a move for Stewart Lockhart to another colony. Noting that it was about time for Weihaiwei's Commissioner to be moved, Lucas argued: 'He has had a difficult and thankless job and in my opinion has earned a move and promotion.'[98] Lucas' suggestion for promotion was agreed by his senior, Ommanney: they even agreed that Stewart Lockhart was ideally suited to run 'a small West Indian Government'.[99] Stewart Lockhart was, naturally, unaware of the secret decision about his future, though Lucas wrote privately on several occasions assuring him that promotion was imminent.[100] A rosy future in the sun seemed assured.

Chapter 9

THE SCHOLAR-COLLECTOR
(1907–1912)

BY the beginning of 1907, Stewart Lockhart had done virtually all he could for Weihaiwei. The administration was organized on a sound footing, and with Johnston, Walter, and the cadet, Carpmael, in the Weihaiwei service, the territory had sufficient staff to ensure its smooth running. The Commissioner felt himself to be in a stalemate. A tight-fisted Treasury, unwilling to advance major expenditure to promote Weihaiwei's growth, and the lack of any security of tenure led Stewart Lockhart to believe that 'progress of any kind is impossible'.[1] Given only half an idea of the home government's views on Weihaiwei's uncertain future, he could do little but keep the territory on a peaceful, even keel. Stewart Lockhart was not alone in being mystified by the home government's policy. Sir John Jordan, British Minister in Beijing, was equally perplexed, writing that he did 'not understand the Wei Hai policy or why there should be such uncertainty',[2] and suggesting that one reason for the lack of decision was the conflicting naval opinion on Weihaiwei. To some extent, he was correct, but as the Colonial and Foreign Offices themselves did not have a fixed policy for the territory, Jordan, like Stewart Lockhart, could only hazard guesses.

The idea of languishing in Weihaiwei for the rest of his career was not one which appealed to Stewart Lockhart. Aware, from Lucas' letters, that he was in line for promotion, he started to pursue this avenue with a vengeance. In 1906, he had unsuccessfully applied for the Governorship of Hong Kong.[3] As is unfortunately customary with a certain number of government papers, his application and the attached minutes were later destroyed pursuant to statute, so one can only surmise as to the reasons for his lack of success. It is significant, however, that when Lucas put forward Stewart Lockhart's name for promotion in 1906, he makes no mention of Hong Kong, but minutes that Stewart Lockhart 'would not be the man for Lt. Governor of Ceylon'.[4] Lucas had followed Stewart

Lockhart's career closely, ever since he was a Hong Kong Cadet, and knew the Scot's strengths and weaknesses better than anyone at the Colonial Office. Lucas was also well aware of what was required for each gubernatorial post in terms of character and ability. Stewart Lockhart's ability as an administrator was not questioned by Lucas, but his decision not to push for Stewart Lockhart to be Governor of Hong Kong requires closer examination. Many in the Far East expected that, one day, Stewart Lockhart would assume responsibility for that colony, and, in 1906, having served his gubernatorial apprenticeship in Weihaiwei, he would seem to have been admirably well qualified to succeed Nathan, who was leaving Hong Kong the following year. As Lucas did not question Stewart Lockhart's ability, one must seek other reasons for his being passed over. In Hong Kong, Stewart Lockhart had suffered many attacks in the Legislative and Executive Councils, particularly from European business men such as Whitehead, who believed him to be too overtly pro-Chinese. Stewart Lockhart's high academic standards and demanding, self imposed, workload cannot have made him universally popular among other officials in the colony, and he was undoubtedly on better terms there with the Chinese business community than with the European one. None of these factors should, in themselves, have debarred Stewart Lockhart from high office in Hong Kong, but they may have been, together, sufficient to make Lucas decide that Stewart Lockhart was less well suited to running a colony with a large European staff than one with a small staff where close contact with the native population was important. Lucas was setting forth options which he believed, first and foremost, to be in the best interests of the British Government, but in doing so, was unwittingly to strand Stewart Lockhart in Weihaiwei.

Whilst awaiting his promised promotion, Stewart Lockhart continued to oversee the smooth running of Weihaiwei, believing that he would 'be sent to some other place before too long'.[5] In such a small territory, once the major ordinances were promulgated and administrative practices established, there was little else to do but keep things 'ticking over'. The official papers reflect the sleepy mood of the territory. With no need, in his mind, to impress the Colonial Office with unnecessary flurries of paperwork, and with no real opportunity to exploit commerce or organize major capital projects, Stewart Lockhart sent progressively fewer and fewer despatches back to London. Indeed, all the papers he sent to the Colonial Office in the years 1907 and 1908 fit into a single, slim file, compared with the ten, fat files emanating from Hong Kong in the same period.[6] Stewart Lockhart undoubtedly had no desire to create additional paperwork for himself when the daily administration of the territory itself created acres of paper.[7] The enormous variety of problems associated with the administration of 150,000 people and the quantities of correspondence created solely by civil litigations in the Magistrates' Courts generated a formidable body of work to be tackled each day. In addition, as the Government's representative, Stewart Lockhart had to receive all visitors of any note, and perform a regular round of public functions which kept him particularly busy in the summer. The Colonial Office, however, saw only what was under its nose and Stewart Lockhart made a grave error in not continually pressing the weight of work in Weihaiwei on London. In running the territory with as little interference from London as possible, he was eventually to play into the hands of those who cared little for him within the Colonial Office, and his career was to suffer accordingly.

Annual Reports became shorter and shorter as Weihaiwei found less and less to tell the outside world. Of the despatches Stewart Lockhart did send to London, few contained any information of import, though the Colonial Office's reaction to some cast an illuminating light on the workings of the diplomatic mind. For example, when Stewart Lockhart sent a description of the award ceremony he had held for the district headmen, during which he had distributed medals, some eyebrows were raised in London. Colonial Office rules stated that all medals should come only from the monarch, a rule which Stewart Lockhart maintained he had not flouted, as the medals 'have been awarded to them by the local authority, as is customary in China where awards of this kind are common'.[8] The star-shaped medals, silver for second class, gold for first, bore the inscription 'Presented by the Government of Weihaiwei', and were distributed by the Commissioner to those who provided assistance to the administration. As a method of thanking Weihaiwei's headmen for their support, it was an excellent ploy, keeping them on their toes and loyal to the

Commissioner. The Colonial Office were in a quandary. To refuse permission to grant further medals seemed petty and yet, technically, Stewart Lockhart was in breach of the regulations by distributing them. It was Lucas who delivered Solomon's judgement. Rather than acknowledge Stewart Lockhart's despatch about the ceremony (in which case, regulations would force the Colonial Office to order the discontinuation of the medals), Lucas decided 'to put the paper by and, if he goes on giving medals, to turn the blind eye'.[9] Of such stuff are governments made.

With no great crises looming on the horizon and the contented companionship of Edith and Margaret, 1907 passed in a haze of cosy domesticity. However, the disbandment of the Chinese Regiment made the beginning of the year rather lonely, for with the loss of the Regiment, Weihaiwei had also lost its hunt. But Stewart Lockhart found time for other pursuits. A visit to Hong Kong in February gave him and Edith the opportunity to enjoy the company of family and friends, though the oppressive climate soon made him long for Weihaiwei;[10] and in May he spent a few enjoyable days staying with Johnston at Wenchuantang. Johnston had settled admirably into his life in the Chinese countryside. Evenings and weekends in his own company enabled him to write *From Peking to Mandalay* whilst continuing his research into Buddhism, in addition to studying the history and culture of Weihaiwei, such as it was, for his book, *Lion and Dragon in Northern China*. He adopted, as far as was practicable, an entirely Chinese lifestyle. Whereas Government House retained cooks who prepared European food, Johnston lived on Chinese food alone, eating with chopsticks, and making no exceptions to his regimen when Stewart Lockhart visited. Not being a total sinophile like Johnston, Stewart Lockhart was forced to admit that, though he enjoyed Chinese meals at Johnston's, he really did prefer European food.[11]

Despite Weihaiwei's remote location, there were clubs and societies to join. As a mark of his contribution to scholarship, the Royal Asiatic Society bestowed upon Stewart Lockhart their highest honour when, in 1906, he was made an honorary member.[12] Perhaps the most unlikely club to which he was elected, however, was the Ends of the Earth Club, based in New York. This somewhat eccentric society was composed of 'good fellows with no axes to grind'[13] and contained an exclusive membership of less than 250. Exactly who proposed Stewart Lockhart's name is unknown, but, once elected, he was in the illustrious company of a group which counted Rudyard Kipling, Arthur Conan Doyle, Lord Charles Beresford, Winston Churchill, and Mark Twain amongst its number.[14] Other clubs were started in Weihaiwei itself, all enthusiastically supported by the Commissioner. Following his arrival in the territory, the Weihaiwei Golf Club had been founded.[15] The same year, he was instrumental in starting the Weihaiwei St Andrew's Society which, as it only admitted 'any respectable Scotchman' as a member, must have been the territory's smallest club.[16] With Stewart Lockhart as President, and any Scot available elected Vice-President — Major Bruce of the Chinese Regiment and Johnston both held the post — the society, somehow, always managed to muster sufficient Scots to hold a St Andrew's night feast each November. Haggis, the centrepiece of any such meal, was mysteriously procured, and the society went to even greater lengths to find the requisite items to make these feasts authentically Scottish events, shipping bagpipes from Tianjin for the occasion.[17]

In the summer other clubs, with a slightly broader membership base, flourished. Particularly popular, because of the strong naval presence, was the Mandarin Duck Sailing Club, named after the Commissioner's badge which featured a pair of these ducks. As Commodore of the club, Stewart Lockhart officiated over the regatta each summer, distributing prizes and cheering the teams on.

The placid existence of 1907 flowed into 1908 without a break. Edith ran Government House with admirable efficiency and supervised the garden, now flourishing as a result of Mr Gibbons' flair. Weihaiwei was not, however, all peace and contentment. It is easy, considering the situation in the territory, to think that all of north China was likewise slumbering, though nothing could be further from the truth. The predatory instincts of Japan and Germany had not abated, and the Japanese encroachment of Korea, nominally an independent country, resulted in some wealthy Koreans fleeing to the safety of Weihaiwei.[18] The rumblings of international unrest were never far from Weihaiwei's shores.

In the summer of 1908, Johnston again spent his leave in the interior of China, this time exploring the sites sacred to Chinese

Buddhists for his book on the subject. Carpmael, by now a Passed Cadet, acted as District Officer in Johnston's absence, whilst the long-serving Walter continued in his post as Secretary to Government. As ever, Johnston's absence was keenly felt by Stewart Lockhart, though he was greatly cheered by the presence of his son, Charles, whose ship arrived as part of the naval contingent stationed for the summer in Weihaiwei. It is a measure of the sacrifices made by Stewart Lockhart and many other colonial officers, that he could observe wistfully after Charles' departure that the five members of the Stewart Lockhart family had yet to find the opportunity to spend a single day together.[19] Indeed, it was not until he retired that he had the opportunity to gather his three children under a single roof.

The social and diplomatic high point of 1908 was the first visit to Weihaiwei of Shandong's new Governor, Yuan Shuxun (Yüan Shu-hsün). Such occasions were ones of splendour, and Stewart Lockhart's annual entertainment allowance of £150 did not extend to entertaining successive Provincial Governors in the style to which they were accustomed. Accordingly, each time such a visit was proposed, permission for an additional £100 of expenditure had to be requested from London. Such requests were never refused, though neither were they readily given. Even with a budget of £100, Stewart Lockhart was hard pressed to repay the Governor's hospitality. During the 1908 visit, for example, Governor Yuan gave Weihaiwei's Commissioner the gift of two fur coats, several rolls of silk, a carpet, an embroidered silk picture, and a large antique red vase.[20] All Stewart Lockhart could offer in return was luncheon in the tiny dining room at Government House, where twenty-two people managed to squeeze round the table for the meal.[21] Luncheon was an all male affair comprising European and Chinese guests, and Edith, like a naughty child, watched the proceedings through a key hole. In relating the occasion to her daughter, Mary, she notes, without complaint, the subordinate role she took in her husband's official life, while greatly enjoying the day's pageant.

... in they went ... the officials in their smart coats and hats with their various buttons of rank and some with the peacock's feather ... After lunch was over Dads proposed The King's and the Emperor of China's health and after that read an address of welcome to the Governor in Chinese which rather surprised the Governor and Dads says after that

he seemed quite a different man. I had never heard Dads do it before
... I think they were much surprised at Dads' knowledge of their
language and literature. He could even speak a dialect of Chinese that
the Governor didn't know himself.[22]

The success of the visit was complete, due in no small measure
to Stewart Lockhart's close attention to detail. As Edith quaintly
observed, 'so few people know how to treat them! Dads of
course knows their etiquette so well',[23] and it was this very fact
which meant that visits by and to successive Governors were,
without exception, successful. Such highlights always lightened
Stewart Lockhart's mood and made him feel that, after all, life in
Weihaiwei was worthwhile. Even the lack of promotion ceased
momentarily to trouble him at such times, permitting him
to reflect that 'my present position ... has much to recommend it'.[24]

   This contentment was to remain for a little longer. A fortnight
after Governor Yuan's visit, a coded telegram reading 'Appul-
crano Honeybag Yourself Crewe' arrived on Stewart Lockhart's
desk.[25] Honeybag was the delightfully appropriate code for a
knighthood: he had just been awarded a KCMG. Although the
award was given for long service, the press concentrated far
more on Stewart Lockhart's scholarly abilities and on his cordial
relations with the Chinese, than on his official career. The Hong
Kong press were particularly favourable, devoting almost twice
as much column space to Stewart Lockhart's achievements as
they did to former Governor Nathan, honoured at the same
time.[26] Stewart Lockhart was delighted, understandably, with
his honour, feeling that the knighthood was almost certainly the
next step to a Governorship.

   1909 was the year when opium finally became an illegal
substance, and Britain stopped pretending that the drug was an
acceptable material to trade. Weihaiwei had its own, small
opium farm, run on the same lines as the one in Hong Kong,
and established by Stewart Lockhart on his arrival in the territory as something which generated revenue. The acquisition
of revenue from the addictive misery of others neither attracted
nor alarmed him: for Stewart Lockhart, it was part of his job.
Throughout his career, he never condemned a trade which is
viewed today as immoral and this is not an aspect of his life
which does him any credit. Nevertheless, sadly, it reflects the

view taken by so many people running Britain's Empire in the late nineteenth and early twentieth century. Johnston, like Stewart Lockhart, never found the time or the inclination to condemn the opium trade. In Weihaiwei, it generated revenue, and was therefore a useful governmental tool.

When the Weihaiwei Government was instructed to stop the open sale of opium, an appropriate ordinance was passed with all speed.[27] The abandonment of the British trade in opium was finalized at the International Opium Commission in Shanghai in 1909. Johnston, on long leave, reached Shanghai in February and met all the opium delegates, reporting the news he gathered to Stewart Lockhart, and showing some concern for Weihaiwei's situation. The first opium ordinance, drafted for Weihaiwei by the judiciary in Shanghai, permitted licensed opium smokers to import their own opium: a move which would have negated the fundamental purpose of the opium commission. Johnston warned Stewart Lockhart of the imminent arrival of the ordinance, adding that Clementi, an old friend and colleague from Hong Kong, had informed Johnston that the delegates would find the ordinance objectionable.[28] Amendments, following Johnston's intelligence, were duly made in order to comply with the spirit of the commission which was intended to end all opium trade with China by 1917.[29] The ban on the sale of opium in Weihaiwei in fact had little effect on either revenue or population. Opium continued to be smoked by registered addicts, though on a much smaller scale than previously, and the only effect discernible to Stewart Lockhart was an increase in alcohol consumption as opium consumption decreased.[30] Johnston suggested a novel method to persuade opium smokers to enter the Weihaiwei refuge to cure their addiction:

The best way I can think of to persuade them is to call upon them to find a very large security for themselves — much more than they will find it possible or easy to guarantee: and then tell them that if they go voluntarily into the Refuge the matter of the Security will be allowed to drop.[31]

The ploy had some success, even if it did drive a number of reformed addicts to drink.

Johnston also spent time in Shanghai trying to glean some nuggets of information about the future of Weihaiwei. Sir Cecil

Clementi-Smith felt that, on balance, Britain was likely to continue her retention of the territory, but warned that the Secretary of State, Sir Edward Grey, was personally against retention, and that it was only due to the views of the permanent officials in the Colonial and Foreign Offices in London that Weihaiwei was still being leased.[32] Given that the question of tenure was as unsettled as ever, Stewart Lockhart had little option but to carry on with the tedium of daily administration, making the most of the few opportunities afforded him in north China.

In April 1909, Stewart Lockhart made one of the official visits he most enjoyed: the annual meeting with the Governor of Shandong. It was a pleasure reciprocated by the Chinese. Before the visit Johnston delightedly reported his meeting with the head of Shandong's Foreign Bureau who told him that the Governor and other officials were looking forward to Stewart Lockhart's arrival. Giles, the eminent, if contentious, Chinese scholar who accompanied Johnston to this meeting, assured him that the anticipation was quite genuine: a rare accolade for a British official in China.[33] Stewart Lockhart recalled Johnston from leave to accompany him on his visit, 'as there was no other officer available',[34] and the visit to Jinan was as successful as previous meetings with Shandong Governors had been, despite a cold which prevented Stewart Lockhart from attending the main official banquet.[35] From Jinan, the two men travelled to Tianjin, where they met Yang Shixiang, the former Provincial Governor, who was now Viceroy of Hebei (Chihli). It is a significant mark of the respect and esteem in which Stewart Lockhart was held by the Chinese that such senior officials took such pains to extend much more than common diplomatic courtesies to him. Johnston and Stewart Lockhart then travelled to Beijing where, as guests of the British Legation, they had the opportunity to catch up with some of the gossip from around China. Beijing also afforded the opportunity for sightseeing, and they 'did most of the sights at Peking and also visited the Ming Tombs'[36] where Johnston photographed Stewart Lockhart standing beside the huge animal carvings lining the route to the tombs.

Pleasant though their trip had been, Stewart Lockhart was delighted to return to Weihaiwei.[37] Lack of promotion apart, life had settled into a not unpleasant routine for him, and with Edith and Margaret at his side, he was a reasonably contented man. Johnston was finding life less amenable, however. Desperately trying to find time to complete his book on Weihaiwei, *Lion and Dragon in Northern China*, he complained to Stewart Lockhart that 'Court-work is so exhausting it leaves me every evening fit for nothing but walking and reading.'[38] Shortly after this, disaster struck Johnston's home when a storm caused flooding so severe that the entire valley in front of his house was under water, ruining crops, and reaching the seventh step leading to his front door.[39] It is some indication of Johnston's resilience that the floods only halted his official work for a day.

In the autumn of 1909, the Stewart Lockharts left Weihaiwei for leave in Britain. It was the first time Stewart Lockhart had returned home since he had moved to Weihaiwei, and it also marked their first meeting with Mary since she had settled into English boarding school life. Christmas that year was one of family celebration, but leave was over all too soon, and by February 1910, after just three months' vacation, the Commissioner was back at Government House.

His return to Weihaiwei in 1910 marks the beginning of an intensification of Stewart Lockhart's interest in Chinese art. As the Weihaiwei administration slumbered on, he found he could devote an increasing amount of time to his scholarly pursuits, an interest which went hand in hand with his growing enthusiasm for art. The availability of spare time, however, was only one factor which contributed to his new passion. By 1910, he was financially secure and no doubt felt he could have a modest, but regular, expenditure on art. Until then, he owned only a few dozen scrolls, most of which had been given to him. Many of the scrolls he owned were by contemporary artists, and no more than twelve purported to be from earlier periods. From 1902 until 1910, he had taken no great steps to extend the small collection he had already built up in Hong Kong. In 1910, however, a Hong Kong Chinese, named Tse Tsan-t'ai, appeared in his life, providing Stewart Lockhart with the means to build up an imposing collection of scroll paintings.

Although Stewart Lockhart had known Tse when he was Registrar General, the two men's correspondence did not begin until Stewart Lockhart returned from leave in 1910. He knew Tse's brothers well, and their correspondence started when one of Tse's brothers sent Stewart Lockhart a book of photographs of the sacred mountain Tai Shan (T'ai Shan) and Confucius' birthplace.[40] Tse had suggested that the volume be sent to Stewart Lockhart, and the Commissioner's letter of thanks for the gift began the correspondence. At the time, the Qing dynasty was beginning to disintegrate, and political cartoons with anti-Manchu slogans were appearing in public places throughout China. Stewart Lockhart's instincts as both an historian and a collector invoked a desire to obtain such transient objects and, knowing Tse to be a staunch republican, he continued the correspondence with Tse primarily with the object of acquiring any political cartoons the Chinese might encounter.[41] The irony of the correspondence, which spanned several years, was that Tse supplied virtually no cartoons,[42] but instead became, for some years, a major supplier of Chinese art to Stewart Lockhart.

In his second letter to Stewart Lockhart, Tse asks if he collects Chinese paintings, noting that 'they are the rage now in England and on the Continent'.[43] With a percipience worthy of a Hong Kong trader, Tse points out that Chinese art could still be bought 'dirt cheap', in comparison with its true value.[44] Four pages of his letter are then devoted to describing the strength and beauty of Tse's own collection. Although at no time in the letter did he offer to sell work to Stewart Lockhart, the Scot was hooked, and promptly wrote back to ask if Tse could assist him in finding paintings to add to his collection.[45] Despite warning Stewart Lockhart that he might wait for months before Tse found anything suitable for him, within six weeks of being asked to look out for art in Hong Kong, Tse was writing with considerable enthusiasm that he had found 'eighteen pictures (6 big and 12 small) by famous painters of the Sung, Yuan, and Ming dynasties for $450.00 (£45)'. He added that 'They are all bargains and you are lucky in getting them so cheap.'[46] Stewart Lockhart paid for the eighteen paintings without seeing them, but wanted guarantees from Tse that the works were genuine. His letter to Tse was diplomatic, but reveals Stewart Lockhart's underlying anxiety not to be taken for a fool.

I am much obliged to you for all your trouble and I am glad to know that you think I have succeeded in getting a good bargain. The value of works of art is always much increased by knowing their history and by being able to trace if possible through whose hands they have passed. I shall therefore be still further obliged to you if you will attach to each of the pictures a description of it, stating who was the possessor of it, what it represents and the indications of its being undoubtedly a genuine picture of the artist and period in question. As you are a connoisseur of Chinese pictures, certificates from you attached to each picture will undoubtedly greatly increase both its interest and value.[47]

Stewart Lockhart was certainly sensible in requesting provenances for the paintings he was buying, although these in themselves would not be an absolute guarantee of authenticity. Within the Hong Kong art market, fakes and forgeries were a constant hazard, as galleries even today discover to their cost. Chinese art itself, fraudsters aside, is fraught with problems of authenticity. Many are the result of practices refined throughout centuries of producing paintings. In Chinese painting, it was common for artists of one period to copy the works and styles of earlier periods as a mark of artistic respect, ensuring that the style of a great master would endure for generations. This custom often confused even an expert eye, making it difficult to tell whether a scroll was from the Song (Sung), Ming or Qing dynasties. Stewart Lockhart was aware of the problems of separating the genuine from the fraudulent, the early original from the later copy, despite the fact that European criticism and examination of Chinese painting was in its infancy. He jotted down notes on the authentication of paintings, detailing the problems all collectors encountered: how paper could be artificially coloured to look old, signatures and inscriptions forged, and false seals appended.[48]

Between 1910 and 1921, Stewart Lockhart made a serious study of Chinese art, collecting almost five hundred paintings in the process. The few books published on Chinese painting, such as Strehlneek's *Chinese Pictorial Art*, printed in 1914, were purchased by him as soon as they became available, and any interested Chinese connoisseurs who arrived in Weihaiwei were invited to discuss, as Tse was, the aesthetics of the subject. However, connoisseurs and informative art criticism were thin on the ground in Weihaiwei. The study of Chinese painting was in its infancy in the West, and Stewart Lockhart had therefore to rely on his own eye and accumulated experience to tell him what to purchase. As the years passed, his experience alone helped him to weed out fakes and when, in 1915, he began to compile a catalogue of his collection, one frequently finds, pencilled into the margin, the words 'forgery', 'not genuine', or 'doubtful authenticity' beside individual entries.[49] His judgement on the first paintings he bought from Tse was not good, for in the first batch of eighteen works, which Tse in reply to his enquiries assured him were undoubtedly genuine, were several forgeries. Tse had been less than illuminating about their provenance, unfortunately, explaining glibly that 'I am told that these pictures came from the Hsu and Yip families of Canton. It is impossible to get the history of every picture as the descendants and members of wealthy families do not want people to know that they are selling these pictures as it means loss of face!'[50] Most of the paintings that Stewart Lockhart bought from Tse were purchased between 1910 and 1914, during which time Stewart Lockhart spent over HK$4,000 on some 90 paintings, 46 of which have now been identified as fakes.[51] The first batch purchased from Tse comprised a set of four scenes by Qiu Ying (Chiu Ying) of *The Palaces of Han*, a *Lotus, Stork and Kingfisher* by Zhao Mengqian (Chao Meng-chien), a *Landscape* by Song Xu (Sung Hsü), and an album of twelve flower paintings by Ma Yuanyu (Ma Yüan-yü).[52] Of these, not one of the scroll paintings is genuine, although the flower paintings, which are of eighteenth-century origin, seem to be authentic. From his catalogue notes, it is clear that Stewart Lockhart at times knew he was purchasing paintings which were not genuine,[53] but it is also clear that, ultimately, the authenticity of the work was not absolutely paramount. All his paintings were lovingly retained and indeed, many of the fakes are beautiful works in their own right. The Zhao Mengqian, *Lotus, Stork and Kingfisher*, Stewart Lockhart describes as 'superb',[54] and his judgement in this instance is absolutely correct, even if the painting is not what it purports to be. It is a painting of poetry and beauty and that, to Stewart Lockhart, was more important than any question of authenticity. Most highly prized were the paintings admired by his daughter Mary who, since 1907, had called herself Betty. In his catalogue the code 'B' or 'BX' signified that this was a work which gave her particular pleasure, and it was her shared joy at seeing these works which led him to gift his entire collection of paintings to her before his death. Even when she was not in Weihaiwei, Stewart Lockhart eagerly shared news of new acquisitions with her, writing how he carried them 'in my imagination daily to the 2nd. mile stone and back again'.[55] Typically, his daughter was taught to view the paintings in a Chinese manner where, unlike in the West, a painting would be hung up only for a short time before being rolled up and stored once more. Mary Stewart Lockhart fondly remembered the long, cold winters in Weihaiwei when her father would hang up a few scrolls from his collection every day in order that he might sit back and enjoy them. Time and again, he would explain to Mary how the beauty of the scrolls excited and inspired him, inviting her comments on the works.[56] For several years, the beauty of the paintings was his passion (Stewart Lockhart described it as 'my picture mania'),[57] which explains his willingness to devote such a sizeable slice of his salary — about four per cent each year between 1910 and 1915 — on their acquisition.

Given the number of forgeries Tse sold Stewart Lockhart, and Tse's inability to provide convincing provenances for the works, it is likely that Tse was buying on the open market in Hong Kong and Guangzhou. Tse doubtless made a profit on these deals, but his choice of old masters was questionable, to say the least, and he undoubtedly duped Stewart Lockhart into paying high prices — sometimes as much as HK$200 — for individual works of dubious quality. Tse was himself the victim of the shadier dealers in Hong Kong. In 1934, he asked Stewart Lockhart's help to sell some of his own collection, a sale for which the Scot had the greatest difficulty in finding buyers because of the dubious quality of the scrolls.[58] Stewart Lockhart was fairly quick to realize the hazards involved in purchasing Chinese art in this manner, and accordingly only bought from Tse for a relatively short time.

However, Tse did not merely send paintings by supposedly past masters to Weihaiwei. By 1911, he was supplying Stewart Lockhart with a considerable number of paintings produced in Shanghai in the nineteenth century. Many of these scroll and fan paintings were purchased for as little as HK$4 or HK$5, and Tse gave Stewart Lockhart others as presents.[59] Comprising some fifty works, this group of Shanghai School paintings which, in total, probably cost less than two of the more expensive forgeries, now forms the core of the finest part of the collection. The Shanghai School may be considered to be the first group of truly professional painters in the history of Chinese art. Until the early nineteenth century most Chinese artists were gentleman-scholars or recluses and painted for pleasure rather than for profit. Chinese artists for centuries had held amateur status as a point of honour. However, the artists of Shanghai painted for a living, selling their work to survive, and in so doing were rather looked down upon by nineteenth-century literati and critics. At the beginning of the twentieth century, their work was still dismissed as lacking artistic integrity and strength, and it is only relatively recently that the jewel-like qualities and delicacy of line in their work have been properly appreciated. In what would have been an unfashionable market, Stewart Lockhart used Tse as one of many sources of supply, in the process building up a superb collection of small masterpieces from the Shanghai School.

The advent of the First World War closed up Tse's main avenues of supply, and although the enterprising young man from Hong Kong continued to correspond with him, though with diminishing frequency, the first great burst of picture buying was over for Stewart Lockhart by 1915. The personal esteem in which Stewart Lockhart held his art collection is signified, to a large extent, by the care he lavished upon it. His precious scrolls were stored, rolled, in a magnificent Korean cabinet made from red lacquer and inlaid with mother of pearl. This glorious piece of furniture was presented to him in 1911 by Prince Kim, brother of the Emperor of Korea, who fled to the safety of Weihaiwei when the Japanese abolished the Korean Empire in 1910. Given in recognition of the kindness the exiled Koreans had received at the hands of the Stewart Lockharts, the cabinet had once been part of the Korean imperial collection.[60]

While building up his collection of paintings, Stewart Lockhart did not lessen his devotion to numismatics, and his already impressive collection of coins continued to grow. Since the publication of *The Currency of the Farther East*, the first two volumes of which were reprinted in 1907, Stewart Lockhart had acquired a huge number of numismatic contacts throughout the Far East. Many coins were acquired from fellow collectors. Giuseppé Ros, from the Italian Consulate in Shanghai, was one of many who traded duplicate coins with Stewart Lockhart.[61] The British consular network was also an invaluable source for new or rare items. By 1914, his collection was of sufficient size and importance to merit a published catalogue which went on sale the following year. Printed as an additional volume to their journal by the North China Branch of the Royal Asiatic Society the cumbersomely titled work, *The Stewart Lockhart Collection of*

Chinese Copper Coins, remains a standard numismatic reference book to this day. Illustrations were made from specially cut wooden blocks prepared for his publishers in Weihaiwei and sent to Shanghai after the impressions printed from them had been compared against the actual coins[62] which Stewart Lockhart had so lovingly catalogued over three decades. The coin collection had been a fairly extensive one even before he arrived in Weihaiwei, and his collecting during these later years was devoted to acquiring particularly rare specimens and to filling in gaps; a quite different policy from the haphazard approach he employed in bringing together his collection of paintings. Indeed, from 1910 to 1915, he seems to have developed a passion for collecting almost anything to do with China. Rubbings from archaeological monuments throughout the country were acquired in quantity from a variety of sources ranging from consular officers to railway engineers, and calligraphic scrolls were collected with almost as much fervour as painted scrolls.[63] Instead of notes on Chinese culture and custom, his notebooks are now filled with notes on art and archaeology.[64] Only poetry, it would seem, remained an abiding passion throughout all his years in Weihaiwei.

He obviously had the time in Weihaiwei to indulge his passion for collecting in a way which had not been possible in Hong Kong, but it was not really until 1910 that he took advantage of it. That year marked the emergence of what was to be a driving force for the rest of his time in Weihaiwei; a veritable mania for collecting. It was almost as though, in the absence of promotion, he had to do something to occupy his time. A year later, by 1911, collecting and research filled his life as they had never done before, and at the same time, the Colonial Office dashed any hopes of a further career move for him. In his disappointment, it would seem that Stewart Lockhart threw himself into a world of beauty and excellence. In 1907, he still held high hopes of being given promotion to be Governor of another colony. Indeed, when the question of rendition once more reared its ugly head that year, a lengthy Colonial Office minute recommended that as long as Britain retained Weihaiwei, expenditure should be kept to a minimum, and the salary for the Commissioner be reduced by £600 to £900 per annum when Stewart Lockhart left, noting that 'he has been given hopes of an early transfer'.[65] Despite this hope, nothing over the next two and a half years was offered to Stewart Lockhart. Other men, some of whom had been waiting years for promotion, were pushed ahead of him in the queue, and, as time went on, his own case for promotion diminished. His chances were further diminished when Lucas was moved from the Far Eastern desk in 1907 to the position of Head of Dominions Division which had little influence over affairs in China. With his old ally no longer at the helm in Chinese affairs, men like Harding and Fiddes, who had never had any patience with Stewart Lockhart, held sway. Increasingly, one finds less and less sympathy within the Colonial Office for the retention of Weihaiwei, the 'white elephant'[66] of the Empire, and this annoyance reflects on Stewart Lockhart so that by the end of 1910, London is minuting that he 'will no doubt stay at Weihaiwei for several more years'.[67]

To some extent, Stewart Lockhart must have seen the writing on the wall when an officer formerly junior to him in Hong Kong, May, was promoted over his head to the Governorship of Fiji. Despite Lucas' placation that it was 'not a post that would have been in your special line',[68] Stewart Lockhart was stung into requesting promotion.[69] By this time, in 1911, Lucas was about to retire and there was nothing to restrain the less supportive members in the Colonial Office from freely expressing their views about Stewart Lockhart. Stubbs, a future Governor of Hong Kong, verges on the malicious when discussing Stewart Lockhart's prospects, maintaining that 'he is lucky to have got where he is'.[70] Stubbs' vituperative tone is echoed by others in the office, ranging from the opinion that he would not 'now be fitted for any post of much responsibility',[71] to the hope that he would retire early.[72] With the weight of official opinion so firmly against Stewart Lockhart, the Secretary of State, Crewe, had little choice but to follow the advice of his officials and deliver the final blow by writing to Stewart Lockhart that 'there is little prospect of my being able to offer you suitable promotion before you reach the age of retirement'.[73]

The blow to Stewart Lockhart's pride and self esteem was immense; doubly so, as he could never have known that, at best, he would have been offered a small West Indian colony. His sights had been set on Hong Kong, and although he keenly felt 'the cold neglect of the Colonial Office' in denying him the opportunity to run that colony, he refused to allow himself to become bitter or resentful.[74] Understandably, he personally felt that he could not 'regard the Fates as altogether kind or just',[75] but what is remarkable is how many prominent colleagues shared his incomprehension at the view of him taken by the Colonial Office. May wrote that their attitude towards Stewart Lockhart 'puzzled and annoyed' him,[76] and Sir Henry Blake found London's action equally mystifying.[77] In Hong Kong, Stewart Lockhart had had a glittering career and at that time was 'assumed to be the right man in the right place'.[78] What had changed?

Certainly, Stewart Lockhart's loss of support within the Colonial Office was due in part to Lucas' retirement. Despite the system of competitive examinations for entry into the service, whom one knew undoubtedly held much sway in the higher echelons of the organization. Likewise, as Weihaiwei drifted downhill, with no resources and no Treasury support, so did its Commissioner's reputation. In 1907, however, the Colonial Office had still realized that the inability to turn Weihaiwei into a second Hong Kong was not the fault of the Commissioner.[79] By 1911, the mood had changed dramatically; the hawks held power in London, and Stewart Lockhart's achievements and abilities were buried under the weight of Weihaiwei's failure. Exactly when the successes were hidden — for concealed they were — is difficult to say. Why they were hidden, and why so much animosity was created against him in London, may, however, be explained. Black, the Major-General who was the first military officer to administer Hong Kong in a Governor's absence had, as related earlier, sworn to ruin his career. Stewart Lockhart's own family certainly believed Black succeeded,[80] and Sir Henry Blake also believed it possible, musing: 'can it be that Black had anything to do with it? He was very furious and vindictive and one does not know what influence he may have had'.[81] At this distance, Black's influence is difficult to prove. Certainly, Stubbs' promotion in the Colonial Office to Acting First Class Clerk in 1907, galvanized the anti-Stewart Lockhart faction into action. Meanwhile, Fiddian, who had never supported Stewart Lockhart, was also in the ascendancy, and their combined strength within the London headquarters removed any possibility of further promotion for Weihaiwei's Commissioner. Whether or not it was Black's vendetta which succeeded is now hard to say. All one can conclude from the papers which still survive is that the combined forces of unsupportive officials, given freedom of action by Lucas' departure, sentenced Stewart Lockhart to a further decade mouldering in Weihaiwei, his formidable administrative talents wasted.

Between 1910 and 1912, while Stewart Lockhart appeared to be spending a great amount of time building up his various collections, and while the Colonial Office believed that the administration of the territory was slipping towards a totally comatose state, the officials there were, as ever, kept busy with a daily diet of problems. Johnston retained his enthusiasm for the academic life, adding to his existing fund of knowledge. In 1910, he even used part of his leave to improve his already impressive knowledge of the Mandarin dialect in order that he might understand 'the difficult passages in the *Chih's* which have hitherto stood in the way of my completion of the sacred hills book' which he was eventually to publish as *Buddhist China*.[82] Academic studies, like Stewart Lockhart's collecting, had to be fitted in around the business of the administration. Johnston's workload was not untypical of that shouldered by the other officials in Weihaiwei — he investigated almost 500 civil petitions in less than eight months in 1910.[83] Criminal cases, though fewer in number, were even more time consuming, as the Magistrate had to participate in every part of the case. Johnston saw the problems of the magistrate's position more clearly that most: '*so long* as I have to do police and detective work, and work up the cases which then come before me for judgement, I do not and *cannot* decide them with absolute impartiality from the purely legal point of view'.[84] Although Johnston saw no problems in working this way, it certainly added to the overall workload he was expected to undertake.

Living in such a small European community, it was inevitable that petty arguments and jealousies should surface, and it was to Stewart Lockhart, as head of that community, that everyone turned. Walter, who had been in the territory since 1902, was beginning to find life there intolerable, and his 'enormous and ever-increasing work of Secy. to Govt. a crushing burden', a view with which Johnston had little sympathy.[85] Weihaiwei's two District Officers had little in common, one perennial problem being the thorny question of seniority. As Secretary to Government, Walter was, officially, the more senior officer. Johnston, on the other hand, had greater experience, and complained that Walter 'as far as possible . . . ought to recognise the peculiarity of my position here, and realise that if seniority went by actual length of service he could not be regarded even as my senior far less as my official superior'.[86] Stewart Lockhart was never to find a solution to this particular problem, but his loyalties, although he was always at pains to treat Walter with fairness, undoubtedly lay with Johnston. He and Johnston were close in a way in which he could never be with Walter; they shared their scholarship, and collaborated in academic pursuits. When Johnston published *Buddhist China*, it was Stewart Lockhart who wrote the Chinese characters which decorate the spine of the book, and he in turn asked Johnston for advice on the translation of many of the characters he encountered among his collection of rubbings.[87] Likewise, Johnston's advice was sought when Stewart Lockhart was compiling an index to the 3,567 characters found in the letters of Yuan Mei, a brilliant eighteenth-century scholar and writer, whose writings he had researched and indexed during 1910 and 1911 with the intention of publishing them in their entirety. Unfortunately, no publisher could be found to take on this formidable piece of research, though he kept both the manuscript and his notes.[88] Stewart Lockhart's admiration of Johnston cannot have been hidden from Walter, and one finds Stewart Lockhart praising Johnston's achievements and ignoring Walter's in numerous letters.[89] It was not that Walter was an unsatisfactory officer, far from it, but rather that Johnston was a quite exceptional one, and Stewart Lockhart's bias, however unintentional, was to turn Walter into a vehement critic of the Weihaiwei administration. In the process, he was to damage Stewart Lockhart's reputation irreparably within the Colonial Office.

Fractious officials were only one of the tiresome crosses which Weihaiwei's Commissioner had to bear. At times, the members of the European population there could be equally tiresome. When Johnston published his book, *Lion and Dragon in Northern China*, it was not unexpected that those who lived and worked in Weihaiwei would be interested in what he had written about the place. The local schoolmaster, Beer, was more interested than most, for he had long deplored Johnston's anti-Christian philosophy. Johnston, after all, was never at pains to hide his love of Buddhism. In *Lion and Dragon*, Johnston mentions a case he tried in which he punishes one man for appearing on behalf of another.[90] The man punished happened to be a Christian

convert, and Beer immediately objected to Johnston's punishment, accusing Johnston of being anti-Christian in the belief that
the man was punished for his religion. The matter was brought
to the attention of Stewart Lockhart, who gave Johnston the
right of reply. His Magistrate's answer was lengthy, but brought
several salient points to light:

In China there has hitherto been no recognised legal profession ... If
once litigants were allowed to appoint other people to appear in Court
and plead on their behalf, the result would be the rapid appearance of a
new profession — the Bar ... and it is quite open to question whether
the western system ... will really be of any serious benefit to the
agricultural masses of China.[91]

Johnston saw no difference between his approach and that of a
Chinese Magistrate, and a system of justice along the lines of a
Chinese magistracy is exactly what he and Stewart Lockhart
were trying to achieve in Weihaiwei. Beer was less happy,
maintaining that 'no man could be punished for a breach of
Chinese custom which was not also an offence against British
law'.[92] Predictably, he was given little support in his claims from
Stewart Lockhart. The Chinese identity of Weihaiwei was to be
steadfastly supported in his administration.

The petty arguments, which took up so much of the Commissioner's time, also began to take their toll on Johnston. Convinced that the Colonial Office was never going to promote him,
he started looking for appointments elsewhere. Stewart Lockhart, fully cognizant of Johnston's ability, was openly supportive of his colleague's wishes and tried to get him an appointment in the newly opened University of Hong Kong.[93] This first
of many attempts to get out of Weihaiwei was unsuccessful, but
it was not to deter Johnston from trying to enter academia on
several other occasions. Colonial Office inactivity was threaten-
ing to result in the loss of one of their most talented officials
from the service in China. Sadly, London did not seem to care.

Chapter 10

A THANKLESS TASK
(1911–1918)

DESPITE the disappointments over promotion, Stewart Lockhart had little time to brood. The first census since his assumption of the administration had to be organized in 1911. Carpmael was given the task of its organization, and in due course produced an admirable statistical report of the territory.[1] The population of almost 150,000 comprised fifty-three per cent males, with the eldest resident being aged 103. Their occupations reflected the rural tenor of the area, with farm labourers, fishermen, and carpenters predominating. As adult male literacy was only 11 per cent, and there were only forty literate women in the territory, Stewart Lockhart's continued support for the Anglo-Chinese school was obviously necessary.[2] The image of rural peacefulness sustained, Weihaiwei's census served only to support the Colonial Office's contention that officials there 'have practically no work in an ideal climate'.[3] The reality, of course, was quite different, with Johnston and the other District Officers coping with literally hundreds of individual pieces of administration each year.[4]

Weihaiwei was beginning to settle down for its annual winter slumber, cut off from the rest of the world when, on 10 October 1911, the imperial troops at Wuchang, in the Yangtze Valley, rose up under the leadership of the northern general, Li Yuanhong (Li Yuan-hung). The Wuchang rising gave Chinese republicans the opportunity they needed, and within the month all China was in rebellion. Even sleepy Weihaiwei was affected, with a bold, black lettered flag being hoisted by the republicans over the walled city on 13 November.[5] Stewart Lockhart calmly reported to the Colonial Office that Weihai City had declared for the republicans, and that his only fear was that the territory might be deluged by Chinese fleeing from more troubled areas of Shandong. As a precautionary measure, he therefore stationed police on the frontier to prevent 'undesirable characters coming into the Territory'.[6] His official tone may have been calm, but privately he bubbled to his family, 'we are all alive oh! and have been having some excitement'.[7] Johnston's wry humour likewise surfaced, observing that as the glorious Mrs Walkinshaw had 'openly declared for the Rebels: so the imperialist cause is now hopeless'.[8]

The following months were ones of political confusion in China as a Republic was declared and then a President appointed. Sun Zhongshan became China's first President on 1 January 1912, and top-level government reorganization quickly followed. Sun Baoqi (Sun Pao-ch'i), the last imperial Governor of Shandong was replaced, within a week of Sun Zhongshan assuming power, by Hu Jianshu (Hu Chien-shu).[9] As the revolution spread, and the Emperor abdicated, lawlessness increased. Acts of piracy took place in Weihaiwei's normally peaceful harbour,[10] and a hundred soldiers were brought in from Tianjin, at Stewart Lockhart's request, to guard the boundary against the influx of people fleeing from the brigandage which followed the revolution.[11] The most serious incident in Weihaiwei, however, occurred when Mr Zhao Dingyu (Chao T'ing-yu), the Chinese Magistrate and an imperial appointee, was placed under house arrest in the walled city by revolutionaries. Johnston reacted swiftly to this uneasy situation, entering Weihai City with a small party of police, rescuing Zhao, and taking him to the safety of Port Edward, whilst leaving behind four armed police to guard the Yamen.[12] By the next day, the normally peaceful inhabitants of the city had recovered their composure, and Zhao could return once more to the safety of his Yamen.[13]

The incident illustrated the problems faced by both Stewart Lockhart and Johnston during these months. On the one hand, it was the Commissioner's duty to protect the people in his care, be they republicans or monarchists; on the other, the walled city was technically not within British jurisdiction, though the British had the right, under the terms of the lease, to intervene there if the defence of the territory was under threat. Stewart Lockhart and Johnston both disliked Sun Zhongshan and personally deplored the overthrow of the Emperor, though they realized there was little they could do about the situation. Indeed, at the moment when news of the abdication was released, Stewart Lockhart was keener on obtaining some of the newly printed republican bank notes than knowing about the end of Manchu rule.[14] When, however, he had to consider Zhao's predicament, he had no hesitation in ordering a rescue attempt. Zhao Dingyu was a friend of his and when, following the dramatic events of January 1912, he was allowed to retire gracefully to his home in Suzhou (Suchou), he sent Stewart Lockhart a farewell gift of a scroll he had painted.[15] Aptly titled *Recluse, Plum Blossom, and Crane*, the inscription indicates Zhao's gratitude for his release from official life, which rendered him as happy as the famous recluse, Lin Bu (Lin Pu), whose only companions had been the cranes and the plum blossom.

The occasional threat to his friends aside, Stewart Lockhart viewed the unrest of 1912 with a degree of detachment. He tried hard to keep the peace locally, though he sometimes despaired as his attempts foundered. Although the walled city quickly resumed its placid appearance, sporadic outbreaks of trouble continued along the border with Shandong. In exasperation, after yet another unsuccessful plea for calm, he complained: 'The stupid country bumpkins have got out of hand so will not listen to peace. The result will be that soldiers will arrive in their land and instead of peace create a desert'.[16] Fortunately, the border troubles dissipated with the arrival of the Inniskillen Fuseliers from Tianjin, and by the spring of 1912, Weihaiwei was once more untroubled by the turmoil of mainland China.

It is some measure how little the revolution affected the daily administration of Weihaiwei that Stewart Lockhart could turn his attention to matters which affected him and his officers more directly. In the summer of 1910, Stewart Lockhart's daughter, Mary, had returned to Weihaiwei to complete her education under the care of a governess already employed to educate young Margaret. With a child and a young adult in the house, the accommodation provided by the government seemed more unsatisfactory than ever. Stewart Lockhart had accordingly asked the Colonial Office for HK$10,000 in order to enlarge Government House with the addition of four bedrooms, all with dressing rooms and bathrooms. For once, and no doubt to his great surprise, his request was passed without complaint,[17] and building work took place throughout 1911.

Emboldened by London's attitude, Stewart Lockhart turned his attention to the question of salary increases and promotion for his two long serving junior colleagues, Johnston and Walter, but in this matter, the Colonial Office was less forthcoming.[18] In 1911, Walter had been on long leave in Britain, during which time he had visited the Colonial Office. Whether or not Stewart Lockhart knew of this visit is unclear, but what he certainly cannot have known was what Walter had told officials there. Walter had been in Weihaiwei since 1902 and frequently complained about his lot; something which infuriated Johnston.[19] Stewart Lockhart, on the other hand, had always been supportive of Walter and, whilst he and Walter were never on the close terms he shared with Johnston, he had never shown Walter anything but kindness and hospitality. The Walters were frequent guests at Government House, often sharing the Christmas festivities with the Commissioner and his wife,[20] and joining in family birthday parties and picnics. Stewart Lockhart certainly considered Walter and his wife to be family friends, and would therefore have been horrified to discover Walter's duplicity. Although no minutes of Walter's meeting with the Colonial Office exist, the ever malicious Stubbs was later to report, with some considerable glee, that 'Mr Walter told me that if the Commissioner worked himself there wouldn't be nearly enough work to go round.'[21] Johnston had, for some time, been warning Stewart Lockhart about Walter's vindictive tongue, though Stewart Lockhart had always chosen to ignore such warnings, suspecting Johnston of over-reaction.[22] Whatever Walter's motives, although he doubtless felt that ingratiation within the Colonial Office was the only way to succeed, his comments were the final nail in the coffin of Stewart Lockhart's career as far as London was concerned. The next minute on the subject declared that 'the only things left to the Commissioner must be to go out to lunch and to write Chinese Odes — both strong points of Sir J. L.'.[23] Walter seems likewise to have succeeded in damaging Johnston's reputation during his visit, and the judgement served on him in London, following Walter's meeting was that Johnston was 'of ill-balanced mind ... at one time restrained with difficulty from becoming a Buddhist monk and ... a man who likes living in the wilds'.[24] The tales told by Walter, 'a good officer',[25] were to block Johnston's progress as effectively as Stewart Lockhart's had been blocked. Walter's poisoned chalice did, however, have the desired effect of giving him the promotion out of Weihaiwei he so obviously wanted. A kindly and supportive Colonial Office appointed him Colonial Secretary in British Honduras within a matter of months of his returning to Weihaiwei.[26]

Walter's lies and invective had other, long-term, effects. His view that the Commissioner did little work resulted in a decision to remove Carpmael from Weihaiwei.[27] In 1913, with Johnston on long leave, and one consular official, Moss, already seconded to help in the territory, Stewart Lockhart was hard pressed to find a second officer to assist him there.[28] He had to appeal personally to his old friend, Jordan, in Beijing for another officer,[29] and it was with some reluctance that Jordan seconded another consular officer, Jamieson, to Weihaiwei.[30] Having two officers seconded at a time when the consular service was already overstretched caused Jordan little pleasure. Indeed, Johnston was finally refused an extension of his leave at the end of that year because there was not a single Mandarin-speaking official available to replace him in the entire British service in China.[31]

Walter's condemnation of Stewart Lockhart was damning, but was it justified? As we have seen, as the years slid by in Weihaiwei, Stewart Lockhart certainly devoted a large amount of time to his personal collections and research. Commissioner's despatches dwindled in number after 1904, and few new ordinances were promulgated annually. Even when the administration was reorganized, the Colonial Office received only a minimal amount of information about the changes. Weihaiwei's Commissioner preferred to get on with his work without interference from London. All too quickly, without a secure tenure, Weihaiwei's commercial prospects vanished and this, coupled with Treasury stringency, meant that virtually no development could be planned. Stewart Lockhart did what he could with the limited resources available to him, but one cannot create a power-house from thin air. Aware that Weihaiwei would one day revert to China, laws were deliberately kept to a minimum and existing Chinese structures maintained. Therefore, once the administration was put on a sound footing, the day-to-day running of the territory, with all which that entailed, was his major preoccupation in winter. This was hardly an arduous task, but it was one which occupied his working day fully, and in summer, the necessary social duties he had as head of the territory did 'make a serious interruption to the day's work'.[32] Walter's comments about Stewart Lockhart and

Johnston were indisputably malicious, but, like all the best gossip, they had a grain of truth at their foundation. Stewart Lockhart was not grossly overworked: neither was he an idle wastrel. Years of disappointment at the hands of the Colonial Office certainly wore him down. Disillusioned, he made the fundamental error of pushing the case for Weihaiwei's development with increasing infrequency; usually only as part of an Annual Report. It is easy, with hindsight, to decry this omission on his part, but given that in Weihaiwei concerted lack of support from London wore a once vigorous and resourceful administrator down into a man of inaction, one can perhaps understand why Stewart Lockhart acted in the way he did, and deplore Walter's maliciousness. Stewart Lockhart found the Colonial Office's attitude to Weihaiwei incomprehensible and the Colonial Office believed him to be inefficient. Faults lay on both sides, but only the Commissioner suffered.

What only Stewart Lockhart knew was that, in the dark days of 1913 which followed Walter's treachery, Johnston had decided to quit his career in the service. Johnston planned, at the end of his fifteen months' leave, to apply for as long an unpaid extension as he would be permitted to take in order to settle his future before he finally resigned.[33] Thus, shortly before Walter moved from Weihaiwei, Johnston set off, apparently for the last time, on leave from the territory. In a final attempt to influence Colonial Office opinion he visited London during his leave, the first time he had been 'home' since arriving in China fifteen years earlier.[34] On his first attempt to see someone at the office, he received quite different treatment from that meted out to Walter, and was dismissed by a doorman![35] May, also in London, intervened on Johnston's behalf, but with only limited success, for when Johnston was eventually granted an interview, it was with one of the most junior officials, Harris, who appeared to know little about the territory. The only information Johnston could glean from Harris was that he and Stewart Lockhart were regarded as 'permanent fixtures' in Weihaiwei.[36] This, alone, was enough to confirm in Johnston's mind the fact that there was no future for him in the Colonial Service. Completely disillusioned, Johnston returned to China, where he was delivered a further blow by Jordan, who informed him that his extension of leave could not be granted due to the shortage of qualified officials. Jordan, however, held out the carrot which was to keep Johnston in the service. Macartney, the long serving consul in Kashgar in Afghanistan, was due to retire, having devoted twenty-eight years of his life to this desolate outpost. Jordan, prompted by Stewart Lockhart, proposed to appoint Johnston to the post the minute Macartney left, provided Johnston agreed to remain in Weihaiwei in the short term.[37] Johnston grasped the opportunity eagerly, for Kashgar seemed to offer everything he wished for; remoteness, contact with the native people of the area, and the chance to run things his way. The fates, rarely kind to those in Weihaiwei, turned their cruel finger from Stewart Lockhart to Johnston, however. Macartney, stuck in Kashgar because of the outbreak of World War One, remained there until 1918,[38] depriving Johnston of promotion, and marooning this talented officer for several years more in Weihaiwei.

Most of the population in Weihaiwei were, in the main, quite unaffected by the quarrels and disillusionment of the officials working in the territory. Even for Stewart Lockhart, there was still much to amuse. Many incidents were related to his daughter, Mary, such as Edith's horrified reaction when their senior houseboy, filled with republican fervour, arrived at Government House with his queue chopped off.[39] But revolution was not the only cause of civil upheaval in the territory. Johnston reported with great glee the following incident:

War took place yesterday on the sea shore between the *Ladies* of the 2 villages! Apparently the men looked on and smiled. One of the wounded ladies was brought to me in a basket, but there is nothing much the matter with her. However I have explained to representatives from both villages that suffragette outrages — though permissible perhaps in a semi-barbarous country like England — cannot be tolerated in a civilised country like China: so I have sent 3 police to live in each village at the expense of the villagers until they sign a Bond to keep the peace.[40]

Life in Weihaiwei revolved around such parochial excitements; so much so that the advent of the First World War brought hardly a murmur from the officials there. Indeed, in all the official papers to London in 1914,[41] the only incident given any comment is the loss of German-held Jiao Xian to the Japanese in the November of that year. 'A side-show to World War I',[42] one suspects this was only reported because the mules for the British force which supported the Japanese siege were embarked from Weihaiwei.[43] Stewart Lockhart was to have plenty of time to brood on the world situation, however. In March 1914, Edith had taken Margaret to England, with the intention of seeing her settled into boarding school before she returned to her husband in Weihaiwei. The outbreak of war made that return journey too dangerous to contemplate, and it was four years before she would be reunited with her husband. Charles, on active naval service, could send only infrequent messages to his parents, and Mary was in Shanghai in 1914, taking singing lessons before setting off for Paris to complete her training. As with Edith, the war was to prevent Mary travelling, and she returned to Weihaiwei in 1915 to spend the war years with her father. But for most of 1914, Stewart Lockhart was deprived of the company of his family, as well as that of Johnston, who was on resumed leave for much of the year.

Given that, days before the outbreak of war in Europe, people were still talking in terms of 'this war-scare',[44] it is not surprising that Weihaiwei, with its remote position, was initially so little affected by the news. Stewart Lockhart obviously felt the lack of family keenly from the outset of the war, and it was not long before Britons, even in far-off China, were made aware of the slaughter and sacrifices in Europe. Mary Stewart Lockhart's friends wrote poignant letters to her there about children being born without seeing their fathers, and of the terrible human cost. Within a few weeks of the war starting, one friend was to write sadly, 'there are so many young widows already'.[45] Stewart Lockhart despaired of the slaughter, but despaired even more that in far-flung Weihaiwei there was little he could do to contribute to the war effort.

However, it was not long before events in Europe took a sufficiently serious turn for the home government to call on Weihaiwei to assist with the war effort. In 1916, the army decided to recruit 150,000 labourers from north China to service the forces in France. As Weihaiwei was Britain's naval base in north China, it was decided that the Chinese Labour Corps, as they were to be known, were to embark from there.[46] Stewart Lockhart was galvanized into action, rejoicing in the contribution that 'his' territory was at last able to make.

The Chinese were, in effect, hired as coolie labour for the front, and with Weihaiwei as the point of exit it is perhaps not surprising that ninety per cent of the Labour Corps came from Shandong Province.[47] The quarters built a decade earlier for the labourers embarking for the Transvaal gold mines were cleaned and repaired to house labourers awaiting transit. Stewart Lockhart set these initial arrangements in motion, but the War Office then sent out their own representative, T. J. Bourne, to Weihaiwei to supervise the hiring and transportation of the coolies to Europe. Moss was seconded to act as Bourne's interpreter, leaving Johnston and Stewart Lockhart to run Weihaiwei. As a result, Johnston was moved to Port Edward, effectively leaving the majority of Weihaiwei's population to their own devices.[48] The consequences of this move are most clearly discernible in the sharp fall in civil cases, which more than halved in two years.[49] The local population had neither the time nor the inclination to travel to Port Edward to resolve their disagreements, except in the most serious of instances, so most began to ignore the divisional magistrate system. This was probably just as well, for Johnston would have been hard pressed to hear the number of cases which both magistrates combined had once undertaken.

Offered a three-year contract and regular pay, coolies flocked to Weihaiwei from the surrounding countryside. Bourne organized a regular series of steamers to transport the labourers[50] on their forty-day trip to the battlefields of France via the Pacific and Canada.[51] In addition to wages for their duties which included quarrying, loading and unloading trains, road maintenance, and lumber work, the Labour Corps were given smart blue serge uniforms and the 'standard coolie ration' of one and a half pounds of rice, half a pound of dried or fresh fish or meat, the same weight in vegetables, and half an ounce of tea in return for a ten-hour working day.[52] The huge influx of Chinese labourers, attracted by Britain's apparently tempting offer, initially caused some problems in Port Edward, though they were generally of a minor nature. Despite numbers being so great that Bourne at one point had to halt enlistment until more ships arrived, Stewart Lockhart could report that although 'there have been some "incidents" in the depot . . . the Weihaiwei Government . . . has dealt with them efficiently', no mean feat, considering that 44,000 coolies embarked from Weihaiwei for France.[53] The coolies worked some distance from the front line, and it was never the intention that they should be asked to face the full brunt of battle. Even so, two thousand lost their lives during the final eighteen months of the war.[54] Their contribution to Britain's war effort was not, however, forgotten, and with the advent of peace, the Secretary of State wrote with some satisfaction of his 'thanks for the assistance rendered' adding that 'The Labour force, recruited through the efforts of the staff at Weihaiwei, has performed services of great value.'[55]

The war years brought their share of triumphs and tragedies to everyone in Weihaiwei. Johnston marked the advent of war in characteristically eccentric style with the death of the Quork. One of Mary Stewart Lockhart's favourite characters, he related the Quork's demise to her with due gravity.

A floating mine drifted ashore near the Promontory: she saw it and thought it was a box of chocolates or a case of gin (she wasn't quite sure which, but she *hoped* it was gin). So she began to hack at it with a knife which she had stolen from the Governor of Tsingtau when she was looting his house. Unfortunately for her, the idea that it was chocolates or gin was quite erroneous . . . her last words just before she exploded were 'I meant well'.[56]

Buried in a matchbox by a Chinese Magistrate, the loss of the Quork symbolized the end of an era.

Johnston's wicked wit doubtless helped him retain his sanity. Living conditions in Weihaiwei, despite Colonial Office opinion to the contrary, were not ideal. Government House — a palace in comparison with the District Officer's accommodation at Wenchuantang — was still without gas, electricity or modern sanitation, but at least it had fresh garden produce and meat was readily available from Port Edward. Until 1916, when he was moved back to Port Edward, Johnston lived without stimulating company in fairly basic conditions. Shortly before his move, he discovered that his houseboy was stealing his provisions.[57] A distressing incident, it was followed by far worse when Johnston suffered a gastric infection of sufficient severity to put him out of action for a few weeks; the cause of it was bad water drawn from the well beside his house, and food supplies decaying in the heat during the forty-mile journey from Port Edward.[58] With neither clean running water nor fresh food, the healthy climate which the Colonial Office proclaimed as one of the chief advantages of living in Weihaiwei was scant consolation.

Life was equally unsettled for Stewart Lockhart. The war deprived him of his wife, whose welfare naturally caused him anxiety when the German Zeppelin attacks began to threaten England. His son, Charles was the cause of mixed emotions: anxiety for his safety, pride for his contribution to the war. There were consolations, of course, the primary one being the presence of Mary, who had always been his favourite child. From 1915 until the middle of 1918, she spent most of her time with her father in Government House, only leaving to visit Shanghai when her naval boyfriend, David Joel, to whom she became betrothed in 1916, received leave. Mary adored her father and Johnston equally, admiring their scholarship and enjoying their companionship, and fitted well into their close company. On the odd occasions when she left the territory, Stewart Lockhart would seek solace in Johnston's friendship, realizing that 'association with him always does me good'.[59]

Despite the concern Stewart Lockhart undoubtedly felt about the war and the internal strife in China, his absorbing daily thoughts were the Colonial Office's snub over promotion. Approaching his fifty-fifth birthday, he still felt sufficiently alert to cast round for other employment. It is some measure of his unhappiness that he considered leaving the service in which he had worked for so long. As early as 1913, when the establishment of a Chair of Chinese was being considered at the University of Edinburgh, he was prepared to apply for the post.[60] Unfortunately, it was to be several years more before the university finally gathered the resources to found the chair. The academic life of his home city would have suited him admirably, but he was undeterred when the appointment fell through, and cast around for other suitable alternatives.

Having established that he was in a position to retire early without the early retirement affecting his pension, and in the process giving the Colonial Office the false impression that he was about to retire early,[61] Stewart Lockhart set out to look for another appointment in academic life. By 1914, he would have been quite happy to leave Weihaiwei, but what he did not want to do was to stop working: he was fully aware that his mind needed to be occupied.[62] The golden opportunity seemed to arrive just before the outbreak of war when he heard that a Chair of Chinese was proposed at the School of Oriental Languages in London.[63] He applied as soon as he heard the news, forwarding his application, as he had to do because of his seniority in the service, through the Colonial Office in London. The testimonials appended in support of his application, praising his knowledge of Chinese literature and his fitness for the post, form an impressive list.[64] Amongst those who lent their support were Jordan, British Minister in Beijing; Satow, the former occupant of that post; Bourne, Judge in the Supreme Court in Shanghai; Parker, Professor of Chinese at Manchester; Wu Dingfang (Wu Ting-fang), Minister of Railways for the Chinese Government, but better known by his Cantonese name, Ng Choy, who was also the first non-European member of Hong Kong's Legislative Council; Sir Kai Ho Kai, the Hong Kong medical philanthropist; Sir Poshan Wei Yuk, another leading member of Hong Kong society; Reverend Pearce, of the London Missionary Society; Sir Charles Lucas, the retired head of the Dominions Division of the Colonial Office; Sir Cecil Clementi-Smith, former Governor of Ceylon and High Commissioner of Borneo and Sarawak; Reginald Johnston; Sir Henry Blake; and Sir Charles Addis, Chairman of the Hongkong and Shanghai Bank. In all, sixteen eminent men were prepared to support his application in the strongest terms. It is doubtful whether any other scholar of Chinese could have mounted such formidable support at that time, and the testimonials and their authors served to emphasize how completely misguided the Colonial Office's assessment of Stewart Lockhart was. On receiving the impressive testimonial in London, even the civil servants who had been so damning in their view of him previously had to admit that they had 'heard that Sir J. Lockhart was a magnificent Chinese scholar'.[65] In the event, the London post, postponed by the war and finally demoted to a readership, was never gained by Stewart Lockhart, but the enormous and impressive support given to his application must have cheered him greatly.

A Chair of Chinese would, in many ways, have been the ideal career move for him. He had, and was continuing to build, a huge fund of knowledge on China. One avenue of scholarship led to another, and a large part of the war years were spent researching the life and work of the eleventh-century poet, Su Dongbo (Su Tung-po). His work on this poet began in earnest in 1913, shortly after he had completed his work on the Yuan Mei letters, and with characteristic thoroughness Stewart Lockhart studied not only Su's poetry but also his life, Confucian and

Buddhist beliefs, and travels, aided greatly in this last respect by Johnston's visits to China. The fruits of the research were never published. As with so much of his research, it was so highly specialized as to be beyond the bounds of the broad, general work being undertaken by other scholars, Johnston's *Buddhist China* being a typical example; it was therefore virtually unpublishable in book form. At the same time, it contained too great a volume of notes and information to squeeze into a single paper in a journal. In many ways, the letters of Yuan and the poems of Su Dongbo fell into the same pattern from that point of view.

Stewart Lockhart's knowledge of Chinese was impressive, and perhaps he received one of his highest compliments when he was asked to contribute to a quite different exercise for publication. Ku Hung-ming asked him to translate Ku's own memoirs from Chinese into English, a task willingly undertaken by the Scot who used a pseudonym for the published work which was instantly recognizable to all his friends: Ardsheal.[66]

The war effectively ended all hopes of an academic career for Stewart Lockhart. By the time it was over, he was too old to consider new responsibilities and, despite the companionship and love of Johnston and Mary, his verve for life was disappearing. Age had begun to catch up with him. Gout was a troublesome ailment from 1912 onwards, and each winter colds and influenza hit him with increasing severity. The combination of staff shortages and the war denied him leave between 1913 and 1917. By the end of 1917, the strain was beginning to show and, for the first time since his typhoid attack at the start of the century, he was forced to take sick leave. Because he was, in any case, due long leave, consent was given for him to take six months away from the territory, and Johnston accordingly acted in his stead from November 1917 until May 1918. Stewart Lockhart restored his physique with a restful journey to Japan with Mary, which they then followed with a more arduous journey to America.[67]

In Stewart Lockhart's absence, Johnston took the opportunity to pillory the Colonial Office in a lengthy despatch about their inadequate support of Weihaiwei over successive years.[68] The despatch, written with Stewart Lockhart's knowledge, was the result of years of resentment at being deprived of the promotion he desired. Johnston felt, by this time, that nothing he could say or do would make his situation worse, having 'been left on the shelf here so long'.[69] Unknown to Johnston, the Colonial Office, who by now viewed him as 'a clever crank',[70] had already decided that he would make an excellent Commissioner in succession to Stewart Lockhart, whom they expected to retire at any time.[71] Johnston could never have realized the strength of the prejudice and bias against Stewart Lockhart when he wrote his despatch. He had hoped to spur the Colonial Office into some positive, if belated, action over Weihaiwei. Instead, the Colonial Office absolved themselves from blame by claiming that Johnston's despatch opened their eyes to the awful state of Weihaiwei 'to an embarrassing extent'[72] and suggested that the blame for this state of affairs lay squarely with Stewart Lockhart. They concluded that it was he who 'has been to blame for letting the territory slide into its present disgraceful condition without more vigorous protests'.[73] The Commissioner's numerous minutes, and pleas in Annual Reports on the subject forgotten entirely, he was now the scapegoat for years of Treasury squeezes and Colonial and Foreign Office indecision. This unreasoned prejudice was to be found only in London; Stewart Lockhart's standing amongst those who knew him was as high as ever, though many echoed Lucas' musings that 'you have had a thankless task . . . but you have done your bit . . . and will . . . look back hereafter at a good piece of work successfully carried out'.[74]

The war years were not ones entirely of sadness, though the plaudits were certainly slow in coming. There was great excitement when, in 1916, both Johnston and Stewart Lockhart were awarded honorary degrees by the fledgling University of Hong Kong.[75] Stewart Lockhart wrote to the university, expressing his delight at the honour, which he said he would have to accept in absentia, as the ceremony was to be held in December that year. December came and went without any further intimation from the university, and Stewart Lockhart was therefore astonished when, in January the following year, a friend from Edinburgh sent him a newspaper cutting containing no intimation of his receipt of an honorary degree from Hong Kong.[76] Stewart Lockhart immediately wrote to Sir Charles Eliot, Vice-Chancellor of the university, demanding to know what on earth the institution thought it was doing. Eliot's reply was less than satisfactory, as it was only at that stage that it was explained that honorary degrees were not conferred in absentia.[77] Both Johnston and

Stewart Lockhart were, understandably, dismayed, for the chances of either of them being in Hong Kong at a time which coincided with the appropriate university ceremony were indeed slim. In fact, Stewart Lockhart received his honour in 1918, but Johnston had to wait until 1929 to receive his.

As the First World War at last drew to a close in 1918, life in Weihaiwei took on a lighter tone. His sixtieth birthday was celebrated in some style with Mary and Edith, and was an excuse for the neighbouring Chinese gentry to present him with quantities of calligraphy to mark the occasion.[78] His wife had no sooner returned, however, than he lost the companionship of Mary who left Weihaiwei in June 1918 to marry her naval boyfriend, David Joel, in Ceylon. Johnston celebrated the long overdue award of a CBE that spring, and Stewart Lockhart began to look forward to peace. Like so many Britons at the end of the war, he loathed the Germans with vehemence, demanding full retribution for the four years of misery caused by the 'Hun bullies'.[79] In his fast approaching old age, Stewart Lockhart was beginning to become increasingly less tolerant of people and policies. In one particularly tetchy letter to Mary, he manages to declare his preference for the company of children to that of adults and his disgust at *The Spectator* for 'its unreasoned attack on Lloyd George', as a result of which he stopped his subscription to the magazine: at the same time he gives his daughter a lecture on religious tolerance.[80] His mental energies seemed to be renewed, though the earlier lucidity of argument, in this instance at least, degenerates into an illogical lecture:

Most people seem to forget that the views they hold on religion are all merely speculation and may be entirely wrong . . . I think people shd. be tolerant and disinclined to throw bricks at neighbours. I did not show your letter on this subject to Mother. I never discuss religion with her which shows that the absence of discussion does not interfere with one's affection.[81]

In this lecture on religious tolerance he was, at least, being consistent with his own beliefs. Though a Confucian himself, he did not let his Confucianism interfere with his support of Christian institutions in Weihaiwei, encouraging them and showing positive interest in what the Church was trying to do in the territory.[82]

Apart from the odd, peculiar outburst, which was only ever made to the people close to him, Stewart Lockhart continued to believe with a passion in the type of administration he and Johnston practised, in which government and people were bound closely to each other. Weihaiwei may have been a tiny territory, and could easily have been ruled in a completely autocratic fashion, particularly as the home government had a negligible input into its running. On some occasions, it is true that he behaved as though he were monarch of the territory, though this was always done in a manner befitting a Chinese administrator: the father and mother of his people. In 1915, for example, he brought the entire village of Lin Jia Yuan (Lin Chia Yuan) before him to berate them about their misconduct.[83] The villagers had been arguing with the Government of Weihaiwei since 1911 over some land. Having lost the battle on appeal, they committed the unforgivable crime of going over the head of the local administration to appeal for a third retrial directly to the High Court Judge from Shanghai, who was in Weihaiwei to hear a quite different case. Stewart Lockhart was at his sternest in rebuking them: 'your improper conduct has exhausted the patience of this Government and ... any repetition of it will be dealt with without leniency.'[84] His stern speech seems to have been sufficient, for the villagers ceased to seek an overturning of the earlier decision. Despite his sternness, Stewart Lockhart scorned the aloofness, and the pomp, found in so many other British colonies, reserving a particular distaste for the system of British rule in India; a system, he felt, which would 'be changed some day soon'.[85]

The armistice ending the war was celebrated in every outpost of the British Empire, and Weihaiwei played its part with sports and parties. The largest ceremony was reserved for Weihaiwei's new pier, begun in 1916 to ease the embarkation of the Labour Corps to Europe.[86] Although the pier had been in use for some time, it was formally opened on 18 November 1918. It was named the Victory Pier by Edith, who cut the ribbon and declared the pier open, whilst Stewart Lockhart and a guard of honour drawn from the Weihaiwei police force, the Marines, and the 18th Indian Infantry, added some colour to the ceremony.[87] As a memento of the ceremony, Edith was presented with a miniature junk specially made in Shanghai in silver and inscribed in remembrance of the occasion;[88] and the official party and guests then departed for Government House for 'a special brew of Rum Punch which seemed to be much appreciated'.[89]

Having spent so long in England, Edith returned to Weihaiwei with some misgivings. Despite a lifetime in the Far East, she shared none of her husband's sinological interests and missed her friends in Britain. Shortly after her arrival in Weihaiwei, she began to press Stewart Lockhart to retire and return to his home country.[90] It was a move he, surprisingly, resisted. Despite the lack of intellectual stimulation and the unchallenging nature of his work there, he was very fond of the place, loving its countryside and 'its peace and quietness'.[91] He steadfastly resisted Edith's pressure for a further two and a half years, often resorting to purely domestic argument to support his resistance, and declaring that, in any case, 'I hate moving and dread the idea of house-hunting'.[92]

There was also, he felt, much work still to be done. He had hoped that Weihaiwei's paltry economy would be boosted at least temporarily with the return of coolies repatriated from France at the end of the war. However, Qingdao (Tsingtao) was used in preference because of its rail link which enabled the men to be returned to their home areas with greater speed than would have been possible from Weihaiwei, with its limited communications.[93]

The situation in the interior of Shandong reflected the turmoil elsewhere in China. Imperialists and republicans continued to struggle for the upper hand throughout the years of the First World War. Both Stewart Lockhart and Johnston followed events closely, and were not alone in despairing of China ever recovering her sanity.[94] In common with the British Legation in Beijing,[95] both men supported Yuan Shikai (Yüan Shih-k'ai), and had been passionately opposed to Sun Zhongshan and the southern rebels who carried on his cause after his death. Stewart Lockhart's opinion of Sun as a dangerous revolutionary had not changed since he had crossed him in Hong Kong, and he believed that only Yuan would bring about China's desired stability. Of course, Yuan failed, and when he declared himself Emperor, Johnston and Stewart Lockhart lost all sympathy with his cause, noting that his death in 1916 was not 'a matter of much regret'.[96] Their concern, first and foremost, was with China and they watched with sadness as the Japanese, formerly so admired as a race by Johnston and Stewart Lockhart, encroached more and more deeply into Chinese territory.[97] In Weihaiwei, the unsettled state of China was felt at the end of the war when piracy and attacks by bands of brigands on her borders reached sufficient severity for Stewart Lockhart to call in troops to protect the territory.[98] Captain Binny and sixty-three men from the 18th Indian Infantry were stationed along the border at the end of October 1918. Their presence, if nothing else, startled the 'country bumpkins who are not accustomed to the sight of Indians'[99] sufficiently to keep the peace.

At the same time Indian troops were being sent to protect Weihaiwei, moves were being made to draw Johnston into the very centre of Chinese history. By the end of 1918, Johnston was to be offered a post which took him from sleepy Weihaiwei to Beijing, into the Forbidden City itself. Reginald Johnston, CBE, was about to become, of all things, an imperial tutor.

Chapter 11

LINGERING ON
(1918–1921)

IN 1918, Johnston took his leave, travelling as usual in the interior of China. His hankering for employment outside Weihaiwei was as strong as ever, but luck seemed to be against him. He had unsuccessfully applied for the Chair of Chinese at Columbia University at the end of 1917,[1] and, as a man who felt he had 'been at Weihaiwei far too long for the good either of himself or the community',[2] he also tried to obtain the post of Vice-Chancellor at the University of Hong Kong, available because of Eliot's imminent retirement.[3] The University took some time to make a decision on the matter, and although Johnston did not get the appointment, by the time he heard this news he had been offered, in any event, the post of imperial tutor.

Johnston's leave began at the end of August, and for two months he travelled to some of his favourite areas in the interior of China before arriving in Shanghai at the end of October to spend a month there.[4] For Johnston to spend so much of his leave in a city was unusual, and there is no indication in his letters about his motive for doing so. The first three weeks in Shanghai were apparently spent in a whirl of social activity, seeing old friends, and catching up with some reading at the Royal Asiatic Society's library there. What he did not disclose, even to Stewart Lockhart, was that, on his arrival in the city, he had been approached by Li Jingmai (Li Ching-mai), a man close to the throne, whom Johnston had met in Weihaiwei when Li fled there immediately following the collapse of the Manchu dynasty.[5] Johnston met Li at a dinner party in Shanghai on 26 October, at which Li asked him to meet the following day to discuss 'a matter of importance'.[6] The matter was of sufficient secrecy for Johnston to be forced to omit it from his letters to Stewart Lockhart from Shanghai; only when he returned to Weihaiwei could the full story be revealed.

Although China was now a republic, it was a country which also still had an emperor. The abdication settlement of February

1912 had been a curious arrangement whereby the Emperor retained his imperial title for life, retained two of his imperial palaces, complete with court, and was given the equivalent of one million pounds annually for household expenses.[7] Although the Emperor and his family were to be subsidized by the state, he was effectively treated as 'a foreign sovereign on Chinese soil',[8] though his movements were, in practice, confined to the limits of the Forbidden City, much reduced in scale since the emergence of the republic, but still forming a sizeable estate — a miniature city — in the heart of Beijing.[9] Thus China had a monarchy which survived in name only, while at the same time warring republican factions tore the country apart in their quest for power. By 1918, China had as her President a man with strong monarchist ties. President Xu Shiqang (Hsü Shih-ch'ang) was a former imperial tutor[10] who, in concert with his intermediary, Li Jingmai, wanted to prepare the Emperor for the day when a constitutional monarchy could be given to the Chinese people.[11] Although there were no plans for an attempted restoration in the short term, Li informed Johnston that 'it is considered very desirable that the boy-emperor should be educated in such a manner as to fit him for the position which it is hoped that he may some day ... occupy'.[12] It was therefore planned to give the emperor a supplement to his traditional Chinese education by teaching him the premier modern language, English, in addition to topics, such as Constitutional History and Political Science, which would be of use to him should a constitutional monarchy be founded.[13] Li and Xu knew from the outset exactly what type of man they wanted for the post of tutor. It would not have been politic, obviously, to advertise their ulterior motives, and it had been decided that the incumbent should be regarded as an imperial tutor, brought in to teach the Emperor English. Secretly, however, Li knew that the post required someone who could teach English Constitutional History, Modern History, and Politics, and who could also, as importantly, demonstrate 'a fair knowledge of the history and literature of China ... and take a sympathetic and appreciative interest in Chinese cultural traditions'.[14] In every sense, Johnston was ideal for the post. Li had met him in Weihaiwei, made enquiries into his past career, and had every confidence in his abilities and suitability for the position. Precisely when the decision had been made to appoint such a tutor is unknown, but it seems to have been one made in haste and in secret. President Xu was not elected until 4 September 1918, and Li approached Johnston a mere six weeks later, presumably to avoid any leakage of the plans which might put a stop to them.

Johnston returned to Weihaiwei with no amount of glee. However, he was not so overwhelmed by the offer that he did not first suggest to Stewart Lockhart that he might wish to take the appointment himself, and deferred sending secret telegrams to Li and to the Colonial Office until Stewart Lockhart had made a decision on the matter.[15] Stewart Lockhart rightly felt that Johnston was the better man for the position, and the secret messages were delayed but a few hours while he informed Johnston of his point of view.

Although Johnston was not required to take up his appointment until the beginning of March, he left Weihaiwei a month earlier in order to settle in Beijing before his duties commenced. In accepting the post as imperial tutor, Johnston remained a Colonial Office Official. This was Johnston's idea, and gave him a degree of security in the event of things not working out in Beijing; the Colonial Office, with an eye to the possible influences Britain might have with one of their subjects so close to the Emperor, lost no time in approving Johnston's demand.[16] Justifiably confident that his colleague would keep in close touch with him, Stewart Lockhart joined the rest of Weihaiwei in bidding Johnston fond farewells and every success. Despite the honour and the sense of historical occasion, Johnston's irreverence continued to surface, and he mused before he left as to whether he would be permitted, in the time honoured fashion of the British educational system, to cane the emperor, 'or would the *tawse* be more suitable?'[17]

Johnston indeed remained in close contact with Stewart Lockhart throughout his time in the imperial post, providing him with news and gossip from the heart of the imperial court. Johnston had plenty of opportunity to write letters, for his original three-year contract stipulated two months' annual holiday each year and only two to three hours' work each day.[18] He quickly settled down to court life, despite the enormous amount of ceremony involved. Each day, the Emperor was carried to the schoolroom on a large chair, draped in imperial yellow, and accompanied by a large retinue of attendants.[19] Very quickly, Johnston was warning Li that 'the highly artificial life that the emperor leads must be detrimental to his health, physical, intellectual and moral'.[20] He believed particularly that the eunuchs who populated the court in large numbers were damaging both to the Emperor and to the court, and for this reason, made several efforts to persuade the imperial princes that he should be allowed to take the Emperor to the Summer Palace, where he would be free of the eunuchs' pervasive influence.[21] Johnston was to get his way eventually, but it was to take time.

Stewart Lockhart likewise kept Johnston informed of the small events in Weihaiwei. Johnston's departure had done nothing to soften Colonial Office opinion of their Commissioner in the territory. Hoping that he would retire imminently, London voiced the opinion that he 'had better do so as soon as we have settled the future of WHWei'.[22] Although under pressure from his wife, Stewart Lockhart was still resisting the idea of retirement, being reluctant to stop working and leave his amenable corner of China. Weihaiwei was almost becoming civilized and now had a lively social programme. Regattas, gymkhanas, amateur dramatics and sports filled the summer months, and the long winters were now alleviated by concerts and the arrival of the latest modern wonder, the cinema. Winter evenings could henceforth be spent watching on screen the stars of the silent movies: people like Charles Hawtrey and Charlie Chaplin.[23] These social gatherings often had their comic moments, though none more comic than the Empire Day picnic in 1920. Almost the entire European population of the territory must have been present, for the celebrations were for two hundred guests, there at the invitation of the Commissioner. Parties set off to Half Moon Bay in holiday mood for the event, Stewart Lockhart arriving in the Government launch, *Alexandra*, with all the necessary provisions. In full view of the assembled party, a sudden swell hit the launch at the moment the crockery for the picnic was being transferred from launch to beach. Much of it was never retrieved from the sea, forcing Stewart Lockhart to send one of his more humble despatches to the Colonial Office to explain the loss of large quantities of government property, and request their replacement.[24]

In 1919, the University of Hong Kong invited him to take up the post Johnston had unsuccessfully applied for a year earlier, that of Vice-Chancellor of the university. It was an appointment he regretfully declined. A few years earlier he might have grasped the opportunity with eagerness, but he now felt that he was too old for such a challenging position, and suggested they look to a younger man for the appointment.[25]

Weihaiwei rarely reflected the turmoil elsewhere in China, and seemed to be stuck in a time warp. Even the local schools reflected the lack of change in the territory, with Stewart Lockhart reporting that it was not until 1920 that the old pre-republican method of teaching had given place to 'more modern methods'.[26] Generally, the Chinese organizations in Weihaiwei reflected attitudes which had vanished several years earlier in more advanced parts of China. The education of girls in the territory showed little improvement, with only one hundred girls, in a school population of over four and a half thousand, being educated at even the most rudimentary level.[27] Stewart Lockhart could have done far more to promote female education in Weihaiwei, just as he could have done more for middle grade education, and yet he made little attempt, apart from supporting the Anglo-Chinese school, to do so. In this sense, his attitude towards the maintenance of an existing order was a negative one, though it is only fair to point out that, in a peasant economy, it was almost impossible to persuade farmers to keep any of their children at school for longer than necessary, let alone educate the female members of the household, there being no tradition of women's education in China. Despite a literacy rate of only seventeen per cent, the standard of literacy in Weihaiwei was indeed accepted as being on a par with that of the rest of China.[28]

Under British rule, the peasants of Weihaiwei had flourished, at least in the material sense. Harvests had been good, and prosperity had been maintained in the peaceful territory. Then, in 1919 and 1920, tragedy struck north China, and its effect was felt even in Weihaiwei. The first major disaster was famine, which hit the whole of north China in 1919. Crops failed, and an estimated 100,000 people in the territory were in need of food.[29] Stewart Lockhart used his influence amongst the Chinese of the South to raise money for famine relief, eventually securing a respectable HK$65,730 by this method, and using the money to purchase grain imported from Dalian.[30] The grain supplies did much to stave off the worst of the starvation, but the situation was still sufficiently serious for Stewart Lockhart to have to request further funds from the Colonial Office in the spring of 1920, as an estimated 10,000 people were still destitute.[31] Fortunately, the following harvests succeeded, though it was some time before Weihaiwei considered itself to be returned to agricultural prosperity.[32]

Famine was not the only problem to be faced in what must have seemed to be twenty-four months of disaster. Anthrax hit the mule population in the autumn of 1919, decimating Weihaiwei's main mode of transport.[33] At the same time, a severe cholera epidemic broke out amongst the human population. North China had been haven to many epidemics and plagues over the years, but this was the first time that Weihaiwei had suffered badly. As people were already beginning to be weakened by famine, the disease swept through the villages of the territory. Entire villages were decimated, and many others had their populations halved. Though no final accurate count was made of the deaths, village headmen's reports finally gave rise to the belief that over 5,000 people perished in the epidemic.[34]

Little could have been done to save those who contracted cholera, but earlier epidemics in the vicinity of Weihaiwei had persuaded Stewart Lockhart that a rethink of sanitary measures was overdue. In 1918 he took the opportunity of inviting the Public Works Department from Hong Kong to report on the sanitary condition of the island, which was causing particular concern.[35] Dysentery had been a severe problem on the island in that and the previous year, causing misery to large numbers of the people working there. Even the normally healthy Johnston had contracted it and had been confined to the sanatorium.[36] In September 1918, two members of Hong Kong's Public Works Department arrived in Weihaiwei and stayed six weeks in order to complete their report. [37] The island was overcrowded and, in the main, unsanitary. The report recommended that only drastic measures could remedy the situation and remove the fear of dysentery from every visitor arriving in the area. Before the arrival of these officials the situation had indeed become so severe that Stewart Lockhart had had the majority of the Chinese living on the island removed to the mainland for fear of a further epidemic.[38] His fears seemed to have justified this drastic action, for the final report recommended the demolition of most of the island's houses, including the whole of the east village.[39] With their narrow streets, thatched roofs, and no running water, the Chinese houses on the crowded island were condemned. Swiftly demolished, they were replaced by new buildings which, although the sanitary conditions still left a lot to be desired by modern standards, at least were built along more spacious streets in accordance with building regulations.[40] Even the new sanitary arrangements were primitive, consisting of two buckets per household for night soil, and morning and evening collections of the same.[41] This, however, was a great improvement on previous practice, and gives some idea of the dreadful conditions endured by many in the territory.

Sanitation was something Stewart Lockhart could take positive steps to improve. Natural disasters were, on the other hand, impossible to control, and he could only ensure that he minimized the suffering as much as possible during such tragedies. Other aspects of life were equally frustrating, but no more within his control. Perhaps with his passion for numismatics, he found the state of the Chinese currency more interesting than frustrating, but, if this was the case, he was one of the few people who did. Internal unrest ensured that currency values fluctuated throughout China on a daily basis by 1919. One writer found himself infuriated by this state of affairs when he went to the Post Office in Weihaiwei to purchase a four cent stamp, and found he could pay for it in a variety of values:

If he presented a banknote, and purchased twenty-five four cent stamps, a dollar met the cost. If he paid in small silver coins, the stamp cost five cents — i.e., he obtained two four-cent stamps for a ten-cent piece. If he used copper cent coins, he was compelled to pay six of them for each four-cent stamp.[42]

After so many years in China, Stewart Lockhart knew how to take such trivial annoyances in his stride. If anything, the unusual state of China's currency gave him the impetus to extend his already large collection, and in his final years in China he continued to buy both coins and paintings with considerable enthusiasm. Perhaps the most important coin he purchased during these years, and certainly one of the most important in the entire collection, was acquired from a Hongkong and Shanghai Bank employee from Tianjin, A. R. Lowson. For many years, Lowson had purchased sets of coins minted in Tianjin for Stewart Lockhart, and he wrote on a casual basis if anything interesting appeared on the numismatic scene. In 1919, Lowson sent Stewart Lockhart the message: 'I saw a Chinese coin the other day — a gold one — of which I enclose a poor tracing and a few notes by our Interpreter'.[43] Lowson was holding the coin on option until Stewart Lockhart could consider whether or not he wished to make the purchase. Stewart Lockhart had no hesitation in approving the sale, for in doing so he was buying a unique piece of history. In 1915, the republican President of China, Yuan Shikai, had declared himself Emperor. His empire was short lived, and almost universally despised, but in celebration of his reign, Yuan had had 2,000 gold coins minted, and it was one of these Stewart Lockhart had been offered by Lowson. Of the many thousands of coins Stewart Lockhart bought in China, this was the jewel of his collection.

Paintings were also purchased, though not in the quantity they had been during the days of Tse's agency. As his taste refined, so did the quality of the paintings he bought. Monochrome works were now a particular favourite, especially those with bamboo as a subject. Living as he did in north China, he was in the part of the country where bamboo painting might almost have been considered a specialization, and Stewart Lockhart took advantage of this situation to buy at least twenty fine scrolls of bamboo during his final years in Weihaiwei, as well as several other monochrome studies.[44]

Dealing with the disasters of 1919 and 1920 must have taken its toll on a man who had, by now, spent forty years in China. Edith continued to press her husband to retire and return to Britain, and the pressure she brought to bear became all the greater when her mother died in England in the summer of 1920.[45] Due long leave the following year, Stewart Lockhart decided that at last the time had come for him to say farewell to the Far East, and the decision taken, his friend Johnston was one of the first to know.[46] He not only wanted to let Johnston know as a courtesy before the news became public; he also wanted to give his colleague the opportunity to succeed him in Weihaiwei, and asked Johnston if he wished to have his name put forward to the Colonial Office for the post. After years of suffering Colonial Office intransigence, Johnston was cautious:

I should certainly like to be *offered* it, because it would show the C. O. thought me worth promoting, and the fact that I had been offered it might be useful to me later on if circumstances made it necessary for me to go to them cap in hand for a billet. Whether I accepted it or not would largely depend on whether they intended to reduce the salary and status.[47]

Johnston, in any event, was more than happy in Beijing. He had become the owner of a small estate five hours' ride from the capital which had been paid for by President Xu as a gift.[48] In addition, a generous salary was increased by regular monetary gifts from the Emperor which, in Johnston's first year as tutor, had amounted to a total of £3,050, a sum far in excess of anything the Colonial Service could offer.[49] Such riches enabled Johnston to purchase a real luxury, a Ford motor car which he proudly used to take himself through the streets of Beijing.[50]

News of the imminent retirement of the Commissioner of Weihaiwei was greeted at the Colonial Office with relief, but without any change in attitude towards him: '18 years of WHWei under Treasury control would drive an energetic man to suicide or resignation. Sir J. Lockhart has taken refuge in apathy'.[51] Whilst welcoming the opportunity Stewart Lockhart's retirement gave London to do as it wished with the territory, the Colonial Office was also left in rather a quandary. Its first choice as a replacement for the Commissioner, Johnston, was now safely ensconced in Beijing, and it was not in Britain's interests to move him, even if he had been prepared to leave his post as imperial tutor. Weihaiwei's other long serving Secretary to Government, Walter, was now happily serving King and country on the other side of the world, as Administrator of Dominica. The last member of Weihaiwei's 'permanent' staff, the cadet Carpmael, had suffered a nervous breakdown and could not therefore be considered for the post.[52] The question of who would succeed Stewart Lockhart was thus left in abeyance for the time being, and it was decided to send Reginald Stubbs to the territory to report on its future as soon as possible. Stubbs, a decade earlier, had been one of the 'hawks' who had so successfully kept Stewart Lockhart in Weihaiwei following Lucas' retirement. Now Governor of Hong Kong, he was instructed to seek out Johnston in Beijing, in addition to visiting Weihaiwei, to ascertain his views on the territory.[53]

In 1919, Weihaiwei had once more been the subject of speculation, with the question of its rendition being raised at the

Paris conference which followed the end of World War One. Having spent so many years in an indecisive limbo, one would have expected, when the question of rendition was once more raised following Japan's acquisition of Jiao Xian, that the Colonial Office would have been only to happy to hand its white elephant back to China. However, it did not take long for some of the brighter minds in the Colonial Office to point out that, in raising the question of Weihaiwei's rendition, Britain was running the risk of also raising the question of her unequal treaty by which she acquired the New Territories at the same time as she had Weihaiwei. As one official noted, 'some day F. O. will discover that our retention of Hong Kong itself is incompatible with the principle of the League of Nations but that dog is asleep just now'.[54] Therefore it was quickly decided that although British rule had resulted in Weihaiwei being 'somewhat unduly depreciated' with its development having 'suffered severely from a too parsimonious administration',[55] it was better to retain the territory rather than risk losing Hong Kong's hinterland in the process of returning Weihaiwei to China. Stewart Lockhart, unaware of the international machinations taking place, could only share Johnston's hope that Stubbs would recommend that the mainland at least be returned to China; neither man believed for a moment that the Admiralty would be prepared to give up the island and therefore their harbour and naval base.[56] Their views on Britain's unequal treaties with China were shared by other, long serving officials in China. When Jordan was asked his views on rendition, he astounded and shocked the Colonial Office, by suggesting that *all* British occupied territories held in China under unequal treaties should be returned: he was swiftly persuaded to change his official views on this subject.[57]

Questions about Weihaiwei's future, however, were not going to disappear. The Paris Conference was followed a year later by the Washington Conference, which opened in November 1921. Once more, the question of Weihaiwei was to be raised, and once more, to remain unsettled. It was, of course, to be a further decade before Britain finally sorted out her views on the territory.[58] In the meantime, people like Johnston and Stewart Lockhart could only sit helplessly on the sidelines and wonder at 'British international morality'.[59]

Thoughts of rendition, except when he was called upon to express them officially to the Colonial Office, or in private

musings to Johnston, were only infrequently on Stewart Lockhart's mind. He was too preoccupied with the final move from
the territory and the handing over of power to be involved in
international decisions. Also there was still work to be done. The
census of 1921 had to be organized, and its appearance demons-
trated how little Weihaiwei had changed over the last decade.[60]
The population showed only a slight increase and the profile of
occupations was almost identical to that listed in the census of
1911. The census apart, Stewart Lockhart had little else to occupy
him officially. He was handing over the territory to Blunt, a
consular official who had already served under him, and who
was more than capable of the tasks ahead. Indeed, the last few
months in Weihaiwei were filled with a task as arduous and
demanding as any official duty he had ever been called upon to
undertake: he was packing to go home.

Stewart Lockhart's final months in China were not ones of
romantic memories or of visits to loved places. They were
months filled with packing cases and trunks, to the virtual
exclusion of all else. One wonders at Edith's tolerance in permitting her husband to overrun Government House with boxes,
though one suspects she was given little option. The most
important coins had long been kept in their own cabinet, in
which they are displayed to this day, and this had to be sealed
with wax in preparation for the long sea journey. However, only
the best coins were kept there; literally thousands of others had
to be put in wooden boxes to be shipped home. Scroll paintings
were removed from the Korean Cabinet, and likewise packed,
the larger ones being put in specially made tin tubes for the
journey home. The local carpenter was kept busy for months
making everything from iron boxes to new picture frames.[61] As
well as the main collections of art and coins, hundreds of
rubbings were stored in wooden chests, as were the calligraphic
scrolls and numerous examples of porcelain he had acquired in
his forty years in China. Of course, in addition to all these items,
Stewart Lockhart's papers had to be transported home. These
consisted of official papers by the ream, album upon album of
political cartoons, endless books of notes from a lifetime's
research, letters, manuscripts, and his notes on Confucius, the
research he cherished most of all.[62] His library alone took weeks
to pack. This was one of the first tasks undertaken — presumably
to make room for all the packing cases arriving for everything

else.[63] Nothing, it seems, was to be lost from his career in China. Even the ephemerae of everyday life were kept, from concert programmes to menu cards.

The final month in the territory offered even less respite, as everyone wanted to wish the Commissioner their personal farewell and give him their personal gift. As had happened in Hong Kong nineteen years earlier, many groups presented him with farewell addresses. It is some indication of the relative poverty of Weihaiwei that the only address which came anywhere close to the luxurious appearance of those given in Hong Kong was that presented by the British staff in the territory, which was embossed in gold on blue satin.[64] The rest were modest affairs, but this made the sentiments none the less sincere. Obviously, no one was going to accuse Stewart Lockhart in their farewell of being a vicious tyrant, even if that had been the case, but even so, the strength of feeling — the sheer love — which appears again and again in these addresses is astonishing. Endless care was taken to select the appropriate gift, and one of the nicest was the present selected by the Chinese staff in the government and the teachers of the Anglo-Chinese school. Knowing Stewart Lockhart's love of Chinese literature, they selected the *Book of Odes*, one of his favourites, and took from it the descriptions of the fourteen musical instruments mentioned in its pages. The musical instruments were reproduced in silver in miniature by a local silversmith who was chosen especially to remind Stewart Lockhart of his years in Weihaiwei.[65] Perhaps the most appropriate gift was, in fact, the simplest. The local Chinese Chamber of Commerce presented him with a bowl of pure water, symbol of an honest administration and a pure and incorruptible mandarin.[66] Its significance was not lost on Stewart Lockhart.

The Chinese of the territory were well aware that they were losing not only an incorruptible mandarin, but also a good friend. Stewart Lockhart produced fierce loyalty in those Chinese who knew him, whether as a colleague or administrator, a loyalty perhaps best illustrated by an anecdote from the hand of one of the Police Inspectors in Weihaiwei: 'I once told a Chinese at Weihai that you were Scotch, and I was trying to explain in my poor Chinese the difference in Scotch, Irish and English. Could get the latter in Chinese but not the two former ... Later the fellow reported me for calling you a foreigner.'[67] Such indignation on the part of a native of the territory at a supposed slur on Stewart Lockhart's name and reputation is, in many ways, a more telling compliment to his administration than any official eulogy.

Feelings generally ran high amongst those who had served in Weihaiwei that Stewart Lockhart had had a raw deal from the Colonial Office over the years, and Blunt restated this point when he sent copies to London of all the addresses given to Stewart Lockhart before he left to return to Britain:

I venture to suggest that it is inconceivable that the deep and universal regret felt by the Chinese population of this Territory upon Sir J. H. Stewart Lockhart's retirement is, in itself, as high a tribute to British administrative methods and as helpful to British prestige as would have been more material progress.[68]

Even the hard bitten officials at the Colonial Office were to admit that they found the addresses 'touching'.[69] A few months after Stewart Lockhart left Weihaiwei, London's view of his administration, which had so vehemently opposed his methods for so many years, finally changed. However belatedly, the Colonial Office, somewhat to its surprise, came to the conclusion that the Government of Weihaiwei during the past 20 years had been carried on 'with such a combination of deference to Chinese custom with British justice and incorruptibility that the inhabitants have come to regard the British occupation as a sort of golden age'.[70] It was a view which those who had known Stewart Lockhart had been firmly convinced of for years. Lucas described Stewart Lockhart's years in Weihaiwei with his customary lucidity when he wrote 'I fear I did not promote your personal interests when it was arranged that you should go to Weihaiwei but it is impossible to forsee how things will turn out and you took admirable care of your charge.'[71]

In deference to their hospitality to successive members of the China Squadron over a period of almost twenty years, HMS *Cairo* was placed at the Stewart Lockharts' disposal to transport him and Edith on the first stage of their journey home.[72] As the government launch took them from the territory for the last time, Stewart Lockhart would have been inhuman had he not felt some tinge of sadness. Yet in leaving Weihaiwei, he was leaving not only his home, but the place which had at times seemed like a millstone round his neck. Instead of becoming the stepping stone to the ultimate prize, the Governorship of Hong Kong, it had weighed him down, ending what should have been a glittering career. He was to be poignantly reminded of the glories of Hong Kong when he stopped there on his way back to Britain. Newspapers had heralded his departure from Weihaiwei with praise for his dealings with the Chinese, pointing out that 'though its existence was something that no Chinese official could be expected to relish, Weihaiwei has ever been on friendly terms with its neighbours, for which fact Sir James Lockhart's own personality and tact were largely responsible'.[73] This friendship with the Chinese had been one of the most important parts of both his official and his unofficial life, and it is significant that although small parties and meals were held in the Stewart Lockharts' honour when they reached Hong Kong at the beginning of May 1921, it was only the Chinese community who celebrated their arrival in any great style. A lavish tea party was held at the Hongkong Hotel at which Stewart Lockhart was presented with an embroidered scroll. Some of his old friends, like Ho Kai, had long since died, but many of the other guests, including Sir Robert Ho Tung, had known Stewart Lockhart for almost his entire career in China and their presence was a tribute to a lifetime's friendship. The guest list read like a Who's Who of the Hong Kong Chinese community, a testament to their admiration of this rather extraordinary Scot.[74] It was not the last time important Chinese would congregate in his honour, but it was to be his final celebration in Hong Kong.

Chapter 12

THE CONFUCIAN COMES HOME
(1921–1937)

THE Stewart Lockharts were returning to Britain with little idea of what they were going to do or where they were going to stay. The first priority was to visit family and friends, and to be reunited with all their now grown up children. A huge family gathering was organized for their return to Britain in June, the reuniting of so many relatives quite overwhelming Stewart Lockhart. The company of his children on their own took longer to achieve than the family gathering had, however, particularly as Mary and Charles had their partners' commitments to consider. Not until December did the Stewart Lockhart family with all three children meet to celebrate Christmas dinner in Scotland.[1] The first time all three children had been together with their parents under the same roof, the occasion was the cause of great celebration.

After so many years working in China, Stewart Lockhart and his wife were in no mood to settle down immediately. They spent the first six months of retirement in Britain, catching up with family affairs and renewing old acquaintances, before taking an extended holiday by themselves. After a brief sojourn through Europe the beginnning of 1922 was spent in Switzerland where Stewart Lockhart tried out his skills at skiing.[2] Further trips were made to Switzerland during the following two winters, during which time Stewart Lockhart learned to ski with a certain degree of skill.[3] From May 1921 until the end of 1923 was a time of relaxation for Stewart Lockhart, and was the longest period in his life when he undertook no research or any other work. A house was not found until the beginning of 1924 when the Stewart Lockharts purchased a comfortable property at Cresswell Gardens in south-west London, and only then did Stewart Lockhart once more turn his attention to things Chinese.

From the time he left Weihaiwei until he settled in his London home, Stewart Lockhart had not ignored Chinese matters entirely. Johnston had kept in regular contact, providing news and information from Beijing. As the Emperor grew up, Johnston undertook increasingly fewer tutorial duties and instead became an unofficial adviser to the crown,[4] and for these duties the Emperor continued to heap rewards upon the Scottish tutor. In 1922, Johnston wrote of his astonishment at being given an honour accorded to few foreigners, namely his designation as a mandarin of the second rank. In addition, he was presented with a sable robe by the Emperor; this was the first time such an honour had been bestowed on a foreigner.[5] A year later the Emperor promoted Johnston to a mandarin of the first rank, in celebration of the imperial marriage.[6] Despite the honours pressed upon him, Johnston was well aware of the lack of stability in his post. He wrote frequently of the 'parlous state' of China, and feared for the Emperor's safety as the war-lords took an ever increasing hold on the country.[7] Of Weihaiwei, there was little news, though British indecision was beginning to irritate the Chinese, with Johnston reporting that 'there is a strong (and in my opinion justifiable) feeling that the hitch is due to British obstinancy and greed', much of which he personally blamed on the Admiralty.[8] In return for Johnston's news and gossip, Stewart Lockhart sent a steady supply of books on various Chinese topics to Johnston in Beijing, ever mindful of his friend's interests, though often adding some particularly pro-Christian text to stimulate Johnston's Buddhist beliefs.[9]

While Johnston was teaching the Emperor how to play tennis and cycle[10] Stewart Lockhart was busy unpacking his trunks of papers, books, paintings and coins. Cresswell Gardens was filled with mementos of China, and his library there was to become a haven of Chinese scholarship.[11] With a firm base in Britain, Stewart Lockhart resumed his study of Chinese literature and history, beginning each day by reading passages of Chinese in bed.[12] Gradually, he began to involve himself in committee work and in organizations related to China. One of the first to which he was elected was the China Association, of which he became a member in 1924.[13] Old friends from China days were not forgotten, either. Jordan wrote regularly until his death in 1925, though his letters are often tinged with sadness as he viewed events in China, a country that he now felt was 'past praying for'.[14] Other retired colleagues, notably Parker, Addis, and Lucas were frequent correspondents, swapping news about the land in which they had all been so intimately involved.

Although he was officially retired from the service, Weihaiwei continued to intrude on his life. Jordan wrote of his hopes in 1922 that rendition of the territory was 'to take place ... within ten months and may be earlier',[15] but these hopes were to be unfulfilled for a further eight years due to a combination of British indecision and the instability of the Chinese government which made it difficult, at times, to know to whom to give the territory back.[16] Given Stewart Lockhart's unparalleled experience of the territory, it is not surprising that the Colonial Office was to look to him on several occasions for advice on matters regarding rendition.[17] The question of land ownership in Weihaiwei was one of particular concern to those Europeans living there, with several, including the headmaster of the European School, Beer, demanding to know what compensation the British Government would offer them should the territory be returned to China. Three years after he retired, Stewart Lockhart was still being asked by the Colonial Office if he could 'throw any light' on freehold grants given to those living in the territory. Given the volume of correspondence he had retained about Weihaiwei, Stewart Lockhart was rarely stuck for a reply.[18]

Occasionally, news from Weihaiwei came in a most indirect manner. The last Governor of Shandong Province before the revolution, Sun Baoqi, became the Premier of China in 1923. Sun was one of the great survivors, having come close to assassination at the outset of the revolution. Indeed, it was only the threats on his life which had persuaded him to declare Shandong Province independent in 1911, though 'he made it clear that he did not believe in "independence" and in breaking with the Imperial Government'.[19] Despite being a royalist at heart, Sun had continued to serve China, in the process meeting Johnston frequently in Beijing. Johnston and Stewart Lockhart had made a visit together to see Sun just before the revolution, and Sun obviously had fond memories of both men, making a point of enquiring after Stewart Lockhart when he met Johnston.[20] Johnston had plenty of time for such meetings, as he now had virtually no tutorial duties to perform. Indeed, he was sufficiently conscience stricken about accepting a salary for doing so little, that he offered to resign on several occasions, but the

Emperor would have none of it.[21] With freedom to move around Beijing, Johnston was a fund of news about affairs in China, and it was he who broke the sad news to Stewart Lockhart that Sly, one of the longest serving junior officers in Weihaiwei, and a man who had driven everyone insane with his constant chatter, had committed suicide.[22] Weihaiwei was obviously hard on her officers, or perhaps unlucky with them, losing both Sly and Carpmael on mental health grounds.

Jordan's death in 1925 gave Stewart Lockhart his first committee work since his return from China when he was appointed to replace Jordan on the Governing Body of the School of Oriental Studies at the University of London.[23] The duties were not particularly onerous, but whereas a decade earlier, Stewart Lockhart would have taken everything offered, and more, he now paced his life rather more carefully, and in taking up this appointment, let his membership of the Folklore Society lapse.[24] Events in China continued to cause concern, with Johnston risking life and limb to save the Emperor, banished from the Forbidden City. Johnston reported the events with characteristic cool.[25] The Emperor's move to the Japanese Legation in Beijing effectively marked the end of Johnston's duties at the imperial court, for when the young Emperor suddenly moved to Tianjin the move took place against Johnston's wishes and advice. The Scot noted, somewhat ruefully that it was doubtful whether he would ever wish to join the exiled court there.[26] Although Johnston was to keep in contact with the Emperor for the rest of his life, his days as imperial tutor were over forever, halted as suddenly as they had begun.

Between 1924 and 1926, life took on a very leisurely pace for Stewart Lockhart. As much time as possible was spent with his family, and he undertook little new research. Despite the slackening pace, the three countries which had dominated his life, Scotland, Hong Kong and Weihaiwei, continued to be a prominent part of his London days. He retained his Scottish connections with as much vigour as ever, having joined the London Highland Club on his return to Britain. It was not long before this enthusiastic Scot was running the society, becoming its President in 1926, and again in 1927.[27] Weihaiwei once more sprang into his life in 1926 when a rather bemused Johnston announced that the Colonial Office had asked him to administer the territory and prepare for its rendition.[28] Arriving in Weihaiwei in April the following year, Johnston was delighted at the posting.[29] Even though he had despaired of becoming stuck in the territory for so many years, he was now being given the opportunity not only to run Weihaiwei himself, but to do what he had believed for so long was the right course of action: to give the area back to China. Hong Kong friends frequently corresponded with Stewart Lockhart, though the social divisions within the Chinese of the colony continued to appear even in these letters. The newly knighted Sir Shouson Chow took no small delight in pointing out that his knighthood made him 'the only living knight of pure Chinese descent', a side swipe at Sir Robert Ho Tung who was of mixed parentage.[30] Stewart Lockhart always trod these diplomatic minefields with great tact, reckoning that on such occasions, no comment was the best course of action.

It was not until the year 1927 that Stewart Lockhart once more began to involve himself fully in the field of Chinese scholarship. At this time he started writing reviews for both the *China Review* and the *Journal of the Royal Asiatic Society* on a regular basis, making full use of his extraordinary breadth of knowledge.[31] The dissemination of this knowledge, mainly through the medium of book reviews, brought him recognition from a younger circle of sinologists who had not necessarily known him in his China days. This circle of contacts became even broader when Stewart Lockhart was appointed Secretary of the Asiatic Society in 1927.[32] It was a high honour, and rightly reflected his standing in the field of Chinese studies. Although he had continued to receive news of China from a variety of correspondents, in addition to the occasional *Government Gazette* from Weihaiwei, it was only with Johnston's arrival in the territory that government publications began to arrive with any regularity at Cresswell Gardens. As his interest in China revived, so his acquisition of the volume of papers from that country increased, with specialist publications such as memoranda from the Tientsin British Committee of Information being sent to him in London. Covering a variety of political topics, from the trouble on the upper Yangtze to a discussion of the British concessions in China, these myriad pieces of news seemed to provide a catalyst which spurred him once more into the field of research.[33]

By 1929, Stewart Lockhart was his old self once more, studying almost any subject he encountered which had some Chinese connection. In that year, his first major publication for several years, the *Index to the Tso Chuan* was printed.[34] The *Index* was in fact only prepared for publication by Stewart Lockhart, having earlier been compiled by Sir Everard Fraser, an official in the Consular Service. Fraser, described as 'one of the most brilliant Chinese scholars who has ever adorned the service',[35] had known Stewart Lockhart since their cadet days when 'both our addresses for service in India were rejected at the same time'.[36] Fraser, like Stewart Lockhart, ended up in China where he was Consul first at Hangu and then, in 1911, in Shanghai, in which post he died in 1922.[37] The *Index*, a prodigious piece of scholarship, had been completed by Fraser before he died, but it required the inevitable revisions and corrections to prepare it for publication, a task Stewart Lockhart gladly undertook.

Age was undoubtedly beginning to take its toll. Gone were the days when Stewart Lockhart could work and play with equal enthusiasm. The ageing process seemed to be constantly under-lined as one close friend after another died. In 1929, he had the sad task of writing Satow's obituary for *The Times*.[38] Few colleagues from China days were now left. Johnston, of course, continued to thrive, but it was a reminder of the passing years when junior colleagues, like Walter, retired.[39] Stewart Lockhart found himself unable to fulfil all the duties required of him. His health began increasingly to let him down, with influenza and bronchitis becoming recurring winter ailments, and it was with some sadness that he had to retire from his presidency of the London Highland Club in 1929.[40]

There were certain tasks which Stewart Lockhart felt unable to refuse, however, and when the University of London asked him to act as the external expert on the Board of Advisers for the Chair of Chinese, he accepted with alacrity.[41] Five years earlier, the university had asked Johnston if he would like to be considered for the Chair, but Johnston was, at that time, unavailable.[42] By 1930, however, the rendition of Weihaiwei had finally taken place,[43] and as soon as he returned to Britain, Johnston visited Stewart Lockhart. Their continued close contact meant that Stewart Lockhart, when asked to advise the university regarding the Chair of Chinese in 1931, unhesitatingly recommended Johnston for the post and, following an interview, Johnston was given the appointment.[44] Johnston had brought back few mementos of Weihaiwei, though he had fulfilled his friend's request and sent Stewart Lockhart the woven silk picture of the Commissioner's badge which had hung, since 1902, in Government House.[45] However, with Johnston appointed to the London Chair and living at Kew, the two men had every opportunity to talk about the old days and now saw more of one another than they had done for years.

Johnston's presence gave Stewart Lockhart a tremendous boost, and gave him another spurt of energy which resulted in further research. In 1930, he began to study the various Chinese translations of the Bible,[46] and at the same time began two projects involving his old adversary, Herbert Giles. Giles had published his *Gems of Chinese Literature* in 1884, a compilation of translations of various Chinese texts dating from the Zhou (Chou) to the Ming dynasties. In 1931, Stewart Lockhart paid tribute to Giles' scholarship by compiling the Chinese texts relating to Giles' publication.[47] Giles gave Stewart Lockhart his blessing on the project, telling him that 'you will indeed have left another footstep which a forlorn and weary brother seeing will take heart again'.[48] Having completed this project, Stewart Lockhart decided to broaden the fields of Chinese scholarship slightly further, making use of translations by Giles and another notable Chinese scholar, Arthur Waley. Over the years Waley had published several translations of Chinese texts. Stewart Lockhart now combined a selection from Giles' *Gems* with several passages from Waley's books, *170 Chinese Poems, The Temple and Other Poems*, and *More Translations from the Chinese*, printing the original Chinese text beside each translation. Stewart Lockhart's edition did not appear until 1934, but it did so to considerable critical acclaim.[49] Giles' health was, by that time, too bad for him to make any comment on the new edition, but Waley was full of praise for the work, which had involved Stewart Lockhart in an enormous amount of reading to locate the precise passages translated by both scholars so many years earlier.[50] Copies of the book were given by Stewart Lockhart to Johnston's students and were used frequently by Johnston in his Chinese poetry classes.[51]

With Johnston in Britain, Stewart Lockhart relied on other sources for information about China. Ho Tung sent regular reports, continuing a correspondence which had already lasted almost fifty years, and was to continue in the next generation between Sir Robert's son, Ho Shai Lai, and Mary Stewart Lockhart. Stewart Lockhart got further information from organizations such as the Chinese Social and Political Science Association of which he was a member.[52] But it was not only China's present state which continued to fascinate him. In 1932, he began researching the history of the Taiping rebellion, corresponding with other scholars who had studied this period.[53] Unpublished and unfinished on his death, this study was to be the swansong of a lifetime's study of China.

Stewart Lockhart's standing in the field of Chinese scholarship ensured that he continued to be asked to represent various bodies, despite his failing health. He took a seat on the Universities China Committee in 1932, an important post as it distributed funds produced by the Boxer Indemnity to promote Chinese scholarship in the academic world.[54] He continued also to work on the Governing Body of the School of Oriental Studies, attending committee meetings and giving Johnston support in his appointment. Although immersed in a world of sinologists, his Scottish ancestry was never ignored, and one of his proudest moments was when the Scottish National Portrait Gallery asked him for a portrait photograph for their archives.[55] In many ways, he was as proud of this inclusion as he was of many far higher honours. Johnston, too, returned to his Scottish roots, buying three islands in Loch Craignish as a retreat in 1934. Close to Stewart Lockhart's childhood home, Johnston made a special visit to Ardsheal on his friend's behalf as soon after purchasing his highland estate as possible.[56]

By the winter of 1934, Stewart Lockhart's deteriorating health confined him to bed for increasingly longer periods of time. Despite this, he consented to having his name added to the honorary committee for the great 1935 exhibition of Chinese art held in London.[57] By now, he had withdrawn from all other committee work, resigning from the last public post he held, at the School of Oriental Studies, in January 1935.[58] Nursed by Edith, who now wrote most of his correspondence for him, life was by no means quiet, but it had slowed down to a snail's pace. His body may have begun to fail, but his mind was as active as ever, and even when he was bedridden he continued to welcome guests and stimulating conversation. It was during these years that he translated many of the inscriptions found on his collection of paintings, and he read everything he could find which related to the Taipings, keeping his mind active in total disregard of his degenerating physical state. The blow from which he never recovered was the death of his youngest child, Margaret, in February 1936. It was one thing to see one's contemporaries fade from this world, but the unexpected loss of Margaret hit him severely. For the next twelve months, Stewart Lockhart's health deteriorated badly. Still mourning his daughter, he finally died at home in London on 26 February 1937. Following a private funeral, his daughter Mary commemorated his life by erecting a plaque in his memory in the small church of St Adamnan's, close to Ardsheal where his life had begun.

Many mourned the loss of 'one of the foremost authorities in this country on Chinese affairs',[59] though none more than his immediate family. Edith, in a daze of grief, began to dispose of Stewart Lockhart's library almost as soon as the funeral was over, whilst Mary gathered together as much as she could of her father's collection, storing papers until she decided what to do with them. He had already given her his collection of paintings, which she had grown to love in Weihaiwei, before he died and the collection of coins passed to her on Edith's death in 1950. In 1937, Mary's desire to keep her father's belongings together was the natural result of wanting to keep his memory alive. Following her mother's death, this desire had become a duty: the collection was no longer merely the embodiment of all her father had believed in, it was one of historical significance and import. Mary Stewart Lockhart's devotion and James Stewart Lockhart's magpie instincts together have bequeathed a unique picture of Stewart Lockhart's contribution to history. In preserving her father's collections, Mary Stewart Lockhart ensured his name would live on. Had she not done so, the world of scholarship would have been poorer, but James Stewart Lockhart would not have been forgotten. His contribution to the colony of Hong Kong was to retain Hong Kong's unique identity by upholding Chinese institutions and promoting Chinese society in an otherwise totally British administration. This has determined, to a great extent, its character to this day. In north China, he continued to administer Weihaiwei with the same beliefs developed in Hong Kong, running the territory with a unique combination of British and Confucian principles. This was a strange mixture, but one which resulted in one of the most benign and least intrusive administrations in the whole of the British Empire. Britain's imperial rule contributed a great deal to many countries, introducing democracy and educational systems to territories which had had neither. But in doing so, traditional lifestyles indigenous to those countries under British rule were destroyed. In comparison, Stewart Lockhart's method of administration was a beacon which lit and enhanced traditional values in Weihaiwei.

The Confucian principles he adopted throughout his life in China changed a sharp Scottish thistle into the pliant bamboo, bending to fortune, but always true to himself. It was a unique combination which influenced another generation of British administrators in China: men of influence like Johnston and Clementi. In initiating a new style of administration in China, Stewart Lockhart proved that the British Empire could care for the people in its charge without destroying their racial identity in the process. It is a lesson many could successfully apply to this day to the betterment of us all.

NOTES

Unless otherwise indicated, official papers from Colonial and Foreign Office Series refer to the Public Record Office classes, CO and FO. A full list of series consulted is to be found in the Selected Bibliography.

If the source document is a Governor or Commissioner's despatch, the entry is abbreviated to despatch number, date, series and section.

If notes are undated, the date of the despatch in which the note is found is included after the despatch number. Additional information, for example confidential or secret, is placed after the date, unless these terms are used within the official document as a specific section number designation.

Annual Reports may be quoted either by their eastern print number, or by their despatch number within a CO series. This is because both sources were consulted, and the original, in despatch form, sometimes differs from the printed version.

In both official sources and unpublished letters, the surnames of the writers and recipients only are given. Christian names are, however, included when differentiation is required between two people of the same surname.

The following abbreviations appear in the Notes:

SLPGWC Stewart Lockhart Papers, George Watson's College
SLPNLS Stewart Lockhart Papers, National Library of Scotland
SLPSSP Stewart Lockhart Papers, Stewart Society Papers

Notes to Chapter 1

1. Letter from Blunt to Stewart Lockhart, 22 April 1921, SLPNLS, Vol. 1.

2. E. Grierson, *The Imperial Dream: the British Commonwealth and Empire, 1775–1969* (London, Collins, 1972), p. 17.

3. C. N. Crisswell, *The Taipans: Hong Kong's Merchant Princes* (Hong Kong, Oxford University Press, 1981), p. 19.

4. The various histories of individual independent schools in Scotland provide an invaluable source for such statistics. H. L. Waugh, ed., *George Watson's College: A History and Record 1724–1970* (Edinburgh, George Watson's College, 1970), gives a short analysis of the careers of the most able scholars at Stewart Lockhart's school, c.1870–c.1910, when, out of a total of 40 school prizewinners, 25 entered some form of government service: the majority going either to Africa or India. Similar patterns emerge in other schools of comparable type.

5. Letter from Stewart Lockhart to Mary Stewart Lockhart, 25 May 1913, SLPGWC. These papers are uncatalogued.

6. Much information regarding the Stewart family is to be found in uncatalogued and unattributable notes in manuscript form in the SLPSSP.

7. In contemporary histories, Stewart Lockhart is often referred to as Lockhart. Letters and documents in the various collections of the Stewart Lockhart Papers make it clear that, for most of his working life, he preferred to be known as James Stewart Lockhart. All his children were christened Stewart Lockhart, and he is most properly referred to by the double surname. His daughter, Mary Stewart Lockhart, verified this usage in conversation with the author in 1980.

8. A number of these items were bequeathed by Stewart Lockhart to the National Museum of Antiquities of Scotland, now known as the National Museum of Scotland. They are listed in his Last Will and Testament, SLPGWC.

9. Letter from Mary Stewart Lockhart to the Editor, *The Scotsman*, February 1967, SLPGWC.

10. This was a small, independent school run by a spinster. These establishments educated young boys and were fairly common in the nineteenth century.

11. King William's College, *Register of King William's College* (Isle of Man, King William's College, 1956), p. xix.

12. Several such reports are contained in SLPNLS, Vol. 1.

13. J. Jones, in a certificate of merit for Stewart Lockhart, 9 August 1872, SLPNLS, Vol. 1.

14. Obituary of James Stewart Lockhart, *The Barrovian*, No. 174 (June 1937), pp. 79–80. The donors were 'Messrs. H. J. H. Tripp, H. E. Hobson, J. H. Stewart Lockhart, E. B. Skottowe, W. H. Bell, K. W. Mounsey, A. F. Wheen, I. R. Wheen, C. E. Sparke, G. D. Main'. King William's College, *Register of King William's College*, p. xxiv.

15. Stewart Lockhart, 'Another Link with the Past', *The Watsonian* (1909), p. 109.

16. Letter from Stewart Lockhart to Mary Stewart Lockhart, 30 November 1904, SLPGWC.·

17. In Scotland, the chief senior scholar in a school is often given the appellation 'dux' towards the end of his or her final year. It is a title earned through academic achievement alone.

18. Alexander Martin, in a postscript to Stewart Lockhart, 'Another Link with the Past', *The Watsonian* (1909), p. 109.

19. Waugh, *George Watson's College*, p. 80.

20. His University of Edinburgh pass certificates are in SLPNLS, Vol. 1.

21. Letter from Stewart Lockhart to Mary Stewart Lockhart, 5 July 1918, SLPGWC.

22. India Office, *Results of the Open Competition for the Civil Service of India* (London, 1878), SLPNLS, Vol. 1.

23. See Note 22 above.

24. Marr to Round, 11 October 1878, Enclosure in No. 301, CO 129/183. The exam commenced on 16 September 1878.

25. Sir A. Bertram, *The Colonial Office* (Cambridge, Cambridge University Press, 1930), and H. L. Hall, *The Colonial Office: A History* (London, Longmans, Green and Co., 1937). Both give excellent accounts of the history of this department.

26. Colonial Office, *Notes of Information for Applicants to the Post of Hongkong Cadets* (London, 1878).

27. G. B. Endacott, *A History of Hong Kong* (Hong Kong, Oxford University Press, 1958), p. 95.

28. Colonial Office, *Notes of Information for Applicants to the Post of Hongkong Cadets*.

29. Endacott, *A History of Hong Kong*, p. 108.

30. Sir M. Hewlett, *Forty Years in China* (London, Macmillan, 1943), p. 1.

31. Colonial Office, *Notes of Information for Applicants to the Post of Hongkong Cadets*.

32. H. J. Lethbridge, *Hong Kong: Stability and Change* (Hong Kong, Oxford University Press, 1978), p. 1.

33. Letter from the Civil Service Commissioners to Stewart Lockhart, 24 October 1878, SLPNLS, Vol. 1, and *The Colonial Office List* for 1887, 1889, 1899, 1907, and 1910.

34. Colonial Office, *Results of the Examination for Two Ceylon Writerships and Two Hongkong Cadetships* (London, 1878).

35. Letter from Robert George Herbert to Stewart Lockhart, 25 November 1878, SLPNLS, Vol. 1.

36. In addition to fluent Cantonese, Dyer Ball also spoke Hakka, one of the dialects of Hong Kong, 'well enough to interpret in it', Letter from Stewart Lockhart to Lucas, 7 June 1882, Enclosure in No. 86, CO 129/201.

37. Letter from Robert George Herbert to Stewart Lockhart, 25 November 1878, SLPNLS, Vol. 1.

38. Hong Kong 5608, undated note, CO 129/192.

39. In 1900, there were still fewer than 100 staff employed within the Colonial Office in Whitehall. See Hall, *The Colonial Office*, p. 25.

Notes to Chapter 2

1. Colonial Estimates, No. 134 Hong Kong, 1881, CO 129/189.

2. Letter from Stewart Lockhart to Lucas, 7 June 1882, Enclosure in No. 86, CO 129/201.

3. See E. H. Parker, *John Chinaman. And a Few Others* (London, John Murray, 1901), for information about a Briton in Guangzhou during this period. A yamen was the office or official residence of a Chinese mandarin and was a term sometimes adopted by British officials in China to describe their official residences.

4. I. Bird, *The Golden Chersonese* (London, 1883; Repr., London, Century, 1983), has excellent descriptions of Guangzhou in 1879.

5. Letter from Stewart Lockhart to Mary Stewart Lockhart, 20 April 1909, SLPGWC.

6. Parker, *John Chinaman. And a Few Others* , p. 208 ff.

7. Stewart Lockhart, undated note in a blue album in which he kept his most valued letters, SLPGWC.

8. Parker, *John Chinaman. And a Few Others*, p. 208.

9. Parker, *John Chinaman. And a Few Others*, p. 209.

10. See Note 9 above.

11. Recalled by Mary Stewart Lockhart in conversation with the author in 1980.

12. Letter from Stewart Lockhart to Lucas, 7 June 1882, Enclosure in No. 86, CO 129/201.

13. Meade to Lucas, 23 April 1883, Enclosure in Telegram 21, CO 129/208.

14. R. F. Johnston, *Twilight in the Forbidden City* (London, Victor Gollancz, 1934), pp. 181–2.

15. Notes on the subject are found in several vols. throughout SLPNLS.

16. Final Cadet Examination Results for Stewart Lockhart, Enclosure in No. 6, CO 129/194.

17. J. H. Stewart Lockhart, *A Manual of Chinese Quotations: Being a Translation of the Ch'eng Yü K'ao* (Hong Kong, Kelly and Walsh, 1893), Introduction.

18. Translation in a notebook, SLPNLS, Vol. 36.

19. Sir John Pope Hennessy (1834–1891), barrister and Member of Parliament, Governor of Labuan (1867), the Gold Coast (1872), Bahamas (1875), Hong Kong (1877), and Mauritius (1883–1889). His turbulent character is well documented by his grandson, J. Pope-Hennessy in *Verandah: Some Episodes in the Crown Colonies, 1867–1889* (London, Century, 1984).

20. Pope-Hennessy, *Verandah*, above, p. 185.

21. See Note 20 above.

22. E. J. Eitel, one of Hong Kong's first historians, was German by birth, but was made a naturalized Briton by a special Governor's Ordinance in 1880. A missionary, he became Director of Chinese Studies under Governor Kennedy in 1875, and was also the Colony's first Inspector of Schools. Disliked and mistrusted by many of the British in Hong Kong, Pope Hennessy's appointment of Eitel as his private secretary in 1880 did little to temper prevailing public opinion.

23. 'Correction of a false rumour', 28 October 1881, translation of a clipping from an unnamed Chinese newspaper, SLPNLS, Vol. 35.

24. Letter from Stewart Lockhart to Lucas, 7 June 1882, Enclosure in No. 86, CO 129/201.

25. Part of a translation in a notebook containing translation exercises in Stewart Lockhart's hand, SLPNLS, Vol. 35.

26. Parker, *John Chinaman. And a Few Others*, p. 210.

27. Letter from Addis to Stewart Lockhart, 14 September 1889, SLPGWC.

28. K. Newton, 'An Evening in a Library', (London, undated), typescript, pp. 3–4, SLPGWC.

29. Recalled by Mary Stewart Lockhart in conversation with the author in 1980. She was an invaluable informant about her father's collection of Chinese art and artefacts and the information she was able to provide appears reliable in view of the verification obtained, where available, from other sources.

30. Note amongst some translations in a notebook, 27 July 1880, SLPNLS, Vol. 36.

31. No. 13, 12 February 1881, CO 129/192.

32. Minute from Wingfield to Lucas, undated, in No. 13, 12 February 1881, CO 129/192.

33. Old Au had taught Stewart Lockhart well, as the cadet passed two of the five papers with credit. The examination saga is contained in No. 6, 28 September 1881, CO 129/194.

34. Lucas to Meade, 10 November 1881, Minute in No. 6, CO 129/194.

35. Stewart Lockhart to Secretary of State, 9 April 1883, SLPNLS, Vol. 1.

36. See Note 35 above.

37. The secretariat was composed of the Governor, Colonial Secretary, Registrar General, Attorney General, Surveyor General, Colonial Treasurer, Auditor General, Harbour Master, Chief Justice, Registrar (Supreme Court), Interpreter (Supreme Court), Magistrate, Interpreter (Police Court). These were the main posts within the administration in the 1870s and 1880s. The list can never be definitive as posts were, from time to time, combined, and cadets and assistants also frequently accounted for varying numbers. The justiciary were, of course, not government officials in the strict sense, but their salaries were taken into account by the home government when judging budgets, and they were crucial to the running of the colony.

38. Letter from Nathan to Stewart Lockhart, 11 June 1906, SLPNLS, Vol. 1.

39. E. J. Eitel, *Europe in China: The History of Hong Kong* (Hong Kong, 1895; Repr., Taipei, Ch'eng-wen Publishing, 1968), p. 522.

40. Eitel, *Europe in China*, above, p. 529.

41. A. Ireland, *The Far Eastern Tropics* (London, Archibald Constable and Co., 1905), p. 27.

42. Pope-Hennessy, *Verandah: Some Episodes in the Crown Colonies, 1867–1889*, p. 200.

43. Pope-Hennessy, *Verandah*, above, p. 22.

44. Wingfield to Lucas, 25 February 1880, Minute in No. 4, CO 129/187.

45. Pope-Hennessy, *Verandah: Some Episodes in the Crown Colonies, 1867–1889*, p. 72.

46. Bowen to Secretary of State, 23 May 1883, Copy, SLPNLS, Vol. 2.

47. Eitel, *Europe in China: The History of Hong Kong*, p. 75.
48. Eitel, *Europe in China*, above, p. 76 ff. Unless otherwise stated, statistics for opium in Hong Kong are taken from this source. It is impossible to obtain accurate figures as, at all times, a great deal of smuggling took place. All figures drawn from duties levied should therefore be treated with circumspection.
49. In the instance of Jardine Matheson, 'by the end of the 1830's they were handling over 6,000 chests each year, producing an annual profit of over $100,000'. Crisswell, *The Taipans: Hong Kong's Merchant Princes*, p. 33.
50. 'Sir George Birdwood on the Opium Question', *The Overland Mail*, 27 January 1882, pp. 19–20.
51. Lord C. Beresford, *The Break Up of China* (London, Harper and Brothers, 1899), pp. 211–12.
52. Bertram, *The Colonial Office*, p. 55.
53. Marsh, Testimonial on Stewart Lockhart, undated, SLPNLS, Vol. 1.
54. Letter from Stewart Lockhart to Mary Stewart Lockhart, 25 October 1908, SLPGWC.

Notes to Chapter 3

1. In a lengthy memo requesting the reorganization of the Executive and Legislative Councils, Bowen requested, amongst other things, that the number of unofficial members on the Legislative Council be increased and that one of them should always be of Chinese origin. No. 4, 14 May 1883, CO 129/208.
2. Endacott, *A History of Hong Kong*, p. 199.
3. Letter from Ku Hung-ming to Stewart Lockhart, 20 November 1887, SLPNLS, Vol. 5.
4. Letter from MacKinnon to Stewart Lockhart, 5 August 1884, SLPNLS, Vol. 5.
5. Sir G. F. Bowen, *Thirty Years of Colonial Government*, S. Lane-Poole, (ed.), (London, Longmans and Co., 1889), Vol. 2, p. 252.
6. Bowen, *Thirty Years of Colonial Government*, p. 268.
7. Sir C. Collins, *Public Administration in Hong Kong* (London, Royal Institute of International Affairs, 1952), p. 119.
8. Bowen hardly mentions the unrest in his memoirs, whereas he discusses in depth the many diplomatic dinners he held in order to retain friendly communications with both sides. The disorders, however, merited much police time and attention and are described in various despatches and memos in CO 129/218.
9. Stewart Lockhart, 'Triads', 4 October 1884, SLPNLS, Vol. 25.
10. Mary Stewart Lockhart in conversation with the author in 1980.
11. No. 146, 4 May 1886, CO 129/226.
12. No. 224, 28 June 1886, CO 129/227.
13. Despatch from Bowen to Herbert, 3 May 1887, Enclosure in Telegram No. 2, CO 129/232.
14. Eitel, *Europe in China: The History of Hong Kong*, p. 574.
15. Stewart Lockhart, translation from an unnamed Chinese newspaper cutting, 24 October (no year), SLPNLS, Vol. 35.
16. Endacott, *A History of Hong Kong*, p. 243.
17. G. Donaldson, *The Scots Overseas* (London, Robert Hale, 1966), p. 206.
18. Letter from Ku Hung-ming to Stewart Lockhart, 20 November 1887, SLPNLS, Vol. 5.
19. See Note 18 above.
20. Stewart Lockhart, 'Memorandum on the Question of a Guarantee from

Chinese Authorities against the infliction of Torture on criminals extradited from Hongkong on their trial by Chinese Authorities', undated, SLPNLS, Vol. 24.

21. 'Rendition of Chinese Criminals', Hong Kong 3886, 27 February 1888, CO 129/240.

22. Curwin to Fiddes, 27 February 1888, Minute in Foreign Office to Colonial Office, CO 129/240.

23. Eitel, *Europe in China*, p. 259.

24. H. F. MacNair, *The Chinese Abroad: Their Position and Protection* (London, 1933; Repr. Taipei, Ch'eng-wen Publishing, 1971), p. 84.

25. See Note 24 above.

26. Stewart Lockhart, 'Notes on Chinese Emigration to Honolulu, Cuba and the Sandwich Islands', undated, SLPNLS, Vol. 27.

27. No. 360, 11 December 1888, CO 129/239.

28. For a history of the District Watch Committee and the development of the Tung Wah Hospital Group and the Po Leung Kuk, see, Lethbridge, *Hong Kong: Stability and Change*, pp. 104 ff.

29. Collins, *Public Administration in Hong Kong*, p. 128.

30. Lethbridge, *Hong Kong: Stability and Change*, pp. 104 ff.

31. Tung Wah Group of Hospitals, *One Hundred Years of the Tung Wah Group of Hospitals, 1870–1970*, (Hong Kong, Tung Wah Group of Hospitals, 1970), preface, Vol. 1. A substantial amount of information about the history of the Tung Wah is drawn from this publication.

32. Tung Wah Group of Hospitals, *One Hundred Years of the Tung Wah Group of Hospitals, 1870–1970*, Vol. 2, p. 18.

33. Lethbridge, *Hong Kong: Stability and Change*, p. 71. Also series CO 129, where references to the problems of prostitution in 19th century Hong Kong appear virtually on a monthly basis.

34. Dyer Ball, *Things Chinese: Being Notes on Various Subjects Connected with China* (London, Sampson Low, Marston and Co., 1892), p. 339.

35. Stewart Lockhart to Bowen, 11 August 1884, Enclosure in No. 282, CO 129/217.

36. See Note 35 above.

37. Various Enclosures in No. 91, 24 March 1886, CO 129/225.

38. See Note 37 above.

39. De Robeck to Meade, undated note in No. 182, 29 May 1886, CO 129/226.

40. O. Chadwick, 'Report on the Sanitary Condition of Hong Kong', Eastern No. 38, 1882.

41. Surveyor General, Colonial Surgeon, and Registrar General.

42. G. B. Endacott, *The Government and People in Hong Kong 1841–1962* (Hong Kong, Hong Kong University Press, 1964), p. 148.

43. Endacott, *Government and People*, above, p. 148.

44. A bibliography of most of Stewart Lockhart's published works is in Lethbridge, *Hong Kong: Stability and Change*, pp. 159–62.

45. J. H. Stewart Lockhart and A. R. Colquhoun, 'A Sketch of Formosa', *China Review*, 13, No. 3, 1884–85, pp. 161–207. The original notes for the article are in SLPNLS, Vol. 34.

46. Letter from Faber to Stewart Lockhart, 20 May 1885, SLPNLS, Vol. 7, and Stewart Lockhart's notes on the club, SLPNLS, Vol. 7.

47. Letter from Stewart Lockhart to Chalmers, 9 February 1887, SLPNLS, Vol. 7.

48. No. 55, 24 February 1886, CO 129/228.

49. Letter from Chalmers to Stewart Lockhart, 11 August 1887, SLPNLS, Vol. 7.

50. Letters from Parker to Stewart Lockhart, various dates, SLPNLS, Vol. 5.

51. Letter from Ku Hung-ming to Stewart Lockhart, 15 July 1887, SLPNLS, Vol. 5.

52. See Note 51 above.

53. Mary Stewart Lockhart, in a blue notebook containing a short biography of Stewart Lockhart, 1966, SLPGWC.

54. Letter From Lethbridge to Mary Stewart Lockhart, 23 August 1972, SLPGWC.

55. Letter from Stewart Lockhart to the Editor, *China Review*, 7 June 1886, SLPNLS, Vol. 37.

56. A copy of the translation is retained in SLPNLS, Vol. 37.

57. J. H. Stewart Lockhart, 'Some Notes on Chinese Folk-lore', *Folk-Lore*, 1, No. 3, September 1890, pp. 359-68.

58. Relevant notebooks, SLPNLS, Vol. 37.

59. Statistics sheet, Victoria Regatta, 1884, SLPNLS, Vol. 70.

60. *Hongkong Telegraph*, 29 September 1887.

61. N. Dunne, *Club: The Story of the Hong Kong Football Club 1886–1986*, (Hong Kong, Hong Kong Football Club, 1985), p. xvi.

62. *The Daily Press*, 20 February 1886, as quoted in Dunne above, p. 6.

63. Stewart Lockhart to Frederick Stewart, 13 October 1887, Enclosure in No. 355, CO 129/234.

64. See Note 63 above.

Notes to Chapter 4

1. *Hongkong Telegraph*, 26 February 1889.

2. Lethbridge, *Hong Kong: Stability and Change*, p. 141.

3. J. W. Budd, 'Notes as to a comparatively modern family history' (manuscript, no place of writing, August 1904), SLPGWC. Mrs Hancock was a Budd by birth.

4. 'Address from the Traders and Inhabitants of Hong Kong to Mr Stewart Lockhart, Protector of Chinese', SLPNLS, Vol. 24. Other congratulatory addresses may be found in the same volume.

5. Jordan to Stewart Lockhart, 4 April 1889, SLPGWC.

6. J. N. Jordan and J. H. Stewart Lockhart, 'China in Transition', undated, SLPNLS, Vol. 2, p. 3.

7. Letter from Miles Lockhart to Edith Stewart Lockhart, 14 June 1890, SLPSSP.

8. Letter from Stewart Lockhart to Edith Stewart Lockhart, 14 June 1890, SLPSSP.

9. Several thousand photographs, partially catalogued and dating from 1880, are retained in the Stewart Lockhart Collection of Photographs, SLPGWC.

10. Letter from Addis to Stewart Lockhart, 23 February 1890, SLPGWC.

11. Danby and Leigh, Plans for a three bedroomed house, 1890, SLPGWC.

12. J. Camplin, *The Rise of the Plutocrats: Wealth and Power in Edwardian England* (London, Constable, 1978) contains several references throughout the book to the Sassoons.

13. Mary Stewart Lockhart, note in F. D. Sassoon, 'Celebrities at Home', undated, SLPGWC.

14. Sassoon, 'Celebrities at Home', SLPGWC.

15. A Correspondent, 'British Ignorance of China', *New Books and New Editions Supplement to the London and China Express*, 17 October 1890, pp. 4–5, SLPNLS,

Vol. 13. This may have been written by Stewart Lockhart; he certainly made several corrections and annotations to the printed text.

16. Stewart Lockhart, undated note in large notebook, SLPNLS, Vol. 36.

17. No. 315, and Enclosures, 29 September 1889, CO 129/242.

18. Robinson to Knutsford, No. 4607, 3 February 1892, Confidential, CO 129/254.

19. Lucas to Wingfield, 1 February 1892, Minute in Telegram 1988, CO 129/254.

20. Several letters in this vein from Lucas to Stewart Lockhart are in SLPNLS, Vol. 11.

21. Eitel, *Europe in China: The History of Hong Kong*, p. 286.

22. *Overland China Mail*, 24 November 1892.

23. Hong Kong,'Petition of the Merchants, Bankers, Professional men, Traders, Artisans and other Ratepayers and Inhabitants of Hong Kong', *Papers on the Subject of a Petition Addressed to the House of Commons Praying for an Amendment of the Constitution of the Crown Colony of Hongkong* (Hong Kong, 1896).

24. Letter from Lucas to Stewart Lockhart, 20 April 1893, SLPNLS, Vol. 11.

25. Enclosure in No. 132, 4 June 1894, CO 129/263.

26. Sir. G. Howe, as reported in *The Independent*, 1 June 1988.

27. Lucas to Wingfield, 6 December 1892, Minute in No. 400, Confidential, CO 129/256.

28. See Note 27 above.

29. The disaster is well documented throughout CO 129/256.

30. No. 10, 15 January 1894, CO 129/262.

31. No. 115, 17 May 1894, CO 129/263.

32. No. 203, 4 September 1894, CO 129/264.

33. No. 219, 26 September 1894, CO 129/264.

34. J. S. Thomson, *The Chinese* (Indianapolis, Bobbs-Merrill Co., 1909), p. 327.

35. No. 219, 26 September 1894, CO 129/264.

36. Thomson, *The Chinese*, p. 327.

37. Tung Wah Group of Hospitals, *One Hundred Years of the Tung Wah Group of Hospitals, 1870–1970*, Vol. 1, p. 6.

38. Sassoon, 'Celebrities at Home', SLPGWC.

39. Ireland, *The Far Eastern Tropics*, p. 33.

40. Lethbridge, *Hong Kong: Stability and Change*, Chapter 5.

41. Most of the correspondence between Wei Yuk and Stewart Lockhart, which underlines the strong friendship between their families, is contained in SLPGWC.

42. Lethbridge, *Hong Kong: Stability and Change*, p. 110.

43. J. H. Stewart Lockhart, *'Report of the Special Committee ... to Investigate and Report on ... the Bill for the Incorporation of the Po Leung Kuk'* (hereafter cited as *Po Leung Kuk Report*), (Hong Kong, Norohana and Co., 1893).

44. Letter from Whitehead to Robinson, 28 June 1893, Enclosure in No. 137, CO 129/259.

45. *Po Leung Kuk Report*, p. 2.

46. *Po Leung Kuk Report*, p. v.

47. The proceedings of the committee, as recorded in the *Po Leung Kuk Report*, are a fascinating insight into the committee's conduct. One can almost hear Whitehead and Stewart Lockhart raging at one another through the proceedings. Whitehead and Ho Kai also had the greatest difficulty being civil to one another at times.

48. *Po Leung Kuk Report*, p. 100.

49. *The Hongkong Weekly Press*, 43, No. 4, 22 January 1896, p. 66.

50. Menu card, 10 June 1893, SLPNLS, Vol. 12.

51. *The Oban Times*, 30 September 1893.

52. *Pitch and Toss, or The Kurile Intelligencer*, 20 January 1894.

53. An enrolment card for Edinburgh University, Session 1889–90, SLPGWC. The relevant notebooks on law, SLPNLS, Vol. 35.

54. Relevant notebooks, SLPNLS, Vol. 28.

55. Stewart Lockhart, draft letter to unnamed Jesuit priest, 1 April 1890, SLPNLS, Vol. 13.

56. Relevant notebook, SLPNLS, Vol. 28.

57. Eitel, *China Review*, 20, No. 5, as quoted in the Kelly and Walsh publicity sheet for *A Manual of Chinese Quotations* (Hong Kong, Kelly and Walsh, 1893), SLPGWC.

58. Letter from Watters to Stewart Lockhart, 14 April 1893, SLPGWC.

59. Letter from Legge to Miles Lockhart, 28 June 1893, SLPGWC.

60. *China Review*, 20–3 (1893–5).

61. *China Review*, 23 (1895), p. 485.

62. Letter from Eitel to Stewart Lockhart, 29 September 1896, SLPGWC.

63. Letter from Giles to Stewart Lockhart, 29 October 1903, SLPGWC.

64. Letter from Giles to Stewart Lockhart, 24 March 1904, SLPGWC.

65. Several letters from Bushells to Parker during the early 1880s survive in SLPGWC.

66. Letter from Bushells to Stewart Lockhart, 29 June 1896, SLPGWC.

67. Letter from Wadman to Stewart Lockhart, 18 July 1892, SLPGWC.

68. J. H. Stewart Lockhart, *The Currency of the Farther East: From Earliest Times up to the Present Day* (Shanghai, Kelly and Walsh, 1895), Vol. 1, preface.

69. Letter from Chalmers to Stewart Lockhart, 12 April 1894, SLPNLS, Vol. 8.

70. Letter from Addis to Stewart Lockhart, 23 February 1890, SLPGWC.

71. J. H. Stewart Lockhart, 'Review of a Catalogue of the Hippisley Collection', undated galley proof, SLPNLS, Vol. 29.

Notes to Chapter 5

1. Letter from Lucas to Stewart Lockhart, 16 August 1897, SLPNLS, Vol. 11.

2. Letter from Addis to Stewart Lockhart, 30 July 1896, SLPGWC.

3. Mary Stewart Lockhart, in conversation with the author in 1982, described her father as a man who was recognized as being courteous and genial in his official duties. When roused, however, he 'blew the roof off', in her words, and she recalled that he was not a man to be crossed on such occasions.

4. No. 94, 27 March 1895, CO 129/266.

5. Captain Superintendent of Police to Governor, 20 March 1894, Enclosure in No. 63, CO 129/262.

6. No. 147, 16 June 1894, CO 129/263.

7. No. 94, 27 March 1895, CO 129/266.

8. Stewart Lockhart, 'Report on the Coolie Strike to the Legislative Council', 26 March 1895, as reported in the *Hongkong Weekly Press*, 41, No. 13, 28 March 1895, p. 227.

9. No. 206, 26 June 1895, CO 129/267.

10. See Note 9 above.

11. Letter from Stewart Lockhart to Sun Zhongshan, 4 October 1897, as quoted in Great Britain, eds., Foreign and Commonwealth Office and the Central Office of Information, *China Reflected: An Anthology from Chinese and Western Sources* (London, 1986), p. 40.

12. Lucas to Fairfield, 4 December 1895, Minute 506, Confidential, CO 129/269.

13. Chamberlain to Robinson, 21 October 1895, Confidential, CO 129/267.

14. Chamberlain to Robinson, 4 December 1895, Confidential, CO 129/269.

15. Letter from Robinson to Stewart Lockhart, 18 February 1896, SLPNLS, Vol. 2.

16. Letter from Stewart Lockhart to Robinson, 20 February 1896, SLPNLS, Vol. 2.

17. Lucas to Wingfield, 31 March 1896, Minute in Confidential 6856, CO 129/271.

18. See Note 17 above.

19. Letter from Lucas to Stewart Lockhart, 11 April 1896, SLPNLS, Vol. 2.

20. Wingfield to Chamberlain, 31 March 1896, Minute in Confidential 6856, CO 129/271.

21. Chamberlain to Robinson, 11 April 1896, Confidential, CO 129/271.

22. Lucas to Chamberlain, 11 April 1896, Confidential 6856, CO 129/271.

23. Chamberlain to Robinson, 4 May 1897, Copy, SLPNLS, Vol. 2.

24. Lucas to Graham, 30 March 1897, Confidential, CO 129/275.

25. Mary Stewart Lockhart, undated note on Stewart Lockhart, SLPGWC.

26. Mary Stewart Lockhart, in a blue notebook containing a short biography of Stewart Lockhart, 1966, SLPGWC.

27. Letter from Blake to Stewart Lockhart, 2 July 1912, SLPNLS, Vol. 5.

28. Lucas to Chamberlain, 21 January 1902, No. 8011, CO 129/310.

29. Letter from P'ang Shau-chun to Brewin, 16 September 1930, SLPNLS, Vol. 30.

30. Letter from Cai Tinggan to Stewart Lockhart, 29 April 1897, SLPNLS, Vol. 6.

31. No. 159, 20 July 1897, CO 129/276.

32. *Hongkong Weekly Press*, 43, No. 4, 22 January 1896, p. 66.

33. See Note 32 above. *Feng shui* is the supersititious belief in the propitious siting of buildings, graves, and so on.

34. Tung Wah Group of Hospitals, *One Hundred Years of the Tung Wah Group of Hospitals, 1870-1970*, Vol. 1, p. 7.

35. *One Hundred Years of the Tung Wah*, above, Vol. 1, pp. 23-4.

36. *One Hundred Years of the Tung Wah*, above, Vol. 1, p. 7.

37. *One Hundred Years of the Tung Wah*, above, Vol. 2, p. 11.

38. Bird, *The Golden Chersonese*, p. 90.

39. Bird, above, p. 89.

40. 'Address from the Chinese Community of Hong Kong to Stewart Lockhart', 19 April 1902, SLPGWC.

41. W. L. Langer, *The Diplomacy of Imperialism, 1890-1902*, 2nd edn. (New York, Alfred Knopf, 1951), p. 46.

42. Langer, above, p. 78.

43. The scramble for territory and concessions is admirably covered by L. K. Young in *British Policy in China 1895-1902* (Oxford, Oxford University Press, 1970). The acquisitions of the New Territories and of Weihaiwei are discussed in greater detail respectively in P. Wesley-Smith, *Unequal Treaty 1898-1997: China, Great Britain and Hong Kong's New Territories* (Hong Kong, Oxford University Press, 1980), and P. Atwell, *British Mandarins and Chinese Reformers* (Hong Kong, Oxford University Press, 1985).

44. Sir J. T. Pratt, *The Expansion of Europe into the Far East* (London, Sylvan Press, 1947), p. 97.

45. Beresford, *The Break Up of China*, p. 1.

46. The MP is unnamed, but quoted in a letter from Hugh Fraser to Stewart Lockhart, 19 March 1901, SLPNLS, Vol. 2.

47. G. N. Curzon, *Problems of the Far East* (London, Longmans, Green and Co., 1894), p. 421.

48. Robinson to Ripon, 9 November 1894, Secret No. 23, CO 537/34.

49. Letter from Lovat Fraser to Stewart Lockhart, 16 May 1899, SLPNLS, Vol. 20.

50. Atwell, *British Mandarins and Chinese Reformers*, pp. 6–11, and Great Britain, *Parliamentary Debates*, 4th Series, Session 1899, various dates.

51. The scale of the scramble for territory by the European powers can be guaged by the number of leasing agreements China signed in just four months in 1898: 6 March, Germany leases Jiao Xian; 28 March, Russia leases Lüshun; 2 April, Britain leases Weihaiwei; 9 April, France leases the bay of Guangzhou; 9 June, Britain leases New Territories.

52. Wesley-Smith, *Unequal Treaty 1898–1997: China, Great Britain and Hong Kong's New Territories*, p. 31.

53. No. 19, 26 January 1898, CO 129/281.

54. Lucas to Stewart Lockhart, 22 June 1898, CO 13111/98, SLPNLS, Vol. 2.

55. See Note 54 above.

56. 'A General Proclamation from the Governor General of Kwangtung Province, 19 July 1898'. Translation enclosed in a letter from Mansfield to Stewart Lockhart, 27 July 1898, Confidential No. 65 of H. B. M. Consulate Guangzhou, SLPNLS, Vol. 3.

Notes to Chapter 6

1. Minutes of the various meetings are in CO 129/287.

2. Letter from Lucas to Stewart Lockhart, 22 June 1898, CO 13111/98, SLPNLS, Vol. 2.

3. Memorandum from Hamilton to Lucas, 14 June 1898, Hong Kong 13111, Secret, CO 129/287.

4. See Note 3 above, and No. 209, 22 July 1898, and replies, CO 129/284.

5. Stewart Lockhart, 'Report on the Extension of the Colony of Hongkong', 8 October 1898, Eastern No. 66, and SLPNLS, Vol. 2.

6. Stewart Lockhart, 'Report on the Extension', (above), Index No. 30.

7. Stewart Lockhart, 'Journal of Inspection through the Newly Leased Territory', 9 August 1898, SLPNLS, Vol. 3.

8. See Note 7 above.

9. See Note 7 above. This custom may have been suggested by Stewart Lockhart, for in Scotland such 'pooroots' (literally, pour outs) were common on special occasions. It is a tradition which continues to the present day when coins are scattered for children to pick up after wedding ceremonies.

10. Stewart Lockhart, 'Journal of Inspection through the Newly Leased Territority', entry dated 18 August 1898, SLPNLS, Vol. 3.

11. Stewart Lockhart, 'Journal of Inspection', (above), entry dated 19 August 1898, SLPNLS, Vol. 3.

12. 'Address from 147 villages in the New Territories to Stewart Lockhart', 8th Moon 1898, SLPNLS, Vol. 2.

13. Stewart Lockhart describes the incident in a letter (undated) to Sercombe Smith: 'when we reached Kam T'in Hu yesterday we found that our chair coolies had been driven from the village. I tried to ascertain the reason for the extraordinary conduct on the part of the villagers, but they refused to furnish any explanation ... In addition to having driven away our chair coolies, the villagers were most discourteous in their reception of our party; not one of the elders deigned to meet me though I carefully explained to the villagers who I

was and the object of my mission . . . Our reception at all other places visited by us has been so good that the behaviour of the Kam T'in Hu inhabitants is all the more extraordinary.' SLPNLS, Vol. 3. Several weeks later, a less than friendly press, including a vehemently anti-British French newspaper, picked up and reported the story with, it seems, some imaginative additions. See Wesley-Smith, *Unequal Treaty 1898–1997: China, Great Britain and Hong Kong's New Territories*, pp. 46–7.

14. Stewart Lockhart, 'Report on the Extension of the Colony of Hongkong', p. 13.

15. Memorandum from Hamilton to Lucas, 14 June 1898, CO 129/287.

16. J. L. Watson, *Emigration and the Chinese Lineage: The Mans in Hong Kong and London* (Berkeley, University of California Press, 1975), pp. 16–17.

17. Despatch No. 242, 27 August 1898, CO 129/284, and Lucas to Stewart Lockhart, 7 October 1898, SLPNLS, Vol. 2.

18. Stewart Lockhart, 'Report on the Extension of the Colony of Hongkong', p. 13.

19. Minute from Lucas to Johnson, 21 November 1898, in No. 269, CO 129/285.

20. Wesley-Smith, *Unequal Treaty 1898–1997: China, Great Britain and Hong Kong's New Territories*, pp. 88–92.

21. Minute from Grindle, 10 January 1919, in CO 1484, Confidential, CO 521/20.

22. Minute from Lucas to Johnson, 21 November 1898, in No. 269, CO 129/285.

23. Balfour to MacDonald, 29 April 1898, Telegram No. 141, FO 17/1340.

24. Letter from Gundry to Sercombe Smith, 13 November 1898, Copy, SLPNLS, Vol. 3.

25. Memorandum from Blake to Stewart Lockhart, 11 March 1899, SLPNLS, Vol. 2, and Telegram, 9 March 1899, CO 129/290.

26. 'Memorandum on the Delimitation of the Northern Boundary of the New Territories', Copy, SLPNLS, Vol. 2.

27. Catalogue Nos. 2 and 3, Stewart Lockhart Collection of Paintings, SLPGWC, and Stewart Lockhart, notes on paintings in an Edinburgh University Notebook, SLPGWC.

28. These disturbances are comprehensively narrated in Wesley-Smith, *Unequal Treaty 1898–1997: China, Great Britain and Hong Kong's New Territories*, pp. 57 ff. The best contemporary account is to be found in Stewart Lockhart, New Territories Diaries, which include verbatim accounts by May, SLPNLS, Vol. 36.

29. Telegram from Blake to Chamberlain, 1 April 1899, CO 129/290.

30. No. 88, 7 April 1899, CO 129/290.

31. Stewart Lockhart, New Territories Diaries, 25 April 1899, SLPNLS, Vol. 36.

32. See Note 31 above.

33. Letter from Assistant Superintendent of Police to Honorary Secretary for Chinese Affairs, 2 June 1924, Copy as Enclosure in CO 33142, SLPNLS, Vol. 5.

34. Wesley-Smith, *Unequal Treaty 1898–1997: China, Britain and Hong Kong's New Territories*, p. 68.

35. No. 246, 7 June 1924, CO 33142, Copy, SLPNLS, Vol. 5.

36. Stewart Lockhart to Blake, undated copy of confidential memo, appended to 'Report on the Extension of the Colony of Hongkong'.

37. *The Daily Graphic*, 8 June 1900.

38. Stewart Lockhart, 'Translations of Miscellaneous Chinese Documents', SLPNLS, Vol. 3.

39. Notes by Stewart Lockhart, explaining the origin of many of the paintings,

are included in his manuscript catalogue of the Stewart Lockhart Collection of Paintings, SLPGWC.

40. Telegram, Hong Kong No. 25829, 8 August 1900, CO 129/300.

41. No. 206, 2 June 1900, CO 129/299.

42. For one of the best of these see Sir M. Hewlett, *The Siege of the Peking Legations* (Harrow, Editors of the Harrovian, 1900).

43. Letter from Michie to Stewart Lockhart, 24 June 1900, SLPNLS, Vol. 5.

44. Letter from Blake to Morrison, 11 June 1900, G. E. Morrison, *The Correspondence of G. E. Morrison; Volume 1, 1895–1912*, ed., Lo Hui-min (Cambridge, Cambridge University Press, 1976), p. 138.

45. No. 3.25, Stewart Lockhart Collection of Photographs, SLPGWC.

46. Thomson, *The Chinese*, p. 218.

47. Nos. 2.25–2.34, Stewart Lockhart Collection of Photographs, SLPGWC.

48. *The Sphere*, 22 March 1902.

49. Lucas to Ampthill, 28 August 1901, Minute in Hong Kong 28308, CO 129/303.

50. Ampthill to Lucas, 29 August 1901, Minute in Hong Kong 28308, CO 129/303.

51. No. 8011, 21 January 1902, Confidential Despatch, CO 129/313.

52. Letter from G. Scott to Stewart Lockhart, 27 March 1902, SLPNLS, Vol. 12.

53. Many of these are still preserved in SLPGWC.

54. 'Translation of Address from the Inhabitants of the Eastern Section of the New Territories', April 1902, SLPNLS, Vol. 24.

55. 'Farewell Address from the Chinese Community of Hong Kong', 19 April 1902, SLPGWC.

56. 'Farewell Address from the Po Leung Kuk', April 1902, SLPGWC.

57. 'Farewell Address from the Executive and Legislative Councils of Hong Kong', 1 April 1902, SLPGWC.

58. Speech by Fung Wa Chun, 19 April 1902, as reported in *The Hongkong Telegraph*, 21 April 1902.

59. *South China Morning Post*, 12 November 1902.

Notes to Chapter 7

1. G. T. Hare, 'Administrative Report on the Civil Administration of the Territory of Weihaiwei', 31 March 1902, Weihaiwei 20426, Secret, CO 521/3.

2. Langer, *The Diplomacy of Imperialism 1890–1902*, p. 454.

3. A. J. Marder, *British Naval Policy 1880–1905: The Anatomy of British Sea Power* (London, Putnam and Co., 1940), p. 309.

4. Hansard, *Parliamentary Debates*, 21 April 1899, p. 230.

5. Convention for the Lease of Weihaiwei, in Major F. C. Turner, 'Military Report and General Information Concerning the Dependency of Wei-Hai-Wei', Confidential Report 083/3990 (Intelligence Division, War Office, 1904), p. 31.

6. Letter from Hosie to Stewart Lockhart, 27 May 1906, SLPNLS, Vol. 1.

7. *The Graphic*, 17 December 1898.

8. Beresford, *The Break Up of China*, p. 79.

9. Letter from Chirol to Morrison, 31 March 1898, Morrison, *The Correspondence of G. E. Morrison*, Vol. 1, p. 76.

10. Captain P. Scott, 'Report on Weihaiwei', 23 February 1902, Copy, p. 1, SLPNLS, Vol. 1.

11. Letter from Windham to Fisher, 12 December 1901, Copy, SLPNLS, Vol. 1.

12. Letter from Stewart Lockhart to Stubbs, 10 December 1920, SLPNLS, Vol. 1, and F. Swettenham, 'Report on Weihaiwei', Eastern No. 72, July 1900.

13. Scott, 'Report on Weihaiwei', p. 1, SLPNLS, Vol. 1.

14. Hare, 'Report on Weihaiwei', CO 521/3.

15. See Note 14 above.

16. Cowan to Chamberlain, No. 9, 13 February 1902, CO 521/3.

17. Minute by Lucas, 14 April 1902, in memorandum from Blake to Onslow, Enclosure in Weihaiwei 20426, Secret, CO 521/3.

18. Merewether to Stewart Lockhart, 12 April 1902, SLPNLS, Vol. 12.

19. No. 35, 5 December 1910, CO 521/11.

20. No. 19, 8 May 1902, CO 521/3.

21. Stewart Lockhart, 'Annual Report for 1902', CO 521/4.

22. Weihaiwei Order in Council, 1901, p. 1, Copy, SLPNLS, Vol. 1.

23. Thomson, *The Chinese*, p. 344.

24. A record of visitors was made in the Commissioner's Visitors Book, SLPGWC.

25. No. 19, 8 May 1902, CO 521/3.

26. Numerous photographs of the territory, 1902–1921, remain in the Stewart Lockhart Collection of Photographs, SLPGWC.

27. R. F. Johnston, *Lion and Dragon in Northern China* (London, John Murray, 1910), pp. 29 ff.

28. Johnston, *Lion and Dragon in Northern China*, p. 3.

29. Johnston, *Lion and Dragon in Northern China*, p. 94.

30. Johnston, *Lion and Dragon in Northern China*, p. 7.

31. Commissioner's Visitors Book, 6 May 1902, SLPGWC.

32. Commissioner's Visitors Book, June to September 1902, SLPGWC.

33. Edith Stewart Lockhart's Visitors Book, July to August 1902, SLPGWC.

34. Album No. 47, SLPGWC.

35. Commissioner's Visitors Book, December 1902 to February 1903, SLPGWC.

36. Letter from Stewart Lockhart to Mary Stewart Lockhart, 14 March 1905, SLPGWC.

37. Stewart Lockhart, 'Annual Report for 1902', CO 521/4.

38. Johnston, *Lion and Dragon in Northern China*, p. 96.

39. See Note 38 above.

40. Johnston, *Lion and Dragon in Northern China*, p. 97.

41. No. 9, 9 April 1907, CO 521/10.

42. Stewart Lockhart, 'Annual Report for 1902', CO 521/4.

43. Atwell, *British Mandarins and Chinese Reformers*, p. 43.

44. Unsigned manuscript, 'Notes on Weihaiwei', April 1934, SLPNLS, Vol. 1.

45. Stewart Lockhart, 'Confidential Report of a Journey in the Province of Shantung Including a Visit to Kiaochou', 26 June 1903, CO 521/4.

46. Hare, 'Report on Weihaiwei', CO 521/3.

47. Lucas, 28 June 1903, Minute in Confidential 25277, CO 521/4.

48. Letter from Stewart Lockhart to Lucas, 28 June 1903, CO 521/4.

49. See Note 48 above.

50. Stewart Lockhart, 'Annual Report for 1902', CO 521/4, and Turner, 'Military Report and Recent Information Concerning the Dependency of Wei-Hai-Wei', p. 18.

51. Johnston, *Lion and Dragon in Nothern China*, p. 94.

52. Letter from Morrison to Roburo, 31 January 1905, Morrison, *The Correspondence of G. E. Morrison*, Vol. 1, p. 288.

53. H. B. Morse, *The Trade and Administration of the Chinese Empire* (Hong Kong, Kelly and Walsh, 1908), p. 223.

54. No. 9, 2 February 1903, CO 521/4.

55. Letter from Stewart Lockhart to Lucas, 28 June 1903, CO 521/4.

56. Letter from Morrison to Roburo, 31 January 1905, Morrison, *The Correspondence of G. E. Morrison*, Vol. 1, p. 288.

57. Johnston, *Lion and Dragon in Northern China*, p. 14.

58. Letter from Satow to Morrison, 24 March 1904, Morrison, *The Correspondence of G. E. Morrison*, Vol. 1, p. 258.

59. Commissioner's Visitors Book, 19 August 1903, SLPGWC.

60. Letter from Satow to Morrison, 24 March 1904, Morrison, *The Correspondence of G. E. Morrison*, Vol. 1, p. 258.

61. Memorandum from Lucas to Chamberlain, 29 August 1903, CO 521/4.

62. Stewart Lockhart, 'Annual Report for 1902', CO 521/4.

63. Memorandum from Stewart Lockhart to Colonial Office, 14 October 1903, Foreign 37912, CO 521/5.

64. Thomson, *The Chinese*, p. 321.

65. Stewart Lockhart, 'Confidential Report on a Journey in the Province of Shantung', CO 521/4, and Eastern No. 84, August 1903.

66. See Note 65 above. Additional information is contained in Stewart Lockhart's diary of the visit, SLPNLS, Vol. 36.

67. Stewart Lockhart, 'Confidential Report on a Journey in the Province of Shantung', for 27 April 1903, CO 521/4.

68. Letter from Stewart Lockhart to Lucas, 28 June 1903, CO 521/4.

69. Much of the correspondence is retained in SLPNLS, Vols. 38–40. Between the years 1902–6 there are more letters to Chinese officials than there are despatches to London.

70. R. F. Johnston, *Account of a Journey in Shantung from Weihaiwei to the Tomb of Confucius* (Weihaiwei, Weihaiwei Press, 1904), p. 1.

71. Nos. 5.1–5.84, 6.1–6.95, 7–14, SLPGWC.

72. Telegram No. 13, 16 May 1902, CO 521/3.

73. Fiddian, 3 June 1903, Minute in Telegram CO 21791, CO 521/3.

74. No. 19, 8 May 1902, CO 521/3.

75. Copies of both publications are bound in an album, SLPNLS, Vol. 67.

76. *Weihaiwei Gazette*, No. 418, 11 April 1903.

77. Fiddian to Risley, 16 February 1903, Minute in No. 1, CO 521/4.

78. Lucas to Ommanney, 21 February 1905, Minute in No. 1, CO 521/8.

79. Stewart Lockhart, 'Annual Report for 1902', CO 521/4.

80. Stewart Lockhart, 'Speech to the Chinese Regiment', 1 January 1903, SLPNLS, Vol. 4. See also A. A. S. Barnes, *On Active Service with the Chinese Regiment* (London, Grant Richards, 1902).

81. Letter from Lucas to Stewart Lockhart, 30 January 1902, SLPNLS, Vol. 11.

82. Stewart Lockhart, 'Annual Report for 1902', CO 521/4.

83. Letter from Stewart Lockhart to Mary Stewart Lockhart, 1 April 1906, SLPGWC.

84. Letter from Anna Lockhart to Stewart Lockhart, 24 July, 1902, SLPSSP.

Notes to Chapter 8

1. No. 61, 7 September 1903, CO 521/5.

2. Minute from Antrobus to Lucas, 30 November 1903, in Weihaiwei 43148, CO 521/5.

3. Johnson to Lucas, 27 November 1903, Minute in No. 61, CO 521/5.

4. G. Woodcock, *The British in the Far East* (London, Weidenfeld and Nicolson, 1969), p. 70.

5. Lucas, 8 April 1904, Minute in Telegram, CO 521/6.

6. No. 30, 9 May 1904, CO 521/6.

7. Letter from Johnston to Chamberlain, 25 November 1898, CO 129/289, and letter from Johnston to the Academic Registrar, University of London, January 1931, enclosing curriculum vitae, SLPNLS, Vol. 13.

8. Letter from Johnston to the Academic Registrar, University of London, January 1931, enclosing curriculum vitae, SLPNLS, Vol. 13.

9. Letter from Stewart Lockhart to Chamberlain, 19 November 1903, Weihaiwei 43148, Private, CO 521/5.

10. Harding to Lucas, 24 February 1905, Minute in CO 5714, Confidential, CO 521/8.

11. No. 65, 27 August 1904, CO 521/6.

12. No. 70, and enclosures, 30 September 1904, CO 521/7.

13. The Grant-in-Aid of £11,250 for 1901–2 had diminished to £6,000 in 1904–5. Stewart Lockhart, 'Annual Report for 1903', CO 521/6.

14. No. 15, 19 February 1904, CO 521/6.

15. Confidential, 17 March 1904, CO 521/6.

16. Letter from Stewart Lockhart to Mary Stewart Lockhart, 30 November 1904, SLPGWC.

17. Letter from Lady Blake to Morrison, 4 June 1904, *Morrison, The Correspondence of G. E. Morrison*, Vol. 1, p. 204.

18. Letter from Stewart Lockhart to Mary Stewart Lockhart, 12 January 1905, SLPGWC.

19. See Note 18 above.

20. Letter from Edith Stewart Lockhart to Mary Stewart Lockhart, October 1906, SLPGWC.

21. See Note 20 above.

22. The bulk of the letters, dating from 1906, are to be found in SLPNLS, Vols. 9, 10, and 10A. A few others have been located in other SLPNLS volumes, and a further small number in SLPGWC. Johnston's letters to Edith and Mary Stewart Lockhart are also retained in SLPGWC.

23. Nos. 4.10–4.23, Stewart Lockhart Collection of Photographs, SLPGWC.

24. Johnston, *Lion and Dragon in Nothern China*, p. 17.

25. Stewart Lockhart, 'Annual Report for 1915', CO 521/17.

26. Letter from Moss to Stewart Lockhart, 7 April 1933, SLPNLS, Vol. 1.

27. No. 24, 22 March 1904, CO 521/6.

28. Stewart Lockhart, 'Annual Report for 1905', CO 521/8.

29. No. 28, 28 April 1906, CO 521/9.

30. Letter from Stewart Lockhart to Mary Stewart Lockhart, 23 January 1905, SLPGWC.

31. Letter from Moss to Stewart Lockhart, 22 March 1934, SLPNLS, Vol. 6.

32. No. 75, 14 November 1904, CO 521/7.

33. No. 1, 7 January 1905, CO 521/8.

34. Fiddian to Lucas, 20 February 1905, Minute in No. 1, CO 521/8.

35. Lucas to Ommanney, 21 February 1905, Minute in No. 1, CO 521/8.

36. Letter from Lucas to Stewart Lockhart, 22 September 1905, SLPNLS, Vol. 11.

37. CO 5714, Confidential, 11 January 1905, CO 521/8.

38. Harding to Lucas, 24 February 1905, Minute in CO 5714, Confidential, CO 521/8.

39. Letter from Nathan to Lucas, 7 April 1905, Enclosure in CO 5714, Confidential, CO 521/8.

40. *The Times of India*, 29 November 1904.

41. Stewart Lockhart, 'Annual Report for 1904', CO 521/8.

42. Cox to Lucas, 25 May 1905, Minute in No. 20, CO 521/8.

43. Fiddes to Lucas, 27 May 1905, Minute in No. 20, CO 521/8.

44. Johnston, 'Secretary to Government's Report for 1904', CO 521/8.

45. Stewart Lockhart, 'Annual Report for 1904', CO 521/8.

46. No. 55, 30 September 1905, CO 521/8.

47. Bertram, *The Colonial Office*, p. 47.

48. Unsigned manuscript, 'Notes on Weihaiwei', April 1934, SLPNLS, Vol. 1.

49. Johnston, *Lion and Dragon in Northern China*, pp. 155 ff.

50. Johnston, *Lion and Dragon*, above, p. 15.

51. See Note 50 above.

52. Johnston, *Lion and Dragon*, above, p. 80.

53. Elgin to Stewart Lockhart, 12 February 1906, Telegram, CO 521/9.

54. No. 15, 13 February 1906, CO 521/9.

55. See Note 54 above.

56. Letter from Johnston to Stewart Lockhart, 26 June 1906, SLPNLS, Vol. 9.

57. Fiddes to Lucas, 17 May 1906, Minute in No. 24, CO 521/9.

58. Lucas to Ommanney, 18 May 1906, Minute in No. 24, CO 521/9.

59. A wealth of information on the reorganized administration is to be found in Johnston, *Lion and Dragon in Northern China*, pp. 98–9.

60. Letter from Johnston to Stewart Lockhart, 26 July 1906, SLPNLS, Vol. 1.

61. Letter from Walter to Stewart Lockhart, 17 July 1906, SLPNLS, Vol. 1.

62. Letter from Johnston to Stewart Lockhart, 26 July 1906, SLPNLS, Vol. 1.

63. Johnston, *Lion and Dragon in Northern China*, p. 99.

64. Stewart Lockhart, 'Annual Report for 1902', CO 521/4.

65. Letters from Johnston to Stewart Lockhart, various dates, SLPNLS, Vols. 9 and 10.

66. Hewlett, *Forty Years in China*, p. 42.

67. Letter from Stewart Lockhart to Mary Stewart Lockhart, 10 February 1906, SLPGWC.

68. See Note 67 above.

69. Letter from Edith Stewart Lockhart to Mary Stewart Lockhart, October 1907, SLPGWC.

70. Letter from Johnston to Stewart Lockhart, 14 September 1906, SLPNLS, Vol. 9.

71. Letter from Johnston to Stewart Lockhart, 9 January 1906, SLPNLS, Vol. 9.

72. Johnston, *Lion and Dragon in Northern China*, facing p. 46.

73. Letter from Johnston to Stewart Lockhart, 27 May 1908, SLPNLS, Vol. 9.

74. Letter from Johnston to Stewart Lockhart, 12 February 1906, SLPNLS, Vol. 9.

75. Letter from Johnston to Stewart Lockhart, 2 May 1910, SLPNLS, Vol. 9.

76. Letter from Johnston to Stewart Lockhart, 7 October 1908, SLPNLS, Vol. 9.

77. Letter from Johnston to Stewart Lockhart, 12 February 1906, SLPNLS, Vol. 9.

78. Letter from Johnston to Stewart Lockhart, 25 May 1908, SLPNLS, Vol. 9.

79. Letter from Johnston to Stewart Lockhart, 27 June 1906, SLPNLS, Vol. 1.

80. The articles are listed in a letter from Johnston to the Academic Registrar, University of London, January 1931, enclosing his curriculum vitae, SLPNLS, Vol. 13.

81. Johnston to Stewart Lockhart, 26 June 1906, SLPNLS, Vol. 9.

82. 'List of Persons detailed at Li Kung Ch'ih to render services to H. H. The Commr. and his staff', SLPNLS, Vol. 24, and Stewart Lockhart, 'Report on a Visit to Kiaochou and Chinan', Eastern No. 104, August 1906.

83. 'Report on the Entertainment of His Honour The Commissioner of Wei Hai Wei by the Governor of Shantung on May 19th 1906', SLPNLS, Vol. 24.

84. 'Report on the Entertainment of His Honour The Commissioner of Wei Hai Wei by the various Civil and Military Officials at Chinanfu on May 21st 1906', SLPNLS, Vol. 24.

85. 'Report of the Conversation between the Commissioner of Wei Hai Wei and the Governor of Shantung on May 19th 1906 when the Commissioner called officially on the Governor', SLPNLS, Vol. 24.

86. Colonial Office Print, Eastern No. 104, p. 11.

87. R. Walter, 'Weihaiwei', in R. C. Forsyth, ed., *Shantung: The Sacred Province of China* (Shanghai, Chinese Literature Society, 1912), p. 109.

88. See Note 87 above.

89. Stewart Lockhart, 'Speech to Schoolmasters and Students', Speech No. 8, 31 July 1913, SLPNLS, Vol. 46.

90. Numerous minutes regarding Weihaiwei's future are to be found throughout CO 521/9.

91. Letter from Satow to Stewart Lockhart, 31 January 1906, SLPNLS, Vol. 11.

92. Letter from Lucas to Stewart Lockhart, 15 August 1906, SLPNLS, Vol. 4.

93. Lucas to Ommanney, 19 July 1906, Minute in No. 36, CO 521/9.

94. See Note 93 above.

95. Admiralty to Commander in Chief, 9 October 1906, Telegram No. 138, Confidential, Copy, SLPNLS, Vol. 4.

96. Letter from Lucas to Stewart Lockhart, 7 December 1906, SLPNLS, Vol. 4.

97. Letter from Stewart Lockhart to Lucas, 15 November 1906, SLPNLS, Vol. 4.

98. Minute from Lucas to Ommanney, 19 July 1906, in No. 36, CO 521/9.

99. Minute from Lucas to Ommanney, 13 December 1906, in Weihaiwei 46163, Private, CO 521/9.

100. Lucas to Stewart Lockhart, various letters, 1906–1907, SLPNLS, Vol. 11.

Notes to Chapter 9

1. Letter from Stewart Lockhart to Jordan, 26 July 1907, SLPNLS, Vol. 6.

2. Letter from Jordan to Stewart Lockhart, 1 August 1907, SLPNLS, Vol. 6.

3. Register of Letters Received, 1906, CO 770/1.

4. Minute from Lucas to Ommanney, 13 December 1906, in Weihaiwei 46163, Private, CO 521/9.

5. Letter from Stewart Lockhart to Mary Stewart Lockhart, 28 February 1907, SLPGWC.

6. CO 521/10 and CO 129/332–342 respectively.

7. Over 600 volumes exist, covering Stewart Lockhart's term in the territory, in the Commissioner's Files for Weihaiwei, CO 873. This compares with only eighteen in Weihaiwei Original Correspondence, CO 521, sent to the Colonial Office for the same period.

8. No. 9, 9 April 1907, CO 521/10, and Stewart Lockhart, 'Presentation of Medals to Headmen', Speech No. 2, 26 November 1906, SLPNLS, Vol. 46.

9. Minute from Lucas to Hopwood, 15 May 1907, in No. 9, CO 521/10.

10. Letter from Stewart Lockhart to Mary Stewart Lockhart, 28 February 1907, SLPGWC.

11. Letter from Stewart Lockhart to Mary Stewart Lockhart, 4 May 1907, SLPGWC.

12. Letter from Ferguson to Stewart Lockhart, 19 May 1906, SLPNLS, Vol. 1.

13. *Ends of the Earth Membership Booklet*, 1906 (no place of publication, or publisher), SLPNLS, Vol. 1.

14. See Note 13 above.

15. Weihaiwei Golf Club, *List of Rules*, (Weihaiwei, 1902), p. 1, SLPNLS, Vol. 65.

16. Weihaiwei St Andrew's Society Booklet, SLPNLS, Vol. 44.

17. Letter from Stewart Lockhart to Addis, 27 November 1903, SLPNLS, Vol. 69.

18. Letter from Johnston to Stewart Lockhart, August 1908, SLPNLS, Vol. 9.

19. Letter from Stewart Lockhart to Mary Stewart Lockhart, 19 October 1908, SLPGWC.

20. Letter from Stewart Lockhart to Mary Stewart Lockhart, 25 October 1908, SLPGWC.

21. Letter from Edith Stewart Lockhart to Mary Stewart Lockhart, 25 October 1908, SLPGWC.

22. See Note 21 above.

23. See Note 21 above.

24. Letter from Stewart Lockhart to Mary Stewart Lockhart, 25 October 1908, SLPGWC.

25. Crewe to Stewart Lockhart, 9 November 1908, Telegram Foreign No. 62, SLPNLS, Vol. 4.

26. *South China Morning Post*, 12 December 1908.

27. Confidential Despatch, 5 July 1909, CO 521/11.

28. Letter from Johnston to Stewart Lockhart, 19 February 1909, SLPNLS, Vol. 9.

29. Collins, *Public Administration in Hong Kong*, p. 143.

30. No. 10, 15 April 1910, CO 521/11.

31. Letter from Johnston to Stewart Lockhart, 2 May 1910, SLPNLS, Vol. 9.

32. Letter from Johnston to Stewart Lockhart, 8 February 1909, SLPNLS, Vol. 9.

33. Letter from Johnston to Stewart Lockhart, 9 March 1909, SLPNLS, Vol. 9.

34. Commissioner Confidential Despatch, 3 May 1909, CO 19802, CO 521/11.

35. Letter from Stewart Lockhart to Mary Stewart Lockhart, 20 April 1909, SLPGWC.

36. See Note 35 above.

37. See Note 35 above.

38. Letter from Johnston to Stewart Lockhart, 21 May 1909, SLPNLS, Vol. 9.

39. Letter from Johnston to Stewart Lockhart, 'Thursday', SLPNLS, Vol. 9.

40. Letter from Tse to Stewart Lockhart, 19 February 1910, SLPGWC.

41. See Note 40 above.

42. A collection of cartoons was, however, amassed. The bulk of them, pasted into albums, are retained in SLPNLS, Vols. 51–53.

43. Letter from Tse to Stewart Lockhart, 11 April 1910, SLPGWC.

44. See Note 43 above.

45. Letter from Tse to Stewart Lockhart, 2 May 1910, SLPGWC.

46. Letter from Tse to Stewart Lockhart, 20 June 1910, SLPGWC.

47. Letter from Stewart Lockhart to Tse, 1 July 1910, SLPGWC.

48. Stewart Lockhart, 'Notes on Chinese Art', undated, SLPNLS, Vol. 14.

49. Stewart Lockhart, 'Catalogue of Collection of Chinese Paintings', SLPGWC.

50. Letter from Tse to Stewart Lockhart, 11 July 1910, SLPGWC.

51. S. M. Airlie, *An Ardent Collector: An Exhibition of the Stewart Lockhart Collection* (Edinburgh, Merchant Company Education Board, 1982), pp. 9–11.

52. Catalogue nos. 4, 1, 6, and 31 respectively, Stewart Lockhart Collection of Chinese Paintings, SLPGWC.

53. A fact confirmed by his daughter, Mary, in conversation with the author in 1982.

54. Catalogue no. 1, Stewart Lockhart, 'Catalogue of Collection of Chinese Paintings', SLPGWC.

55. Letter from Stewart Lockhart to Mary Stewart Lockhart, 17 October 1912, SLPGWC.

56. Mary Stewart Lockhart, in a blue notebook containing a short biography of Stewart Lockhart, 1966, SLPGWC.

57. Letter from Stewart Lockhart to Mary Stewart Lockhart, 21 May 1913, SLPGWC.

58. Letter from Tse to Stewart Lockhart, 19 November 1934, SLPNLS, Vol. 12.

59. Letter from Tse to Stewart Lockhart, 6 March 1911, SLPGWC.

60. Mary Stewart Lockhart, in a blue notebook containing a short biography of Stewart Lockhart, 1966, SLPGWC.

61. Letter from Ros to Stewart Lockhart, 24 May 1913, SLPGWC.

62. Many of the blocks are retained in SLPGWC.

63. The calligraphic scrolls and several trunks of rubbings, uncatalogued, are in SLPGWC.

64. See especially SLPNLS, Vols. 14, 25, 27, 30, and 33.

65. Minute from Harding to Fiddes, 6 December 1907, in No. 35, CO 521/10.

66. Minute from Stubbs to Fiddes, 9 September 1910, in Confidential File dated 1 August 1910, CO 521/10.

67. Minute from Harding to Collins, 19 December 1910, in No. 32, CO 521/11.

68. Letter from Lucas to Stewart Lockhart, 23 December 1910, SLPNLS, Vol. 11.

69. Letter from Stewart Lockhart to Secretary of State, 8 August 1911, Confidential, CO 521/12.

70. Minute from Stubbs, 30 August 1911, in Confidential File dated 8 August 1911, CO 521/12.

71. Minute from Risley to Collins, 28 August 1911, in Confidential File dated 8 August 1911, CO 521/12.

72. Minute from Collins, 30 August 1911, in Confidential File dated 8 August 1911, CO 521/12.

73. Despatch from Crewe to Stewart Lockhart, 1 September 1911, No. 27919/11, CO 521/12.

74. Letter from Stewart Lockhart to Mary Stewart Lockhart, 25 February 1912, SLPGWC.

75. Letter from Stewart Lockhart to Mary Stewart Lockhart, 1 December 1912, SLPGWC.

76. Letter from May to Stewart Lockhart, 28 August 1912, SLPNLS, Vol. 5.

77. Blake to Stewart Lockhart, 2 July 1912, SLPNLS, Vol. 5.

78. See Note 77 above.

79. Minute from Harding to Fiddes, 16 December 1907, in No. 35, CO 521/10.

80. Mary Stewart Lockhart, in a blue notebook containing a short biography of Stewart Lockhart, 1966, SLPGWC.

81. Letter from Blake to Stewart Lockhart, 2 July 1912, SLPNLS, Vol. 5.
82. Letter from Johnston to Stewart Lockhart, 29 December 1910, SLPNLS, Vol. 9.
83. Letter from Johnston to Stewart Lockhart, 12 August 1910, SLPNLS, Vol. 9.
84. See Note 83 above.
85. See Note 83 above.
86. Letter from Johnston to Stewart Lockhart, 19 September 1910, SLPNLS, Vol. 9.
87. Letter from Johnston to Stewart Lockhart, 23 January 1913, SLPNLS, Vol. 9.
88. Yuan Mei manuscript and notes, SLPNLS, Vol. 23, and letters from Johnston to Stewart Lockhart throughout 1910 and 1911, SLPNLS, Vol. 9.
89. Letter from Stewart Lockhart to Heatley, 15 September 1912, 'Johnston is . . . as enthusiastic a student as ever. I need hardly tell you what a great help he is to me in the work of the administration', SLPNLS, Vol. 13.
90. Johnston, *Lion and Dragon in Northern China*, p. 104.
91. Letter from Johnston to Stewart Lockhart, 1 May 1911, SLPNLS, Vol. 9.
92. Letter from Beer to Stewart Lockhart, 6 May 1911, SLPNLS, Vol. 9.
93. Letter from Lugard to Stewart Lockhart, 17 July 1911, SLPNLS, Vol. 12.

Notes to Chapter 10

1. No. 31, 15 August 1911, CO 521/12.
2. See the various reports and files on the subject in CO 873/199–217, and the Annual Reports for the territory between 1904 and 1906, for the start and progress of the school. It is also mentioned in annual reports thereafter. See also R. Walter, 'Weihaiwei', in Forsyth, ed., *Shantung*, pp. 103–5.
3. Minute from Stubbs to Collins, 16 September 1911, in No. 35, CO 521/12.
4. Several instances of the daily workload are quoted in a letter from Johnston to Stewart Lockhart, 12 August 1910, SLPNLS, Vol. 9.
5. Stewart Lockhart kept the flag, now in SLPNLS, Vol. 1.
6. Stewart Lockhart, 14 November 1911, Confidential Despatch, CO 521/12.
7. Letter from Stewart Lockhart to Mary Stewart Lockhart, 12 February 1912, SLPGWC.
8. Johnston to Stewart Lockhart, 10 November 1911, SLPNLS, Vol. 9.
9. Commissioner Confidential Despatch, 13 January 1912, CO 521/13.
10. No. 1, 13 January 1912, CO 521/13.
11. No. 6, 2 February 1912, CO 521/13.
12. 'Report by Secretary to Government', 23 January 1912, Enclosure in No. 4, CO 521/13.
13. No. 7, 10 February 1912, CO 521/13.
14. Letter from Stewart Lockhart to Mary Stewart Lockhart, 13 February 1912, SLPGWC.
15. Catalogue no. 147, Stewart Lockhart, 'Catalogue of Collection of Chinese Paintings', SLPGWC.
16. Letter from Stewart Lockhart to Mary Stewart Lockhart, 25 February 1912, SLPGWC.
17. No. 32, 4 November 1910, CO 521/11.
18. No. 14, 4 April 1912, CO 521/13.
19. Letter from Johnston to Stewart Lockhart, 12 August 1910, SLPNLS, Vol. 9.

20. Commissioner's Visitors Book, SLPGWC.

21. Minute from Stubbs to Collins, 25 April 1912, in No. 14, CO 521/13.

22. Letter from Johnston to Stewart Lockhart, 12 August 1910, SLPNLS, Vol. 9.

23. Minute from Stubbs to Collins, 16 August 1912, in No. 42, CO 521/13.

24. Minute from Stubbs to Collins, 25 April 1912, in No. 14, CO 521/13.

25. See Note 24 above.

26. No. 46, 12 August 1913, CO 521/14.

27. Minute from Stubbs to Collins, 25 April 1912, in No. 14, CO 521/13.

28. No. 46, 12 August 1913, CO 521/14.

29. Several letters between Stewart Lockhart and Jordan cover this subject in 1913, SLPNLS, Vol. 1.

30. No. 58, 21 October 1913, CO 521/14.

31. No. 69, 22 October 1913, CO 521/14.

32. Minute from Risley to Collins, 10 February 1913, in Weihaiwei 4425, CO 521/13. The enormous amount of correspondence in the Commissioner's files for Weihaiwei, CO 873/7 ff., likewise bears testament to the piles of papers and work he and his officers undertook.

33. Letter from Johnston to Stewart Lockhart, 6 March 1913, SLPNLS, Vol. 9.

34. Letter from Johnston to Stewart Lockhart, 10 October 1913, SLPNLS, Vol. 9.

35. Letter from Johnston to Stewart Lockhart, 1 December 1913, SLPNLS, Vol. 9.

36. Letter from Johnston to Stewart Lockhart, 9 December 1913, SLPNLS, Vol. 9.

37. Letter from Johnston to Stewart Lockhart, 12 April 1914, SLPNLS, Vol. 9.

38. C. P. Skrine and P. Nightingale, *Macartney of Kashgar: New Light on British, Chinese, and Russian Activities in Sinkiang, 1890–1918* (Hong Kong, Oxford University Press, 1987), p. 259.

39. Letter from Stewart Lockhart to Mary Stewart Lockhart, 19 December 1912, SLPGWC.

40. Letter from Johnston to Stewart Lockhart, 8 May 1913, SLPNLS, Vol. 9.

41. CO 521/15.

42. A. Feuerwerker, *The Foreign Establishment in China in the Early Twentieth Century* (Ann Arbor, University of Michigan, 1976), p. 9.

43. E. M. Gull, *Facets of the Chinese Question* (London, Ernest Benn, 1931), p. 139.

44. Letter from Idina Sackville to Mary Stewart Lockhart, 1 August 1914, SLPGWC.

45. Letter from Idina Sackville to Mary Stewart Lockhart, 16 October 1914, SLPGWC.

46. Telegram dated 16 October 1916, enclosed in Confidential 49281/1916, CO 521/17.

47. MacNair, *The Chinese Abroad*, p. 235.

48. No. 44, 20 December 1916, CO 521/17.

49. 'Annual Report for 1920', Eastern No. 1097, p. 4.

50. Letter from Stewart Lockhart to Mary Stewart Lockhart, 14 February 1917, SLPGWC.

51. MacNair, *The Chinese Abroad*, p. 235.

52. Secretary of State to Governor of Hong Kong, 29 September 1916, War Office 46369/1916, Copy of paraphrase Telegram, CO 521/17, and E. M. Gull, 'The Story of the Chinese Labor Corps', *Far Eastern Review*, 15, No. 4, April 1918, pp. 125–35.

53. Letter from Stewart Lockhart to Mary Stewart Lockhart, 17 December 1917, SLPGWC, and Gull, 'Chinese Labor Corps', p. 135.

54. MacNair, *The Chinese Abroad*, p. 236.

55. Secretary of State to Stewart Lockhart, 16 November 1918, as reported in *Weihaiwei Government Gazette*, Vol. xi, No. 28, 1918.

56. Letter from Johnston to Mary Stewart Lockhart, 4 December 1914, SLPGWC.

57. Letter from Johnston to Stewart Lockhart, 12 July 1916, SLPNLS, Vol. 10.

58. Letter from Johnston to Stewart Lockhart, 8 August 1916, SLPNLS, Vol. 10.

59. Letter from Stewart Lockhart to Mary Stewart Lockhart, 14 November 1915, SLPGWC.

60. Letter from Johnston to Stewart Lockhart, 23 January 1913, SLPNLS, Vol. 9.

61. Minute by Collins, 30 August 1911, in No. 18, CO 521/12.

62. Letter from Stewart Lockhart to Jordan, 15 May 1914, SLPNLS, Vol. 13.

63. Letter from Stewart Lockhart to Secretary of State, 17 September 1914, SLPNLS, Vol. 13.

64. Colonial Office file 40110, 17 September 1914, CO 521/15.

65. Minute from Risley to Collins, 19 October 1914, in Colonial Office 40110, CO 521/15.

66. Ku Hung-ming, 'Reminiscences of a Chinese Viceroy's Secretary', *Journal of the North China Branch of the Royal Asiatic Society*, 46, 1915, pp. 61–76.

67. No. 2, 3 January 1918, CO 521/19.

68. See Note 67 above.

69. Letter from Johnston to Stewart Lockhart, 10 November 1917, SLPNLS, Vol. 10.

70. Minute from Risley to Collins, 11 April 1916, in No. 8, CO 521/17.

71. Minute from Collins to Macnaghton, 12 April 1916, in No. 8, CO 521/17.

72. Undated Minute from Beckett to Fiddes, in Confidential File dated 10 August 1920, CO 521/21.

73. Minute from Beckett to Grindle, 28 March 1919, in Secret File CO 18353, CO 521/20.

74. Letter from Lucas to Stewart Lockhart, 16 January 1916, SLPNLS, Vol. 11.

75. Letter from May to Stewart Lockhart, 5 October 1916, SLPNLS, Vol. 13.

76. Johnston to Stewart Lockhart, 3 March 1917, SLPNLS, Vol. 13.

77. Letter from Eliot to Stewart Lockhart, 18 January 1917, SLPNLS, Vol. 13.

78. Most of these highly decorated letters are in SLPNLS, Vol. 38.

79. Letter from Stewart Lockhart to Mary Stewart Lockhart, 8 October 1918, SLPGWC.

80. Letter from Stewart Lockhart to Mary Stewart Lockhart, 23 August 1918, SLPGWC.

81. See Note 80 above.

82. Letter from Revd and Mrs Burnett to Stewart Lockhart, April 1921, SLPNLS, Vol. 1.

83. 'Copy of Commissioner's Address to the people of Lin Chia Yuan', 6 December 1915, SLPNLS, Vol. 45.

84. See Note 83 above.

85. Letter from Stewart Lockhart to Mary Stewart Lockhart, 8 October 1918, SLPGWC.

86. No. 4, 25 January 1916, CO 521/17.

87. Letter from Stewart Lockhart to Mary Stewart Lockhart, 21 November 1918, SLPGWC.

88. The silver junk was stolen from the Stewart Lockhart Collection at George Watson's College in 1988.

89. Letter from Stewart Lockhart to Mary Stewart Lockhart, 21 November 1918, SLPGWC.

90. Letter from Stewart Lockhart to Mary Stewart Lockhart, 22 November 1918, SLPGWC.

91. Letter from Stewart Lockhart to Mary Stewart Lockhart, 31 October 1913, SLPGWC.

92. Letter from Stewart Lockhart to Mary Stewart Lockhart, 22 November 1918, SLPGWC.

93. No. 44, 15 August 1918, CO 521/19.

94. Letter from Stewart Lockhart to Mary Stewart Lockhart, 8 September 1918, SLPGWC. Wu Dingfang agreed with Stewart Lockhart that China had been 'to a great extent mismanaged' since the revolution, Wu to Stewart Lockhart, 23 December 1916, SLPNLS, Vol. 12.

95. E. Teichman, *Affairs in China: A Survey of the Recent History and Present Circumstances of the Republic of China* (London, Methuen, 1938), p. 46.

96. Letter from Johnston to Stewart Lockhart, 7 June 1916, SLPNLS, Vol. 10.

97. Letter from Johnston to Stewart Lockhart, 22 May 1916, SLPNLS, Vol. 10.

98. Confidential Despatch CO 59518, 19 October 1918, CO 521/19.

99. Letter from Stewart Lockhart to Mary Stewart Lockhart, 29 October 1918.

Notes to Chapter 11

1. Letter from Johnston to Stewart Lockhart, 17 November 1917, SLPNLS, Vol. 10.

2. Letter from Johnston to Stewart Lockhart, 24 September 1918, SLPNLS, Vol. 10.

3. See Note 2 above.

4. Letter from Johnston to Stewart Lockhart, 28 October 1918, SLPNLS, Vol. 10.

5. Johnston, 25 January 1919, Enclosure in Secret CO 18353, CO 521/20.

6. See Note 5 above.

7. See Note 5 above.

8. See Note 5 above.

9. Johnston, 7 March 1919, Enclosure in Johnston to Li, Copy, SLPNLS, Vol. 10.

10. Letter from Johnston to Stewart Lockhart, 14 July 1920, SLPNLS, Vol. 10.

11. Johnston, 25 January 1919, Enclosure in Secret File CO 18353, CO 521/20.

12. See Note 11 above.

13. See Note 11 above.

14. See Note 11 above.

15. Letter from Johnston to Stewart Lockhart, 27 December 1918, SLPNLS, Vol. 10.

16. Telegram CO 62741, 27 December 1918, CO 521/19.

17. The tawse, a leather belt, was used in place of the cane as a punishment in Scottish schools. Letter from Johnston to Stewart Lockhart, 4 January 1919, SLPNLS, Vol. 10.

18. Secret File CO 18353, 27 January 1919, CO 521/20.
19. Johnston, 7 March 1919, Enclosure in Letter from Johnston to Li, Copy, SLPNLS, Vol. 10.
20. Letter from Johnston to Li, 17 July 1919, Copy, SLPNLS, Vol. 10.
21. See Note 20 above, and Letter from Johnston to Stewart Lockhart, 23 March 1919, SLPNLS, Vol. 10.
22. Minute from Beckett to Grindle, 28 March 1919, in Secret File CO 18353, CO 521/20.
23. Programmes for all these events, and more, are in SLPNLS, Vol. 69.
24. No. 39, 23 July 1920, CO 521/21.
25. Various letters, from the Chancellor of the University of Hong Kong to Stewart Lockhart, and replies, July 1919, SLPNLS, Vol. 5.
26. 'Annual Report for 1920', Eastern No. 1097, p. 6.
27. See Note 26 above.
28. Draft, 1921 Census, p. 1, SLPNLS, Vol. 67.
29. Draft, 1921 Census, p. 4, SLPNLS, Vol. 67.
30. See Note 29 above.
31. Telegram, 13 March 1920, CO 521/21.
32. The Census reported the famine two years before as one of the reasons behind the small increase in population, Draft, 1921 Census, p. 1, SLPNLS, Vol. 67.
33. No. 11, 19 March 1920, CO 521/21.
34. Draft, 1921 Census, p. 1, SLPNLS, Vol. 67.
35. A. E. Wright and R. M. Henderson, 'Report in regard to the Sanitary Condition of the Island of Liu Kung Tao, Wei Hai Wei', Hong Kong, 7 December 1918, CO 521/20.
36. Letter from Johnston to Stewart Lockhart, 4 September 1917, SLPNLS, Vol. 10.
37. Wright and Henderson, 'Report on Liu Kung Tao', p. 1, CO 521/20.
38. Wright and Henderson, 'Report on Liu Kung Tao', p. 2, CO 521/20.
39. See Note 38 above.
40. 'Annual Report for 1918', Eastern No. 999, p. 4.
41. Memorandum from Stewart Lockhart to Secretary of State, 25 January 1919, Enclosure in Wright and Henderson Report, CO 521/20.
42. C. A. M. Smith, *The British in China and Far Eastern Trade* (London, Constable, 1920), p. 63.
43. Letter from Lowson to Stewart Lockhart, 10 November 1919, SLPGWC.
44. Stewart Lockhart, 'Catalogue of Collection of Chinese Paintings', SLPGWC.
45. Letter from Johnston to Stewart Lockhart, 8 September 1920, SLPNLS, Vol. 10.
46. See Note 45 above.
47. See Note 45 above.
48. Letter from Johnston to Stewart Lockhart, 15 September 1920, SLPNLS, Vol. 10.
49. Letter from Johnston to Stewart Lockhart, 2 November 1919, SLPNLS, Vol. 10.
50. See Note 49 above.
51. Minute from Beckett to Fiddes, 10 August 1920, in Confidential File CO 521/21.
52. Confidential Note from Grindle, 23 November 1921, CO 521/22.
53. Minute from Beckett to Fiddes, 10 August 1920, in Confidential File CO 521/21.

54. Minute by Grindle, 10 January 1919, in Confidential File CO 1484, CO 521/20.

55. For both comments see Curzon to Colonial Office, 24 February 1919, Enclosure in CO 12649, CO 521/20.

56. Letter from Johnston to Stewart Lockhart, 21 December 1920, SLPNLS, Vol. 10.

57. Confidential File CO 1484, 16 January 1919, and Enclosures, CO 521/20.

58. Convention for the Rendition of Weihaiwei, *Weihaiwei Government Gazette*, 5 May 1930, Vol. *xxiii*, No. 10 of 1930. For the rendition of Weihaiwei, and the events in the decade leading up to this see Atwell, *British Mandarins and Chinese Reformers*, pp. 124 ff.

59. Letter from Johnston to Stewart Lockhart, 19 July 1919, SLPNLS, Vol. 10.

60. Draft, 1921 Census, SLPNLS, Vol. 67.

61. Invoice from Ah Mee to Stewart Lockhart, April 1921, SLPGWC.

62. Now in SLPNLS, Vol. 66.

63. By January 1921 Stewart Lockhart had told Johnston that all his books were in store, SLPNLS, Vol. 10.

64. 'Address from the British Staff in Weihaiwei to Sir James H. Stewart Lockhart', April 1921, SLPGWC.

65. Now in SLPGWC.

66. 'Address from the Chinese Chamber of Commerce in Weihaiwei', April 1921, SLPGWC.

67. Letter from Whittaker to Stewart Lockhart, 10 January 1935, SLPNLS, Vol. 12.

68. Despatch from Blunt to Churchill, 7 May 1921, CO 31049, CO 521/22.

69. Unsigned Minute in CO 31049, CO 521/22.

70. Beckett, 7 October 1921, Enclosure in CO 49157, CO 521/22.

71. Letter from Lucas to Stewart Lockhart, 24 December 1922, SLPNLS, Vol. 1.

72. Telegram from Duff to Stewart Lockhart, 18 April 1921, SLPNLS, Vol. 1.

73. *North China Daily News*, 26 April 1921, p. 9.

74. The guests included: Sir Robert Ho Tung, Chow Shou-son, Ho Wing, R. H. Kotewall, and Lau Chu Pak. Guest list, 2 May 1921, Hongkong Hotel, SLPNLS, Vol. 1.

Notes to Chapter 12

1. Letter from Johnston to Stewart Lockhart, 5 December 1921, SLPNLS, Vol. 10, and Letter from Joel to Mary Stewart Lockhart, 13 June 1921, SLPGWC.

2. Letter from Johnston to Stewart Lockhart, 5 December 1921, SLPNLS, Vol. 10.

3. Photographs from all these holidays are in the uncatalogued section of the Stewart Lockhart Collection of Photographs, SLPGWC.

4. Letter from Johnston to Stewart Lockhart, 17 January 1923, SLPNLS, Vol. 10.

5. Letter from Johnston to Stewart Lockhart, 15 January 1922, SLPNLS, Vol. 10.

6. Letter from Johnston to Stewart Lockhart, 17 January 1923, SLPNLS, Vol. 10.

7. Letter from Johnston to Stewart Lockhart, 5 December 1921, SLPNLS, Vol. 10.

8. Letter from Johnston to Stewart Lockhart, 17 January 1923, SLPNLS, Vol. 10.

9. Letter from Johnston to Stewart Lockhart, 15 January 1922, SLPNLS, Vol. 10.

10. Letter from Johnston to Stewart Lockhart, 31 January 1924, SLPNLS, Vol. 10.

11. Newton, 'An Evening in a Library', SLPGWC.

12. Mary Stewart Lockhart in conversation with the author in 1980.

13. Letter from Wilcox to Stewart Lockhart, 16 May 1924, SLPNLS, Vol. 62.

14. Letter from Jordan to Stewart Lockhart, 27 April 1924, SLPNLS, Vol. 12.

15. Letter from Jordan to Stewart Lockhart, 3 March 1922, SLPNLS, Vol. 12.

16. Letter from Johnston to Stewart Lockhart, 2 January 1929, SLPNLS, Vol. 10A.

17. Letter from Grindle to Stewart Lockhart, 15 May 1923, CO 22125/1923, SLPNLS, Vol. 1.

18. Letter from Fiddian to Stewart Lockhart, 31 October 1924, CO 47832/24, and Replies, SLPNLS, Vol. 1.

19. Letter from Whitewright to Stewart Lockhart, 1 December 1911, SLPNLS, Vol. 43.

20. Letter from Johnston to Stewart Lockhart, 31 January 1924, SLPNLS, Vol. 10.

21. See Note 20 above.

22. See Note 20 above.

23. Letter from Beavis to Stewart Lockhart, 22 October 1925, SLPNLS, Vol. 13.

24. Letter from Lethbridge to Mary Stewart Lockhart, 23 August 1972, SLPGWC.

25. Letter from Johnston to Stewart Lockhart, 28 February 1925, SLPGWC.

26. See Note 25 above.

27. Programme, London Highland Club, 1926-7, SLPSSP, and for 1927-8, SLPNLS, Vol. 25.

28. Letter from Johnston to Stewart Lockhart, 26 November 1926, SLPNLS, Vol. 10A.

29. Johnston to Stewart Lockhart, 13 May 1927, SLPNLS, Vol. 10A, and *Weihaiwei Government Gazette*, 2 May 1927, Vol. xx, No. 15 of 1927.

30. Letter from Shouson Chow to Stewart Lockhart, 17 February 1926, SLPNLS, Vol. 5.

31. His writings for the *Journal of the Royal Asiatic Society* are in SLPNLS, Vol. 25, and those for the *China Review* in SLPNLS, Vol. 29.

32. Letter from Johnston to Stewart Lockhart, 2 January 1928, SLPNLS, Vol. 10A.

33. A series of pamphlets from various sources, dating from 1926 to 1931, on a variety of topics on China, are in SLPNLS, Vol. 67.

34. E. D. H. Fraser, comp., *Index to the Tso Chuan*, revised and prepared for the press by J. H. Stewart Lockhart (London, Oxford University Press, 1930).

35. Hewlett, *Forty Years in China*, p. 49.

36. Stewart Lockhart, *Index to the Tso Chuan*, preface, p. *iii*.

37. Stewart Lockhart, *Index to the Tso Chuan*, preface, p. *i*.

38. *The Times*, 27 August 1929.

39. Walter retired in 1929, Letter from Johnston to Stewart Lockhart, 14 October 1929, SLPNLS, Vol. 10A.

40. Letter from Stewart Lockhart to Steele-Smith, 11 September 1929, SLPNLS, Vol. 7.

41. Letter from Stewart Lockhart to Worsley, 25 June 1930, SLPNLS, Vol. 13.

42. Letter from Johnston to Stewart Lockhart, 28 February 1925, SLPGWC.

43. Letter from Johnston to Stewart Lockhart, 14 October 1929, SLPNLS, Vol. 10A, and Convention for the Rendition of Weihaiwei, *Weihaiwei Government Gazette*, 5 May 1930.

44. Letter from Stewart Lockhart to Worsley, 21 February 1931, and Worsley to Stewart Lockhart, 28 February 1931, SLPNLS, Vol. 13.

45. Letter from Johnston to Stewart Lockhart, 2 January 1929, SLPNLS, Vol. 10A. The badge is in SLPGWC.

46. Relevant notes, SLPNLS, Vol. 29.

47. Chai Li-ssu (H. A. Giles), *Han Wen Ts'ui Chen: Chinese Texts Collected by Sir James H. Stewart Lockhart* (Shanghai, Commercial Press, 1931).

48. Letter from Giles to Stewart Lockhart, 23 November 1928, SLPNLS, Vol. 29.

49. H. A. Giles and A. Waley, (eds.), *Select Chinese Verses*, new edn., revised by Stewart Lockhart (Shanghai, Commercial Press, 1934).

50. Letter from Waley to Stewart Lockhart, 27 January 1935, SLPNLS, Vol. 12.

51. Letter from Bailey to Stewart Lockhart, 29 January 1935, SLPNLS, Vol. 12.

52. *Directory of the Chinese Social and Political Science Association*, 1932–3, SLPNLS, Vol. 12.

53. Letter from Taylor to Stewart Lockhart, 19 November 1932, SLPNLS, Vol. 12.

54. Letter from Silcock to Stewart Lockhart, 1 January 1932, SLPNLS, Vol. 7.

55. Letter from the Scottish National Portrait Gallery to Stewart Lockhart, 9 March 1933, SLPSSP.

56. Letter from Johnston to Stewart Lockhart, 21 July 1934, SLPNLS, Vol. 10A.

57. Letter from Lambert to Stewart Lockhart, 2 August 1935, SLPNLS, Vol. 44.

58. Letter from Stewart Lockhart to Rossetti, 26 January 1935, SLPNLS, Vol. 12.

59. Stewart Lockhart's obituary, *The Daily Telegraph*, 1 March 1937.

SELECTED BIBLIOGRAPHY

Official Sources

PUBLIC RECORD OFFICE, LONDON

Colonial Office Series
CO 129 Hong Kong, Original Correspondence
CO 537 Hong Kong, Original Correspondence, Supplementary
CO 489 Hong Kong, Register of Out-letters
CO 131 Hong Kong, Sessional Papers
CO 132 Hong Kong, Government Gazettes
CO 521 Weihaiwei, Original Correspondence
CO 770 Weihaiwei, Register of Correspondence
CO 771 Weihaiwei, Register of Out-letters
CO 841 Weihaiwei, Acts
CO 774 Weihaiwei, Government Gazettes
CO 873 Weihaiwei, Commissioner's Files
CO 429 Patronage, Original Correspondence
CO 882 Confidential Print, Eastern

Foreign Office Series
FO 17 China, General Correspondence
FO 228 China, Correspondence
FO 232 China, Indexes to Correspondence
FO 371 China, Political Correspondence

SCOTTISH RECORD OFFICE, EDINBURGH

Register of Sasines
Register of Births, Marriages, and Deaths

PRIVATE PAPERS

Stewart Lockhart Papers, George Watson's College, Edinburgh. Stewart Lockhart Papers, National Library of Scotland, Edinburgh.
Stewart Lockhart Papers, The Stewart Society, Edinburgh.
Nellie Gordon Papers in the possession of V. Gordon-Smith, Edinburgh.
The Archives of the Merchant Company of Edinburgh.

Books, Articles, and Newspapers

Airlie, S. M., 'The Stewart Lockhart Collection of Chinese Art and Artefacts', Dip. A. G. M. S. Thesis (Manchester, 1979).

—— *An Ardent Collector: An Exhibition of the Stewart Lockhart Collection* (Edinburgh, Merchant Company Education Board, 1982).

—— 'List of the Photographs in the Stewart Lockhart Collection', (Edinburgh, 1983).

Allen, C., (ed.), *Tales From The South China Seas: Images of the British in South-East Asia in the Twentieth Century* (London, 1983; Repr., London, Futura, 1985).

Astor House Hotel, *Guide to North China* (Tientsin, Astor House Hotel, 1913).

Atwell, P., *British Mandarins and Chinese Reformers: The British Administration of Weihaiwei (1898–1930) and the Territory's Return to Chinese Rule* (Hong Kong, Oxford University Press, 1985).

Bard, E., *The Chinese at Home* (London, George Newnes, 1906).

Barnes, A. A. S., *On Active Service with the Chinese Regiment* (London, Grant Richards, 1902).

The *Barrovian*

Bartholomew, *World Travel Map: China and Mongolia* (Edinburgh, John Bartholomew and Son, 1988).

Behr, E., *The Last Emperor* (London, Futura, 1987).

Bence-Jones, M., *The Viceroys of India* (London, Constable and Co., 1984).

Beresford, Lord C., *The Break Up of China* (London, Harper and Brothers, 1899).

Bertram, Sir A., *The Colonial Office* (Cambridge, Cambridge University Press, 1930).

Bird, I., *The Golden Chersonese* (London, 1883; Repr. London, Century, 1983).

—— *The Yangtze Valley and Beyond* (London, 1899; Repr. London, Century, 1985).

Bourne, K. *The Foreign Policy of Victorian England, 1830–1902* (Oxford, Clarendon Press, 1970).

Bowen, Sir G. F., *Thirty Years of Colonial Government*, ed. S. Lane-Poole (2 vols., London, Longmans and Co., 1889).

Bruce-Mitford, C. E., *The Territory of Wei-Hai-Wei* (Weihaiwei, no publisher, 1902).

Buckle, G. E. (ed.), *Letters of Queen Victoria* (Series 3, Vol. 3, New York, John Murray, 1931).

Budd, J. W., 'Notes as to comparatively modern family history made August 1904', typed manuscript.

Burke's, *Genealogical and Heraldic History of the Landed Gentry*, P. Townend (ed.), (3 vols., 18th edn.; London, Burke's Peerage Ltd., 1969).

Cameron, N., *Hong Kong: The Cultured Pearl* (Hong Kong, Oxford University Press, 1978).

Campbell, P. C., *Chinese Coolie Emigration to Countries within the British Empire* (London, P. S. King and Son, 1923).

Camplin, J., *The Rise of the Plutocrats: Wealth and Power in Edwardian England* (London, Constable, 1978).

Carrington, C. E., *The British Overseas: Exploits of a Nation of Shopkeepers* (2 vols., Cambridge, Cambridge University Press, 1968).

Carson, R., Berghaus, P., and Lowick, N., (eds.), *A Survey of Numismatic Research 1972–1977* (Berne, International Numismatic Commission, 1979)

Chadwick, O., 'Report on the Sanitary Condition of Hong Kong', Eastern No. 38, 1882.

Chai Li-Ssu *Han Wen Ts'ui Chen: Chinese Texts Collected by Sir James H. Stewart Lockhart* (Shanghai, Commercial Press, 1931).

Cheng, J. Y. S., (ed.), *Hong Kong in Search of a Future* (Hong Kong, Oxford University Press, 1984).

China Mail

China Review

Chirol, V., *The Far Eastern Question* (London, Macmillan and Co., 1896).

Clayton, A., *The British Empire as a Superpower, 1919–1939* (Basingstoke, Macmillan, 1986).

Coates, A., *Myself a Mandarin: Memoirs of a Special Magistrate* (Hong Kong, Heinemann Asia, 1968).

Collins, Sir C., *Public Administration in Hong Kong* (London, Royal Institute of International Affairs, 1952).

Collis, M., *Wayfoong: The Hongkong and Shanghai Banking Corporation* (London, Faber and Faber, 1965).

Colonial Office, *Notes of Information for Applicants to the Post of Hongkong Cadets* (London, 1878).

—— *Results of the Examination for Two Ceylon Writerships and Two Hongkong Cadetships* (London, 1878).

The Colonial Office List

Colquhoun, A. R., *China in Transformation* (London, Harper and Brothers, 1912).

Correspondent, A, 'British Ignorance of China', *New Books and New Editions Supplement to the London and China Express*, 17 October 1890.

Crisswell, C. N., *The Taipans: Hong Kong's Merchant Princes* (Hong Kong, Oxford University Press, 1981).

Curzon, G. N., *Problems of the Far East* (London, Longmans, Green and Co., 1894).

Daily Graphic, The

Daily Telegraph, The

David, H. W. C., and Weaver, J. R. H., *Dictionary of National Biography 1912–1921* (London, Oxford University Press, 1927).

Directory of the Chinese Social and Political Science Association

Donaldson, G., *The Scots Overseas* (London, Robert Hale, 1966).

Drage, C., *Taikoo* (London, Constable, 1970).

Dunne, N., *Club: The Story of the Hong Kong Football Club 1886–1986* (Hong Kong, Hong Kong Football Club, 1985).

Dyer Ball, J. *Things Chinese: Being Notes on Various Subjects Connected with China* (London, Sampson Low, Marston and Co., 1892).

Eitel, E. J., *Europe in China: The History of Hong Kong* (Hong Kong, 1895; Repr. Taipei, Ch'eng-wen Publishing, 1968).

Encyclopaedia Britannica (15th edn.) (Chicago, Encyclopaedia Britannica, 1978).

Endacott, G. B., *A History of Hong Kong* (Hong Kong, Oxford University Press, 1958).

―――― *An Eastern Entrepot* (Overseas Research Publication No. 4; London, HMSO Department of Technical Co-operation, 1964).

―――― *The Government and People in Hong Kong, 1841–1962* (Hong Kong, Hong Kong University Press, 1964).

Endacott, G. B., and Hinton, A., *Fragrant Harbour: A Short History of Hong Kong* (Hong Kong, Oxford University Press, 1962).

Fairbank, J. K., *Trade and Diplomacy on the China Coast* (Harvard, Harvard University Press, 1953).

Fairbank, J. K., Reischauer, E. O. and Craig, A. M., *East Asia: The Modern Transformation* (London, George Allen and Unwin, 1965).

Feuerwerker, A., *The Foreign Establishment in China in the Early Twentieth Century* (Michigan Papers in Chinese Studies No. 29, Ann Arbor, Center for Chinese Studies, University of Michigan, 1976).

Financial Times

Fleming, P., *The Siege at Peking: A Study of the Boxer Rising* (London, Rupert Hart-Davis, 1959).

―――― *Bayonets To Lhasa: The First Full Account of the British Invasion of Tibet in 1904* (London, Rupert Hart-Davis, 1961).

Folk-Lore

Forsyth, R. C., (ed.), *Shantung: The Sacred Province of China* (Shanghai, Chinese Literature Society, 1912).

Fraser, E. D. H., comp., *Index to the Tso Chuan*, revised and prepared for the press by J. H. Stewart Lockhart (London, Oxford University Press, 1930).

Fraser, P., *Joseph Chamberlain: Radicalism and Empire, 1868–1914* (London, Cassell, 1966).

Gibb, A. D., *The Scottish Empire: An Account of Scotland's Part in Building the British Empire* (London, Maclehose and Co., 1937).

Giles, H. A., *Gems of Chinese Literature* (London, Quaritch, 1884).

—— *China and the Chinese* (New York, Columbia University Press, 1902).

See also Chai Li-Ssu.

Giles, H. A., and Waley, A., *Select Chinese Verses*, (new edn.), revised by J. H. Stewart Lockhart (Shanghai, Commercial Press, 1934).

Gooch, G. P., and Temperley, H., (eds.), *British Documents on the Origins of War, 1898–1914* (London, HMSO, 1927).

Gordon, N., 'The Journal of Miss Nellie Gordon, January 1883–December 1890', diary.

Graphic, The

Great Britain, *Parliamentary Debates*, 4th Series, (Session 1899).

—— *A Draft Agreement between the Government of the United Kindom of Great Britain and Northern Ireland and the Government of the People's Republic of China on the Future of Hong Kong* (London, 1984).

—— *China Reflected: An Anthology from Chinese and Western Sources*, Foreign and Commonwealth Office and the Central Office of Information (eds.), (London, 1986).

Grenville, J. A. S., *Lord Salisbury and Foreign Policy: the Close of the Nineteenth Century* (London, Athlone Press, 1964).

Grierson, E., *The Imperial Dream: the British Commonwealth and Empire, 1775–1969* (London, Collins, 1972).

Growler, The

Gull, E. M., 'The Story of the Chinese Labor Corps' *Far Eastern Review*, 15, No. 4, April 1918, pp. 125–35.

—— *Facets of the Chinese Question* (London, Ernest Benn, 1931).

—— *British Economic Interests in the Far East* (London, Oxford University Press, 1943).

Hahn, E., *China Only Yesterday: 1850–1950, a Century of Change* (London, Weidenfeld and Nicolson, 1963).

Hall, H. L., *The Colonial Office: A History* (London, Longmans, Green and Co., 1937).

Hare, G. T., 'Administrative Report on the Civil Administration of the Territory of Weihaiwei, 1899–1901', Eastern No. 75, 1902.

Harrison, B., (ed.), *University of Hong Kong: the First 50 Years 1911–1961* (Hong Kong, Hong Kong University Press, 1962).

Hayes, J., 'The Pattern of Life in the New Territories in 1898', *Journal of the Hong Kong Branch of the Royal Asiatic Society*, 2 (1962), pp. 75–102.

Hewlett, Sir M., *The Siege of the Peking Legations* (Harrow, Editors of the Harrovian, 1900).

—— *Forty Years in China* (London, Macmillan, 1943).

Hicks Beach, Lady V., *Life of Sir Michael Hicks Beach (Earl St Aldwyn)* (London, Macmillan, 1932).

Hong Kong, *Papers on the Subject of a Petition Addressed to the House of Commons Praying for an Amendment of the Constitution of the Crown Colony of Hong Kong* (Hong Kong, 1896).

Hong Kong Government Gazette

Hongkong Telegraph

Hongkong Weekly Press

Hopkirk, P., *Foreign Devils on the Silk Road: the Search for the Lost Cities and Treasures of Chinese Central Asia* (Oxford, 1984; Repr. Oxford University Press, 1985).

Hsü, I. C. Y, *The Rise of Modern China*, (3rd edition.), (Oxford, Oxford University Press, 1983).

International Federation of Library Associations and Institutions, *Standard Practices in the Preparation of Bibliographic Records* (London, International Federation of Library Associations and Institutions, 1982).

Independent, The

India Office, *Results of the Open Competition for the Civil Service of India* (London, 1878).

Ireland. A., *The Far Eastern Tropics* (London, Archibald Constable and Co., 1905).

Jardine, Matheson, and Co., *Jardine, Matheson, and Company: an Historical Sketch* (Hong Kong, Jardine, Matheson and Co., no date).

Jarvie, I. C. and Agassi, J., (eds.), *Hong Kong: a Society in Transition* (London, Routledge and Kegan Paul, 1969).

Jay, R., *Joseph Chamberlain: a Political Study* (Oxford, Clarendon Press, 1981).

Jeffries, C., *The Colonial Empire and its Civil Service* (Cambridge, Cambridge University Press, 1938).

—— *The Colonial Office* (Oxford, Oxford University Press, 1956).

Johnston, R. F., *Account of a Journey in Shantung from Weihaiwei to the Tomb of Confucius* (Weihaiwei, Weihaiwei Press, 1904).

—— *Remarks on the Province of Shantung* (Hong Kong, Norohana and Co., 1904).

—— *From Peking to Mandalay: A Journey from North China to Burma through Tibetan Ssuch'uan and Yunnan* (London, John Murray, 1908).

—— *Lion and Dragon in Northern China* (London, John Murray, 1910).

—— *Buddhist China* (London, John Murray, 1913).

—— *Letters to a Missionary* (London, Watts and Co., 1918).

—— *Twilight in the Forbidden City* (London, Victor Gollancz, 1934).

—— *Confucianism and Modern China: the Lewis Fry Memorial Lectures 1933–1934* (London, Victor Gollancz, 1934).

Joseph, P., *Foreign Diplomacy in China, 1894–1900* (London, G. Allen and Unwin, 1928).

Journal of the Hong Kong Branch of the Royal Asiatic Society

Journal of the Royal Asiatic Society

Journal of the United Service Institution, Simla

Judd, D., *Balfour and the British Empire: a Study in Imperial Evolution, 1874–1932* (London, Macmillan, 1968).

King William's College, *Register of King William's College* (Isle of Man, King William's College, 1956).

Knollys, H., *English Life in China* (London, Smith and Elder, 1885).

Kotewall, R., and Smith, N. L. (eds.), *The Penguin Book of Chinese Verse* (Harmondsworth, 1962; Repr., Harmondsworth, Penguin, 1965).

Ku, H., 'Reminiscences of a Chinese Viceroy's Secretary, *Journal of the North China Branch of the Royal Asiatic Society* 46, (1915), pp. 61–76.

Kubicek, R. V., *The Administration of Imperialism: Joseph Chamberlain at the Colonial Office* (Commonwealth Studies Series; Durham, North Carolina, Duke University Press, 1969).

Kwong, L. S. K., *A Mosaic of the Hundred Days: Personalities, Politics and Ideas of 1898* (London, Harvard University Press, 1984).

Langer, W. L., *The Diplomacy of Imperialism, 1890–1902*, 2nd edition, (New York, Alfred Knopf, 1951).

Lee, S., (ed.), *Dictionary of National Biography* (London, Smith Elder, 1909).

Lemon, A. and Pollock, N., (eds.), *Studies in Overseas Settlement and Population* (London, Longman, 1980).

Lethbridge, H. J., *Hong Kong: Stability and Change* (Hong Kong, Oxford University Press, 1978).

Lo, Y. Y., *The Opium Problem in the Far East* (Shanghai, Commercial Press, 1933).

Lucas, C. P., *A Historical Geography of the British Colonies* (6 vols., Oxford, Clarendon Press, 1888).

—— *The British Empire: Six Lectures* (London, Macmillan and Co., 1915).

—— *The Empire at War* (Oxford, Royal Commonwealth Society, 1916).

Lugard, Lord F. J. D., *The Diaries of Lord Lugard*, M. Perham, (ed.), (London, Collins, 1959).

Macartney, Lady C., *An English Lady in Chinese Turkestan* (Hong Kong, Oxford University Press, 1985).

Macdonald, H. F., (ed.), *A Hundred Years of Fettes: Memories of Old Fettesians 1870–1970* (Edinburgh, Constable, 1970).

MacNair, H. F., *The Chinese Abroad: Their Position and Protection* (London, 1933; Reprinted, Taipei, Ch'eng-wen Publishing, 1971).

Marder, A. J., *British Naval Policy 1880–1905: the Anatomy of British Sea Power* (London, Putnam and Co., 1940).

—— *Fear God and Dread Nought: Years of Power 1904–1914* (Vol. 2; London, Jonathan Cape, 1956).

Merchant Company of Edinburgh, *The Appeal: Old and New Watson's* (Edinburgh, Merchant Company of Edinburgh, 1930).

Mills, L. A., *British Rule in Eastern Asia* (Oxford, Oxford University Press, 1942).

Morris, J., *Pax Brittanica: The Climax of an Empire* (Harmondsworth, Penguin, 1979).

Morrison, G. E., *The Correspondence of G. E. Morrison: Volume 1, 1895–1912*, Lo Hui-min (ed.), (Cambridge, Cambridge University Press, 1976).

Morse, H. B., *The Trade and Administration of the Chinese Empire* (Hong Kong, Kelly and Walsh, 1908).

—— *International Relations of the Chinese Empire* (London, Longmans and Co., 1918).

Moule, A. E., *Half a Century in China* (London, Hodder and Stoughton, c. 1911).

Newton, K., 'An Evening in a Library', (London, undated), typescript.

Nish, I. H., 'The Royal Navy and the Taking of Weihaiwei, 1898–1905', *The Mariner's Mirror*, 54, No. 1, (1967).

—— 'Admiral Jerram and the German Pacific Fleet, 1913–1915', *The Mariner's Mirror*, 56, No. 4, (1970).

North China and Shantung Mission Association, *The Land of Sinim: Quarterly Chronicle of the Church of England Mission in North China and Shantung*, 20, No. 4, (October 1912).

North China Daily News

Oban Times, The

Overland China Mail

Overland Mail

Parker, E. H., *John Chinaman. And a Few Others* (London, John Murray, 1901).

Pelcovits, N. A., *Old China Hands and the Foreign Office* (New York, King's Crown Press, 1948).

Pelissier, R., *The Awakening of China, 1793–1949*, edited and translated by M. Kieffer (London, Secker and Warburg, 1967).

Pitch And Toss, or The Kurile Intelligencer

Pope-Hennessy, J., *Verandah: Some Episodes in the Crown Colonies, 1867–1889* (London, Century, 1984).

Pratt, Sir J. T., *The Expansion of Europe into the Far East* (London, Sylvan Press, 1947).

Sassoon, F. D., 'Celebrities at Home', undated manuscript.

Sayer, G. R., *Hong Kong: 1862–1919, Years of Discretion* (Hong Kong, Hong Kong University Press, 1975).

Schiffrin, H. J., *Sun Yat-sen and the Origins of the Chinese Revolution* (Los Angeles, University of California Press, 1968).

Scotsman, The

Scott, J. (ed.), *Love and Protest: Chinese Poems from the Sixth Century B. C. to the Seventeenth Century A. D.* (London, Andre Deutsch, 1972).

Scott, Capt, P., 'Report on Weihaiwei', 23 February 1902.

Shaw Y. (ed.), *China and Europe in the Twentieth Century* (Institute of English Monograph Series No. 28; Taipei, National Chengchi University, 1986).

Skrine, C. P., and Nightingale, P., *Macartney of Kashgar: New Light on British, Chinese, and Russian Activities in Sinkiang, 1890–1918* (Hong Kong, Oxford University Press, 1987).

Smith, C. A. M., *The British in China and Far Eastern Trade* (London, Constable, 1920).

Smout, T. C., *A Century of the Scottish People 1830–1950* (London, Fontana, 1987).

—— *A History of the Scottish People* (London, Fontana, 1985).

South China Morning Post

Spence, J., *The China Helpers: Western Advisers in China, 1620–1960* (London, Bodley Head, 1969).

Sphere, The

Stephen, L., and Lee, S. (eds.), *Dictionary of National Biography* (London, Smith Elder, 1908).

Stewart, J., of Ardvorlich, *The Stewarts: the Highland Branches of a Royal Name* (Edinburgh, W. and A. K. Johnston and G. W. Bacon, 1954).

Stewart Lockhart, J. H., 'Some Notes on Chinese Folklore', *Folklore*, 1, No. 3, September 1890, pp. 359–368.

—— *A Manual of Chinese Quotations: Being a Translation of the Ch'eng Yü K'ao* (Hong Kong, Kelly and Walsh, 1893).

—— 'Report of the Special Committee connected with the Bill for the Incorporation of the Po Leung Kuk, or Society for the Protection of Women and Girls' (Hong Kong, Norohana and Co., 1893).

—— *The Currency of the Farther East: From Earliest Times up to the Present Day* (3 vols., Shanghai, Kelly and Walsh, 1895–1898).

—— 'Report on the Extension of the Colony of Hongkong', Eastern No. 66, 1898.

—— 'Confidential Report on a Journey in the Province of Shantung', Eastern No. 84, 1903.

—— 'Report on a Visit to Kiaochou and Chinan', Eastern No. 104, 1906.

—— *The Stewart Lockhart Collection of Chinese Copper Coins*, extra vol. 1, *Journal of the North China Branch of the Royal Asiatic Society*, 1915.

with Colquhoun, A. R., 'A Sketch of Formosa', *China Review*, 13, No. 3, 1884–85, pp. 161–207.

Swettenham, F., 'Report on Weihaiwei', Eastern No. 72, 1900.

Szczepanik, E., *The Economic Growth of Hong Kong* (London, Oxford University Press, 1958).

T'ang L. L., *China in Revolt: How a Civilisation Became a Nation* (London, Noel Douglas, 1927).

Teichman, E., *Affairs of China: A Survey of the Recent History and Present Circumstances of the Republic of China* (London, Methuen, 1938).

Thomson, J. S., *The Chinese* (Indianapolis, Bobbs-Merrill Co., 1909).

Times, The

Times of India, The

Traditional Interior Decoration, 2, No. 4, March 1988.

Trendell, A. J. R., *The Colonial Year Book* (3 vols.; London, Sampson Low, Marston and Co., 1890–1892).

Tsang, G. C. C., and Chuang, S. C., *Fan Paintings by Late Ch'ing Shanghai Masters* (Hong Kong, Hong Kong Urban Council, 1977).

Tse T. T., *The Chinese Republic: A Secret History of the Revolution* (Hong Kong, South China Morning Post, 1924).

—— *Ancient Chinese Art: A Treatise on Chinese Painting* (Hong Kong, South China Morning Post, 1928).

Tung Wah Group of Hospitals, *One Hundred Years of the Tung Wah Group of Hospitals, 1870–1970*, The Board of Directors, 1970–71 (eds.), (2 vols.; Hong Kong, Tung Wah Group of Hospitals, 1970).

—— *The History of Education of Tung Wah Hospitals* (Hong Kong, Tung Wah Group of Hospitals, 1963).

Turner, F. C., 'Military Report and Recent Information Concerning the Dependency of Wei-Hai-Wei' (London, Intelligence Division, War Office, 1904).

Turner, J. A., *Kwang Tung: or Five Years in South China* (London, 1894; Reprinted Hong Kong, Oxford University Press, 1986).

Wang, Tseng-tsai, and others, *Chinese History: Modern Period* (Vol. 3, Chinese Culture Series; Taipei, China Academy, 1978).

War Office, General Staff, *Military Reports on the Province of Shan-tung* (London, War Office, 1905).

Watson, J. L., *Emigration and the Chinese Lineage: The Mans in Hong Kong and London* (Berkeley, University of California Press, 1975).

Watsonian, The

Waugh, H. L., (ed.), *George Watson's College: A History and Record 1724–1970* (Edinburgh, George Watson's College, 1970).

Weaver, J. R. H., *Dictionary of National Biography 1922–1930* (London, Oxford University Press, 1937).

Weihaiwei Gazette

Weihaiwei Golf Club, *List Of Rules* (Weihaiwei, Weihaiwei Golf Club, 1902)

Weihaiwei Government Gazette

Weihaiwei Lyre

Weng, W. G., and Boda, Y., *The Palace Museum, Peking: Treasures of the Forbidden City* (London, Orbis, 1982).

Wesley-Smith, P., *Unequal Treaty 1898–1997: China, Great Britain and Hong Kong's New Territories* (Hong Kong, Oxford University Press, 1980).

Who Was Who, 1895–1915 (London, A. and C. Black, 1916).

Who Was Who, 1927–40 (London, A. and C. Black, 1941).

Wight, M.,*The Development of the Legislative Council 1606–1945* (London, Faber and Faber, 1946).

Wilbur, C. M., *Sun Yat-sen: Frustrated Patriot* (New York, Columbia University Press, 1976).

Williamson, J. A., *A Short History of British Expansion* (London, Macmillan and Co., 1964).

Woodcock, G., *The British in the Far East* (London, Weidenfeld and Nicolson, 1969).

Wright, A., *Twentieth Century Impressions of Hong Kong* (London, Lloyd's Greater British Publishing Co., 1908).

Wright, A. E., and Henderson, R. M., 'Report in regard to the Sanitary Condition of the Island of Liu Kung Tao, Wei Hai Wei', Hong Kong, 1918.

Yee, C., *The Chinese Eye: An Interpretation of Chinese Painting*.

Young, L. K., *British Policy in China 1895–1902* (Oxford, Oxford University Press 1970).

INDEX